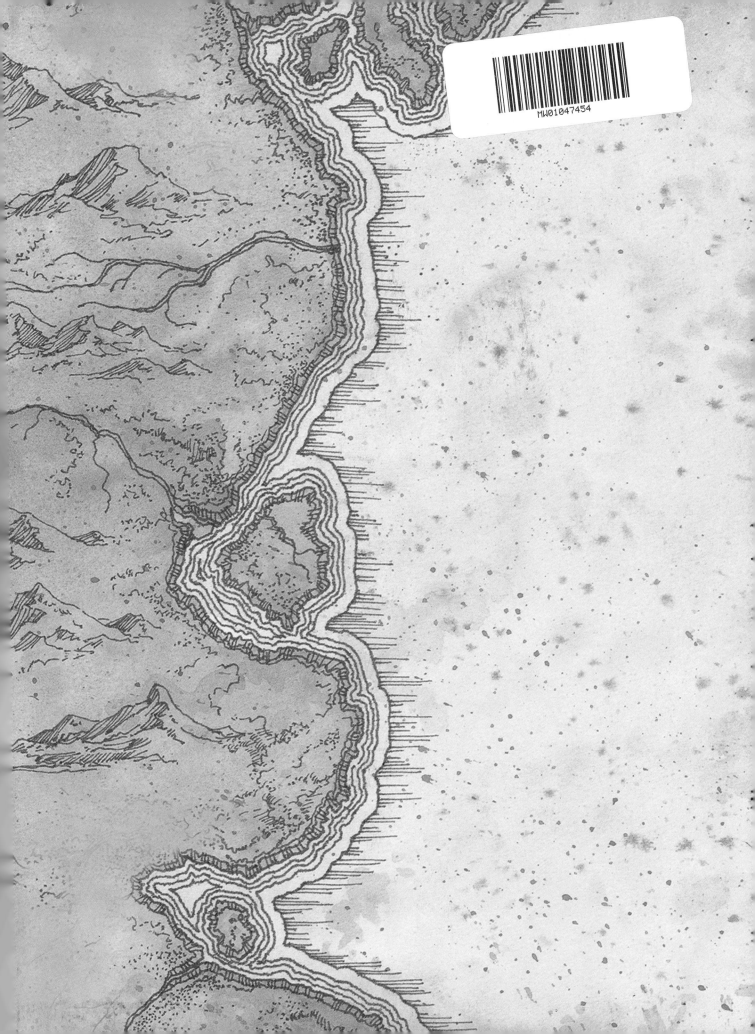

*I*NDIANA

Series Authors

Dr. Richard G. Boehm

Claudia Hoone

Dr. Thomas M. McGowan

Dr. Mabel C. McKinney-Browning

Dr. Ofelia B. Miramontes

Consultants for Indiana History and Geography

Dr. Darrel Bigham
Historic Southern Indiana
University of Southern Indiana

Dorothy W. Drummond
Indiana State University

Series Consultants

Dr. Alma Flor Ada

Dr. Phillip Bacon

Dr. W. Dorsey Hammond

Dr. Asa Grant Hilliard, III

HARCOURT BRACE & COMPANY

Orlando Atlanta Austin Boston San Francisco Chicago Dallas
New York Toronto London

SERIES AUTHORS

Dr. Richard G. Boehm
Professor
Department of Geography
and Planning
Southwest Texas State
University
San Marcos, Texas

Claudia Hoone
Teacher
Ralph Waldo Emerson
School #58
Indianapolis, Indiana

Dr. Thomas M. McGowan
Associate Professor
Division of Curriculum
and Instruction
Arizona State University
Tempe, Arizona

Dr. Mabel C. McKinney-Browning
Director
Division for Public
Education
American Bar Association
Chicago, Illinois

Dr. Ofelia B. Miramontes
Associate Professor
School of Education
University of Colorado
Boulder, Colorado

SERIES CONSULTANTS

Dr. Alma Flor Ada
Professor
School of Education
University of San Francisco
San Francisco, California

Dr. Phillip Bacon
Professor Emeritus
of Geography
and Anthropology
University of Houston
Houston, Texas

Dr. W. Dorsey Hammond
Professor of Education
Oakland University
Rochester, Michigan

Dr. Asa Grant Hilliard, III
Fuller E. Callaway Professor
of Urban Education
Georgia State University
Atlanta, Georgia

CONSULTANTS FOR INDIANA HISTORY AND GEOGRAPHY

Dr. Darrel Bigham
Director
Historic Southern Indiana
Professor of History
University of Southern
Indiana
Evansville, Indiana

Dorothy W. Drummond
Department of Geography,
Geology, and
Anthropology
Indiana State University
Terre Haute, Indiana

MEDIA AND LITERATURE SPECIALISTS

Dr. Joseph A. Braun, Jr.
Professor of Elementary
Social Studies
Department of Curriculum
and Instruction
Illinois State University
Normal, Illinois

Meredith McGowan
Youth Librarian
Tempe Public Library
Tempe, Arizona

GRADE-LEVEL CONSULTANTS AND REVIEWERS

Carol A. Bottoms
Gifted/Talented Coordinator
Greater Clark County
Schools
Jeffersonville, Indiana

Dr. Charles Branham
Assistant Professor
Department of Minority
Studies
Indiana University
Northwest
Gary, Indiana

Sharon R. Bubp
Teacher
General Shanks Elementary
School
Portland, Indiana

Michelle A. Edington
Teacher
Central Elementary School
Huntington, Indiana

Jacky Gholson
Teacher Consultant, Social
Studies K-5
Gary Community School
Corporation
Gary, Indiana

Charles C. Hewett
Teacher
School #96
Indianapolis, Indiana

Barbara Ann Kumbula
Teacher
Wilson Middle School
Muncie, Indiana

Leone B. Little
Chairperson (Retired)
Thomas Carr Howe
High School
Indianapolis, Indiana

Billie D. Moore
Coordinator for
Magnet/Options Programs
Indianapolis Public School
Indianapolis, Indiana

Sheila Oliver
Teacher
Granville Wells
Elementary School
Jamestown, Indiana

Laura Specht
Teacher
Scott Elementary School
Evansville, Indiana

Traci Mansell Strozyk
Teacher
St. John The Baptist School
Newburgh, Indiana

Virginia Terpening
Deputy Director
Indiana Historical Bureau
Indianapolis, Indiana

ISBN: 0-15-306571-0

3 4 5 6 7 8 9 10   032   99

CONTENTS

ATLAS   A1

GEOGRAPHY TERMS   A16

INTRODUCTION

  WHY STUDY INDIANA?   18

    THE POWERFUL IDEAS OF
      SOCIAL STUDIES   19

    READING SKILL • Read Social Studies   21

    THE SUBJECTS OF SOCIAL STUDIES   22

    GEOGRAPHY SKILL • Read a Map   24

  WHERE ON EARTH IS INDIANA?   26

UNIT 1

THE LAND AND EARLY PEOPLE
OF INDIANA   28

  SET THE SCENE WITH LITERATURE
  Canoeing the Wabash with Grandpa
  by Paul Johnson   30

CHAPTER 1

INDIANA'S GEOGRAPHY   32

  LESSON 1 • The Shape of the Land   33

  GEOGRAPHY SKILL • Use Latitude and
    Longitude   36

  LESSON 2 • Rivers and Lakes   38

  LESSON 3 • Weather and Climate   42

  LESSON 4 • LEARN WITH LITERATURE

    The Storm
    written by Marc Harshman
    illustrated by Mark Mohr   46

  THINKING SKILL • Solve a Problem   52

  LESSON 5 • Natural Resources   53

CHAPTER REVIEW   58

Geneva "Gene" Stratton-Porter

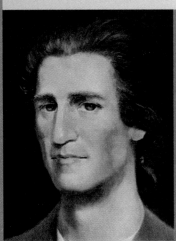

George Rogers Clark

CHAPTER 2

THE EARLY PEOPLE OF INDIANA   60
- LESSON 1 • The Earliest People   61
- CITIZENSHIP SKILL • Work Together in Groups   66
- LESSON 2 • Indian Newcomers   67
- CHART AND GRAPH SKILL • Read a Time Line   71
- LESSON 3 • French Explorers and Traders   72
- GEOGRAPHY SKILL • Follow Routes on a Historical Map   77
- LESSON 4 • The British in Indiana   78
- LESSON 5 • The Americans Fight for Freedom   82
- CHAPTER REVIEW   88

MAKING SOCIAL STUDIES RELEVANT
License (Plate) to Save the Environment   90
STORY CLOTH SUMMARY   92
UNIT REVIEW   94

UNIT 2

PIONEER DAYS   96
SET THE SCENE WITH LITERATURE
The Floating House
written by Scott Russell Sanders
illustrated by Helen Cogancherry   98

CHAPTER 3

FROM TERRITORY TO STATEHOOD   102
- LESSON 1 • The Northwest Territory   103
- LESSON 2 • Conflict Continues in the Northwest Territory   109
- THINKING SKILL • Identify Cause and Effect   115
- COUNTERPOINTS • Indian Land or United States Land?   116
- LESSON 3 • The Nineteenth State   118
- CITIZENSHIP SKILL • Compromise to Resolve Conflicts   123
- CHAPTER REVIEW   124

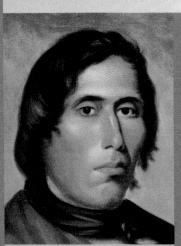

Tecumseh, Shawnee chief

Elizabeth Chapman Conner

CHAPTER 4

PIONEERS IN INDIANA   126
   LESSON 1 • Pioneer Settlements   127
   GEOGRAPHY SKILL • Use a Map to Show
    Movement   133
   LESSON 2 • *LEARN WITH LITERATURE*
    Log Cabin in the Woods
    by Joanne Landers Henry   134
   CHART AND GRAPH SKILL • Read a Diagram   140
   LESSON 3 • New Ways of Travel Bring
    Change   141
   CHART AND GRAPH SKILL • Use a Line
    Graph to See Change   147
  CHAPTER REVIEW   148

MAKING SOCIAL STUDIES RELEVANT
   Conner Prairie   150
STORY CLOTH SUMMARY   152
UNIT REVIEW   154

UNIT 3

PROGRESS AS A STATE   156
   SET THE SCENE WITH LITERATURE
   Escape from Slavery
   by Doreen Rappaport   158

CHAPTER 5

INDIANA GROWS AND CHANGES   162
   LESSON 1 • Indiana in the Civil War   163
   READING SKILL • Tell Primary from
    Secondary Sources   170
   LESSON 2 • Changes on the Farms   172
   LESSON 3 • Manufacturing and the
    Growth of Cities   176
   GEOGRAPHY SKILL • Read Symbols on a
    Product Map   181
   LESSON 4 • Into a New Century   182
  CHAPTER REVIEW   186

Madam C. J. Walker

Virgil ("Gus") Grissom

CHAPTER 6

INDIANA IN THE MODERN WORLD   188
   LESSON 1 • Changing Times   189
   READING SKILL • Tell Fact from Opinion   195
   LESSON 2 • *LEARN WITH LITERATURE*
     When I Was Young In Indiana
     by Dorothy Strattan Hinshaw   196
   LESSON 3 • World War II and After   202
   THINKING SKILL • Understand Point of View   208
   LESSON 4 • Recent Years   209
CHAPTER REVIEW   212

MAKING SOCIAL STUDIES RELEVANT
   Hoosier Hysteria   214
STORY CLOTH SUMMARY   216
UNIT REVIEW   218

UNIT 4

INTO THE TWENTY-FIRST CENTURY   220
SET THE SCENE WITH LITERATURE
On the Banks of the Wabash, Far Away
words and music by Paul Dresser   222
The Star-Spangled Banner
by Francis Scott Key   224

CHAPTER 7

INDIANA TODAY   226
   LESSON 1 • Many Kinds of Hoosiers   227
   GEOGRAPHY SKILL • Use a Population Map   232
   LESSON 2 • How Hoosiers Earn Their Livings   233
   CHART AND GRAPH SKILL • Use a Pictograph   237
   LESSON 3 • Today's Challenges   238
   COUNTERPOINTS • What Is the Best Way
     to Use Indiana's Resources?   242
CHAPTER REVIEW   244

A state citizen

Richard Hatcher

CHAPTER 8

GOVERNMENT IN INDIANA 246
    LESSON 1 • Indiana State Government 247
    CHART AND GRAPH SKILL • Follow a Flow
      Chart 251
    LESSON 2 • Local Governments in Indiana 252
    CITIZENSHIP SKILL • Make Economic Choices 256
    LESSON 3 • Hoosiers and the National
      Government 257
    LESSON 4 • Indiana Citizenship 261
CHAPTER REVIEW 264

MAKING SOCIAL STUDIES RELEVANT
    In Peers We Trust: Teen Court 266
STORY CLOTH SUMMARY 268
UNIT REVIEW 270

FOR YOUR REFERENCE R1

HOW TO GATHER AND
      REPORT INFORMATION R2

ALMANAC
    FACTS ABOUT INDIANA R8
    FACTS ABOUT INDIANA COUNTIES R10
    FACTS ABOUT INDIANA GOVERNORS R14

SOME FAMOUS PEOPLE IN
      INDIANA HISTORY R16

GAZETTEER R20

GLOSSARY R24

INDEX R29

F.Y.I.

LITERATURE, PRIMARY SOURCES, AND DOCUMENTS

Canoeing the Wabash with Grandpa
  by Paul Johnson   30

The Storm
  written by Marc Harshman
  illustrated by Mark Mohr   46

The Floating House
  written by Scott Russell Sanders
  illustrated by Helen Cogancherry   98

The Treaty of Greenville   108

Indiana's First Constitution   121

Log Cabin in the Woods
  by Joanne Landers Henry   134

Escape from Slavery
  by Doreen Rappaport   158

Morgan's Raid   171

When I Was Young in Indiana
  by Dorothy Strattan Hinshaw   196

*On the Banks of the Wabash,
Far Away*
  by Paul Dresser   222

The Star-Spangled Banner
  by Francis Scott Key   224

LEARNING FROM VISUALS

GEOGRAPHY SKILLS
How to Read a Map   24
How to Use Latitude and Longitude   36

How to Follow Routes on a
  Historical Map   77
How to Use a Map to Show
  Movement   133
How to Read Symbols on a
  Product Map   181
How to Use a Population Map   232

CHART AND GRAPH SKILLS
How to Read a Time Line   71
How to Read a Diagram   140
How to Use a Line Graph to
  See Change   147
How to Use a Pictograph   237
How to Follow a Flow Chart   251

BUILDING CITIZENSHIP

READING AND WRITING SKILLS
How to Read Social Studies   21
How to Tell Primary from
  Secondary Sources   170
How to Tell Fact from
  Opinion   195

THINKING SKILLS
How to Solve a Problem   52
How to Identify Cause and Effect   115
How to Understand Point of
  View   208

CITIZENSHIP SKILLS
How to Work Together in Groups   66
How to Compromise to Resolve
  Conflicts   123
How to Make Economic
  Choices   256

FEATURES

COUNTERPOINTS

Indian Land or United States Land?   116

What Is the Best Way to Use
Indiana's Resources?   242

MAKING SOCIAL STUDIES RELEVANT

License (Plate) to Save the
Environment   90

Conner Prairie   150

Hoosier Hysteria   214

In Peers We Trust: Teen Court   266

MAPS

The World: Political   A2

The World: Physical   A4

Western Hemisphere: Political   A6

Western Hemisphere: Physical   A7

United States: Overview   A8

United States: Political   A10

United States: Physical   A12

Indiana: Cities and Highways   A14

Indiana: Land and Water   A15

The United States   24

Indiana   25

Natural Regions of Indiana   35

Latitude and Longitude   36

Indiana Latitude and
Longitude   37

Major Indiana Rivers   39

Where? Indiana's Lost River   41

Growing Season in Indiana   43

Products and Resources of
Indiana   54

Routes of Early People   62

Where? Indiana Mounds   64

Native American Tribes in Indiana   70

Routes of La Salle, 1670–1682   77

The French and British in North
America, 1750   79

Pontiac's War   80

The Proclamation Line of 1763   81

Routes of Clark and Hamilton   84

The Tri-State Tornado, 1925   95

Townships and Sections, 1785   104

Indiana After 1800   110

Where? Prophetstown   111

Major Battles of the War
of 1812   114

Indiana Boundaries, 1800–1816   119

Settlement in Indiana, 1820s   133

Indiana Canals and Roads, 1860   146

Indiana Railroads, 1860   146

Routes to Indianapolis   155

Free African Rural Settlements,
Indiana, 1860   159

Underground Railroad in Indiana   165

The Union and the Confederacy   166

Indiana Products   181

Women's Suffrage in the United
States Before 1920   192

World War II Goods Made in
Indiana   219

Indiana Population   232

Major Corn and Soybean
Growing Regions   234

Indiana Counties   253

Population of the Middle West   271

The United States   R9

CHARTS, GRAPHS, DIAGRAMS, TABLES, AND TIME LINES

Geography Terms   A16

Indiana Within the Western
Hemisphere   26

Unit 1 Time Line   28

Monthly Precipitation in Indiana   44

Chapter 1 Graphic Organizer   58
A Miami Village   68
Miami Government   69
Time Line of Native American
    Settlement in Indiana   71
A French Fort   75
Chapter 2 Graphic Organizer   88
Unit 2 Time Line   96
Cause-and-Effect Chart   115
Chapter 3 Graphic Organizer   124
A Log Cabin   129
A Gristmill   140
Indiana Population, 1810–1850   147
Chapter 4 Graphic Organizer   148

Unit 3 Time Line   156
Number of Farms in Indiana,
    1850–1900   173
Chapter 5 Graphic Organizer   186
Chapter 6 Graphic Organizer   212
Indiana's Economy   234
Indiana Exports   236
Employment in Indiana   237
Chapter 7 Graphic Organizer   244
Branches of the Indiana State
    Government   249
How a Bill Becomes a Law   251
Structure of Unigov   254
Chapter 8 Graphic Organizer   264

ATLAS

CONTENTS

THE WORLD: POLITICAL   A2

THE WORLD: PHYSICAL   A4

WESTERN HEMISPHERE: POLITICAL   A6

WESTERN HEMISPHERE: PHYSICAL   A7

UNITED STATES: OVERVIEW   A8

UNITED STATES: POLITICAL   A10

UNITED STATES: PHYSICAL   A12

INDIANA: CITIES AND HIGHWAYS   A14

INDIANA: LAND AND WATER   A15

GEOGRAPHY TERMS   A16

180° 160°W 140°W 120°W 100°W 80°W 60°W

80°N

ARCTIC OCEAN

Greenland
(DENMARK)

60°N

ALASKA
(U.S.)

CANADA

**NORTH
AMERICA**

UNITED STATES

40°N

Azores
(PORTUGAL)

Bermuda
(U.K.)

Area of inset

*ATLANTIC
OCEAN*

MEXICO

CAPE VERDE

Tropic of Cancer

20°N

*Midway
Islands
(U.S.)*

HAWAII
(U.S.)

*PACIFIC
OCEAN*

VENEZUELA **GUYANA**
SURINAME

COLOMBIA   FRENCH GUIANA
(FRANCE)

Equator

*Galápagos
Islands
(ECUADOR)*

ECUADOR

BRAZIL

*Tokelau
(N.Z.)*   KIRIBATI

PERU

**SOUTH
AMERICA**

**WESTERN
SAMOA**

*American
Samoa
(U.S.)*

*Cook
Islands
(N.Z.)*

*French
Polynesia
(FRANCE)*

BOLIVIA

TONGA

Tropic of Capricorn

PARAGUAY

20°S

*Pitcairn
(U.K.)*

*Easter Island
(CHILE)*

CHILE

URUGUAY

*Niue
(N.Z.)*

ARGENTINA

40°S

*Falkland
Islands
(U.K.)*

*PACIFIC
OCEAN*

*South
Georgia
(U.K.)*

60°S

Antarctic Circle

80°S

180° 160°W 140°W 120°W 100°W 80°W 60°W

UNITED STATES

Gulf of Mexico

*ATLANTIC
OCEAN*

100°W

Tropic of Cancer

BAHAMAS

N

20°N

MEXICO

20°N

CUBA

*Turks and
Caicos (U.K.)*

W   E

S

Anguilla (U.K.)

*Puerto
Rico
(U.S.)*

HAITI **DOMINICAN
REPUBLIC**

St. Martin **(FRANCE AND NETH.)**

*Cayman
Islands
(U.K.)*

JAMAICA

*Virgin Islands
(U.S. AND U.K.)*

ANTIGUA AND BARBUDA
Montserrat (U.K.)

BELIZE

**ST. KITTS
AND NEVIS**

Guadeloupe **(FRANCE)**

DOMINICA

Caribbean Sea

Martinique **(FRANCE)**

GUATEMALA **HONDURAS**

ST. LUCIA

BARBADOS

EL SALVADOR

NICARAGUA

*Aruba
(NETH.)*

*Netherlands
Antilles
(NETH.)*

**ST. VINCENT AND
THE GRENADINES**

PACIFIC OCEAN

GRENADA

**TRINIDAD AND
TOBAGO**

10°N

A2

0   200   400 Miles

**COSTA
RICA**

PANAMA

VENEZUELA

GUYANA

0   200   400 Kilometers
Azimuthal Equal-Area Projection

*Panama
Canal*

10°N

90°W

80°W

70°W

60°W

COLOMBIA

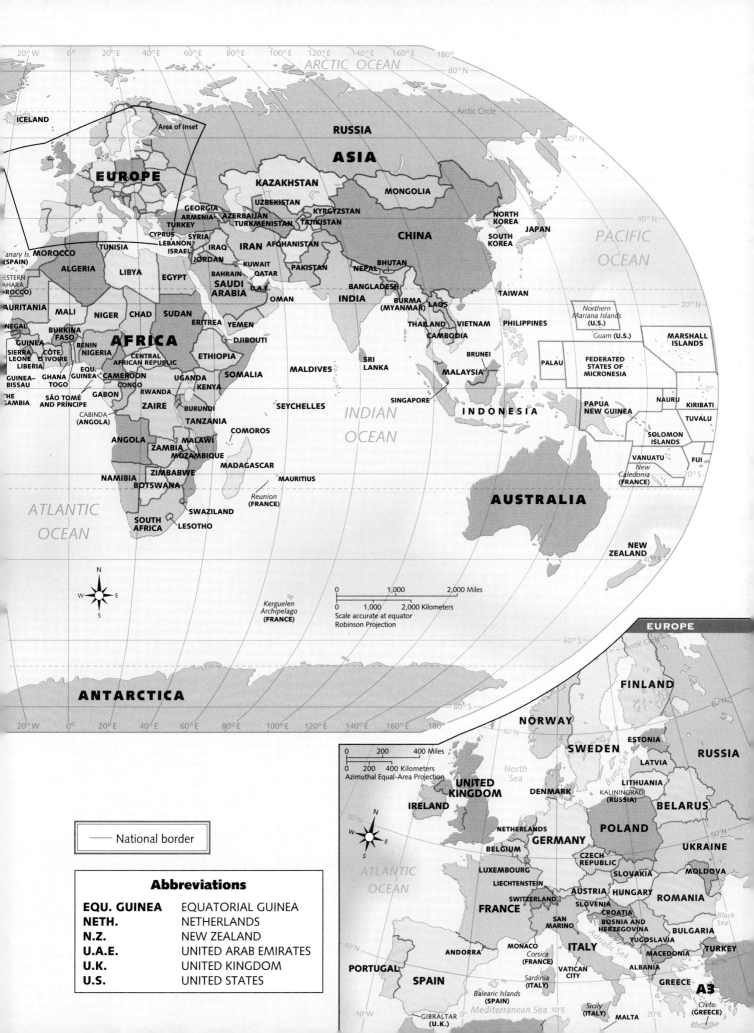

20°W 0° 20°E 40°E 60°E 80°E 100°E 120°E 140°E 160°E 180°

ARCTIC OCEAN

80°N

Arctic Circle

ICELAND

Area of Inset

RUSSIA

ASIA

60°N

EUROPE

KAZAKHSTAN

MONGOLIA

40°N

NORTH KOREA

JAPAN

PACIFIC OCEAN

GEORGIA
ARMENIA AZERBAIJAN KYRGYZSTAN
TURKEY TURKMENISTAN TAJIKISTAN
CYPRUS SYRIA
LEBANON IRAQ IRAN AFGHANISTAN
ISRAEL JORDAN
Canary Is. MOROCCO TUNISIA
(SPAIN)

CHINA

SOUTH KOREA

ESTERN
AHARA
ROCCO)

ALGERIA LIBYA EGYPT

KUWAIT
BAHRAIN QATAR
SAUDI U.A.E.
ARABIA OMAN

PAKISTAN

NEPAL BHUTAN

TAIWAN

20°N

AURITANIA

MALI NIGER CHAD SUDAN

ERITREA YEMEN

INDIA

BANGLADESH

BURMA
(MYANMAR) LAOS

NEGAL
GUINEA
SIERRA
LEONE
LIBERIA

BURKINA
FASO
CÔTE
D'IVOIRE BENIN
NIGERIA

AFRICA

CENTRAL
AFRICAN REPUBLIC

DJIBOUTI

ETHIOPIA

SRI
LANKA

MALDIVES

THAILAND VIETNAM PHILIPPINES

CAMBODIA

Northern
Mariana Islands
(U.S.)

Guam (U.S.)

MARSHALL
ISLANDS

PALAU

FEDERATED
STATES OF
MICRONESIA

GHANA
GUINEA–
BISSAU TOGO
THE
GAMBIA SÃO TOMÉ
AND PRÍNCIPE

EQU.
GUINEA CAMEROON
GABON CONGO

UGANDA
SOMALIA
KENYA

RWANDA

BRUNEI

MALAYSIA

SINGAPORE

NAURU

PAPUA
NEW GUINEA

KIRIBATI

TUVALU

CABINDA
(ANGOLA)

ZAIRE

BURUNDI

TANZANIA

SEYCHELLES

INDIAN

INDONESIA

SOLOMON
ISLANDS

ANGOLA

COMOROS

MALAWI
ZAMBIA
MOZAMBIQUE

OCEAN

VANUATU

FIJI

New
Caledonia
(FRANCE)

20°S

NAMIBIA
BOTSWANA ZIMBABWE

MADAGASCAR

MAURITIUS

AUSTRALIA

ATLANTIC
OCEAN

SOUTH
AFRICA SWAZILAND
LESOTHO

Reunion
(FRANCE)

NEW
ZEALAND

40°S

N
W E
S

0 1,000 2,000 Miles

0 1,000 2,000 Kilometers

Scale accurate at equator
Robinson Projection

Kerguelen
Archipelago
(FRANCE)

60°S

EUROPE

ANTARCTICA

80°S

Arctic Circle

FINLAND

20°W 0° 20°E 40°E 60°E 80°E 100°E 120°E 140°E 160°E 180°

NORWAY

60°N

SWEDEN

ESTONIA

RUSSIA

0 200 400 Miles

0 200 400 Kilometers
Azimuthal Equal-Area Projection

North
Sea

LATVIA

LITHUANIA
KALININGRAD
(RUSSIA)

UNITED
KINGDOM

DENMARK

Baltic Sea

BELARUS

IRELAND

NETHERLANDS
BELGIUM

GERMANY

POLAND

50°N

UKRAINE

LUXEMBOURG

CZECH
REPUBLIC

SLOVAKIA

MOLDOVA

50°N

LIECHTENSTEIN

AUSTRIA HUNGARY

ROMANIA

SWITZERLAND
SLOVENIA

FRANCE

SAN
MARINO

CROATIA
BOSNIA AND
HERZEGOVINA

Black
Sea

BULGARIA

National border

ATLANTIC
OCEAN

N
W E
S

YUGOSLAVIA

MACEDONIA

TURKEY

Abbreviations

EQU. GUINEA	EQUATORIAL GUINEA
NETH.	NETHERLANDS
N.Z.	NEW ZEALAND
U.A.E.	UNITED ARAB EMIRATES
U.K.	UNITED KINGDOM
U.S.	UNITED STATES

40°N

ANDORRA

MONACO
Corsica
(FRANCE)

ITALY

ALBANIA

GREECE

A3

PORTUGAL

SPAIN

VATICAN
CITY

Sardinia
(ITALY)

Adriatic Sea

Balearic Islands
(SPAIN)

Mediterranean Sea 10°E

Sicily
(ITALY)

Crete
(GREECE)

GIBRALTAR
(U.K.)

MALTA

20°E

THE WORLD: PHYSICAL

180° 160° W 140° W 120° W 100° W 80° W 60°

80° N ARCTIC OCEAN

Beaufort Sea

Queen Elizabeth Islands

Greenland

Baffin Island

Great Bear Lake

Mt. McKinley 20,320 ft. (6,194 m)

Mackenzie

Great Slave Lake

Hudson Bay

Bering Sea

Yukon R.

Mt. Logan 19,524 ft. (5,951 m)

NORTH AMERICA

ROCKY MOUNTAINS

Gulf of Alaska

Aleutian Islands

Vancouver Island

Columbia R.

GREAT PLAINS

Missouri R.

Great Lakes

Newfoundland

40° N

APPALACHIAN MTS.

Ohio R.

Azores

Mt. Whitney 14,494 ft. (4,418 m)

Colorado R.

Mississippi

Bermuda

ATLANTIC OCEAN

Gulf of Mexico

Bahamas

Tropic of Cancer

Hawaiian Islands

Yucatán Peninsula

Cuba

Hispaniola

West Indies

Cape Verde Islands

Citlaltepetl 18,701 ft. (5,700 m)

20° N

PACIFIC OCEAN

Caribbean Sea

Galápagos Islands

Orinoco River

Guiana Highlands

Equator

AMAZON

Amazon R.

Polynesia

BASIN

SOUTH AMERICA

ANDES MOUNTAINS

Brazilian Highlands

20° S

Gran Chaco

Paraná River

Atacama Desert

Tropic of Capricorn

Mt. Aconcagua 22,831 ft. (6,959 m)

Pampa

40° S

Patagonia

Falkland Islands

Strait of Magellan

Tierra del Fuego

Cape Horn

60° S

Antarctic Circle

Antarctic Peninsula

80° S

Ross Sea

180° 160° W 140° W 120° W 100° W 80° W 60° W

NORTHERN POLAR REGION

Sea of Okhotsk

ASIA

90° E

60° E

EUROPE

30° E

150° E

120° E

Kamchatka Peninsula

Novaya Zemlya

Severnaya Zemlya

Barents Sea

Baltic Sea

New Siberian Is.

70° N

400   800 Miles

400   800 Kilometers

Azimuthal Equidistant Projection

Norwegian Sea

North Sea

Wrangel Island

ARCTIC OCEAN

North Pole

Svalbard

Bering Sea

Bering Strait

British Isles

BROOKS RANGE

80° N

Iceland

Beaufort Sea

North Magnetic Pole

Queen Elizabeth Islands

Greenland

ATLANTIC OCEAN

Baffin Bay

Arctic Circle

30° W

60° W

A4

NORTH AMERICA

150° W

180°

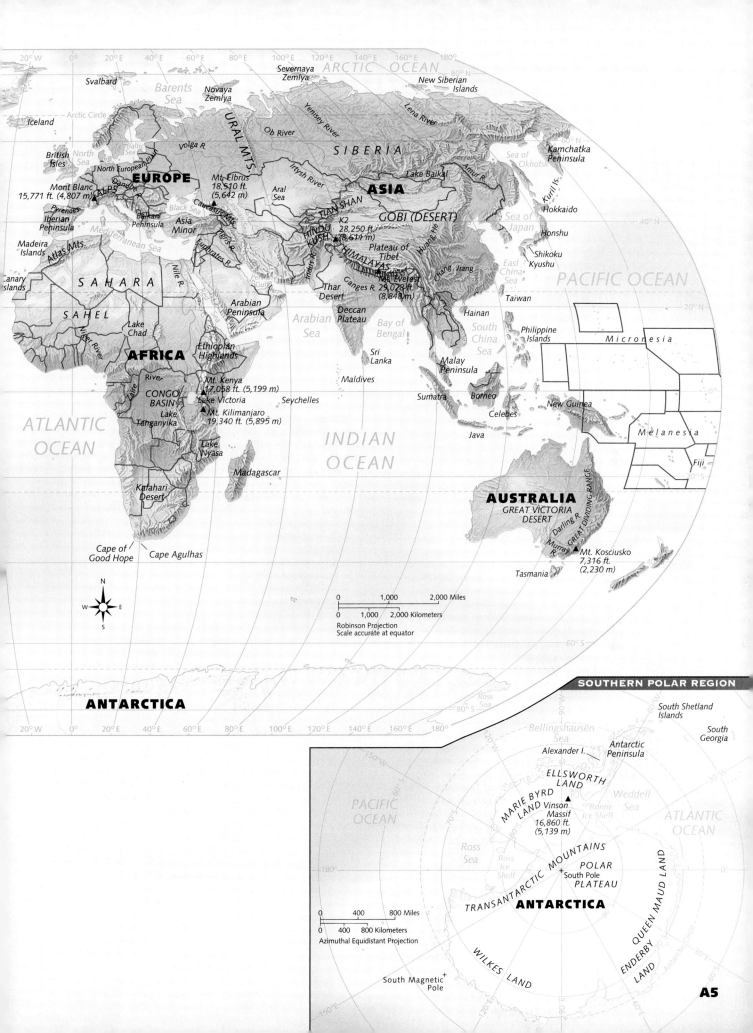

20°W 0° 20°E 40°E 60°E 80°E 100°E 120°E 140°E 160°E 180°

ARCTIC OCEAN

Svalbard

Severnaya Zemlya

Novaya Zemlya

New Siberian Islands

Barents Sea

80°N

Iceland

Arctic Circle

Yenisey River

Lena River

Kamchatka Peninsula

60°N

British Isles

North Sea

Baltic Sea

North European Plain

Ob River

SIBERIA

Sea of Okhotsk

EUROPE

URAL MTS.

Mt. Elbrus
18,510 ft.
(5,642 m) ▲

Irtysh River

Amur R.

Kuril Is.

Mont Blanc
15,771 ft. (4,807 m) ▲

Danube R.

ALPS

Aral Sea

Lake Baikal

ASIA

Hokkaido

Sea of Japan

40°N

Pyrenees

Balkan Peninsula

Black Sea

Caucasus Mts.

TIAN SHAN

GOBI (DESERT)

Honshu

Iberian Peninsula

Asia Minor

HINDU KUSH

K2
28,250 ft.
(8,611 m) ▲

Huang He

Shikoku

Kyushu

Madeira Islands

Atlas Mts.

Mediterranean Sea

Tigris R.

Euphrates R.

Plateau of Tibet

HIMALAYAS

Chang Jiang

East China Sea

PACIFIC OCEAN

Canary Islands

SAHARA

Nile R.

Persian Gulf

Indus R.

Mt. Everest 29,028 ft. (8,848 m) ▲

Thar Desert

Ganges R.

Taiwan

20°N

SAHEL

Arabian Peninsula

Arabian Sea

Deccan Plateau

Bay of Bengal

Hainan

Niger River

Lake Chad

Red Sea

South China Sea

AFRICA

Ethiopian Highlands

Sri Lanka

Philippine Islands

Micronesia

0°

Zaire River

Mt. Kenya
17,058 ft. (5,199 m) ▲

Maldives

Malay Peninsula

CONGO BASIN

Lake Victoria

Seychelles

Sumatra

Borneo

New Guinea

Lake Tanganyika

▲ Mt. Kilimanjaro
19,340 ft. (5,895 m)

Celebes

Melanesia

Lake Nyasa

INDIAN OCEAN

Java

20°S

ATLANTIC OCEAN

Madagascar

Fiji

Kalahari Desert

AUSTRALIA

GREAT VICTORIA DESERT

GREAT DIVIDING RANGE

Cape of Good Hope Cape Agulhas

Darling R.

Murray R.

▲ Mt. Kosciusko
7,316 ft. (2,230 m)

40°S

N
W E
S

Tasmania

0 1,000 2,000 Miles

0 1,000 2,000 Kilometers

Robinson Projection
Scale accurate at equator

ANTARCTICA

Ross Sea

60°S

20°W 0° 20°E 40°E 60°E 80°E 100°E 120°E 140°E 160°E 180°

South Shetland Islands

80°S

Bellingshausen Sea

Alexander I.

Antarctic Peninsula

South Georgia

PACIFIC OCEAN

ELLSWORTH LAND

MARIE BYRD LAND

Vinson Massif
16,860 ft. (5,139 m) ▲

Ronne Ice Shelf

Weddell Sea

ATLANTIC OCEAN

Ross Sea

Ross Ice Shelf

TRANSANTARCTIC MOUNTAINS

POLAR PLATEAU
+ South Pole

QUEEN MAUD LAND

ANTARCTICA

WILKES LAND

ENDERBY LAND

0 400 800 Miles

0 400 800 Kilometers

Azimuthal Equidistant Projection

South Magnetic Pole +

Antarctic Circle

A5

ARCTIC OCEAN

Beaufort Sea

Bering Strait

Viscount Melville Sound

Baffin Bay

Greenland
(DENMARK)

ALASKA
(U.S.)

Fairbanks

Anchorage

Whitehorse

Juneau

Great Bear Lake

Mackenzie River

Foxe Basin

Davis Strait

Arctic Circle

Bering Sea

Gulf of Alaska

Yukon River

Liard River

Yellowknife

Great Slave Lake

CANADA

Lake Athabasca

Hudson Strait

Hudson Bay

Labrador Sea

Edmonton

Calgary

Vancouver

Seattle

Portland

Puget Sound

Boise

Salt Lake City

Great Salt Lake

Reno

San Francisco

Las Vegas

Los Angeles

San Diego

Tucson

Hermosillo

Phoenix

El Paso

Saskatoon

Regina

Winnipeg

Lake Winnipeg

Saskatchewan R.

Peace River

Athabasca R.

UNITED STATES

Columbia R.

Snake R.

Colorado R.

Denver

St. Louis

Memphis

Dallas

Houston

San Antonio

New Orleans

Rio Grande

Missouri R.

Chicago

Indianapolis

Thunder Bay

Great Lakes

Detroit

Cleveland

Ottawa

Toronto

Albany

Quebec

Montreal

St. John

St. Lawrence River

St. John's

Boston

Halifax

Gulf of St. Lawrence

New York City

Philadelphia

Washington, D.C.

Richmond

Norfolk

Raleigh

Atlanta

Charleston

Savannah

Jacksonville

Tampa

Miami

ATLANTIC OCEAN

Honolulu

HAWAII
(U.S.)

PACIFIC OCEAN

Tropic of Cancer

Chihuahua

MEXICO

Durango

León

Guadalajara

Acapulco

Puebla

Mexico City

Monterrey

Tampico

Veracruz

Gulf of Mexico

BAHAMAS

Nassau

Havana

CUBA

JAMAICA

Kingston

BELIZE

Belmopan

GUATEMALA

Guatemala

HONDURAS

Tegucigalpa

San Salvador

EL SALVADOR

Managua

NICARAGUA

COSTA RICA

San José

PANAMA

Panama City

HAITI

Port-au-Prince

Santo Domingo

PUERTO RICO (U.S.)

DOMINICAN REPUBLIC

Caribbean Sea

Maracaibo

Caracas

VENEZUELA

GUYANA

SURINAME

Georgetown

Paramaribo

Cayenne

FRENCH GUIANA (FRANCE)

Medellín

Cali

Bogotá

COLOMBIA

Equator

Galápagos Islands
(ECUADOR)

Quito

Guayaquil

ECUADOR

Iquitos

Trujillo

PERU

Lima

Cuzco

Manaus

Belém

Fortaleza

Recife

Amazon R.

Rio Negro

Negro R.

Tapajos R.

Xingu R.

Tocantins

São Francisco R.

BRAZIL

Brasília

Goiânia

Salvador

Belo Horizonte

FRENCH POLYNESIA
(FRANCE)

Papeete

Lake Titicaca

La Paz

BOLIVIA

Arequipa

Sucre

Campo Grande

Rio de Janeiro

Tropic of Capricorn

Antofagasta

PARAGUAY

Asunción

São Paulo

Curitiba

Salta

San Miguel de Tucumán

CHILE

Paraná R.

Córdoba

Rosario

Pôrto Alegre

URUGUAY

Valparaíso

Santiago

Buenos Aires

La Plata

Montevideo

Rio de la Plata

Concepción

Mar del Plata

Bahía Blanca

Valdivia

ARGENTINA

0   1,000   2,000 Miles

0   1,000   2,000 Kilometers

Miller Cylindrical Projection

—— National border

⊛ National capital

• City

Falkland Islands
(U.K.)

South Georgia
(U.K.)

Punta Arenas

N
W   E
S

A6

150° W   120° W   90° W   60° W   30° W

60° N

30° N

0°

30° S

ATLAS

WESTERN HEMISPHERE: PHYSICAL

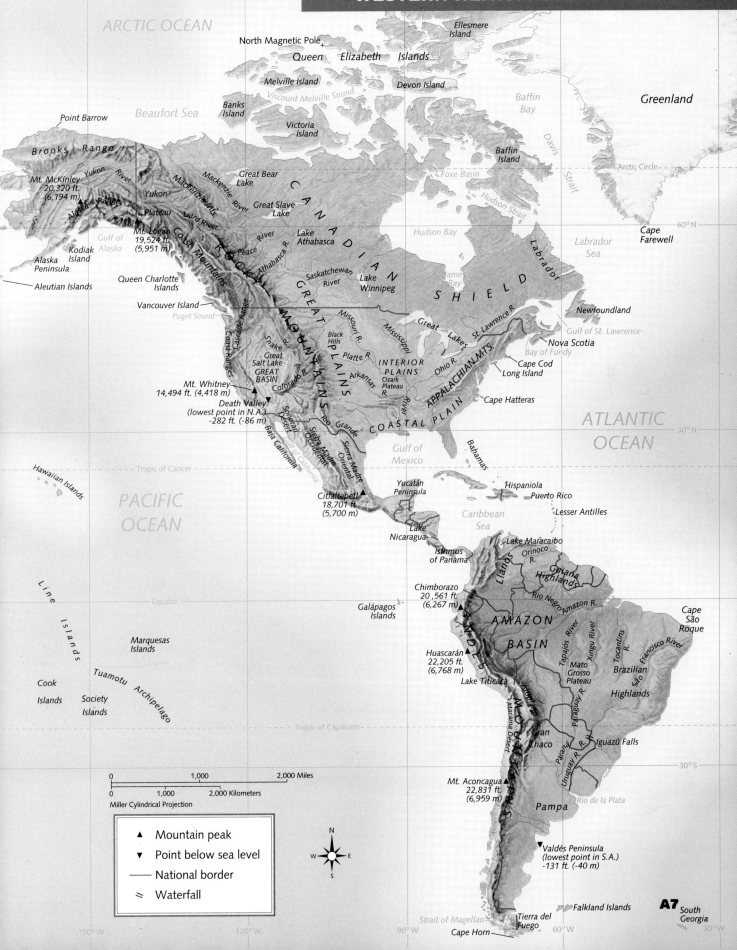

A7 South Georgia

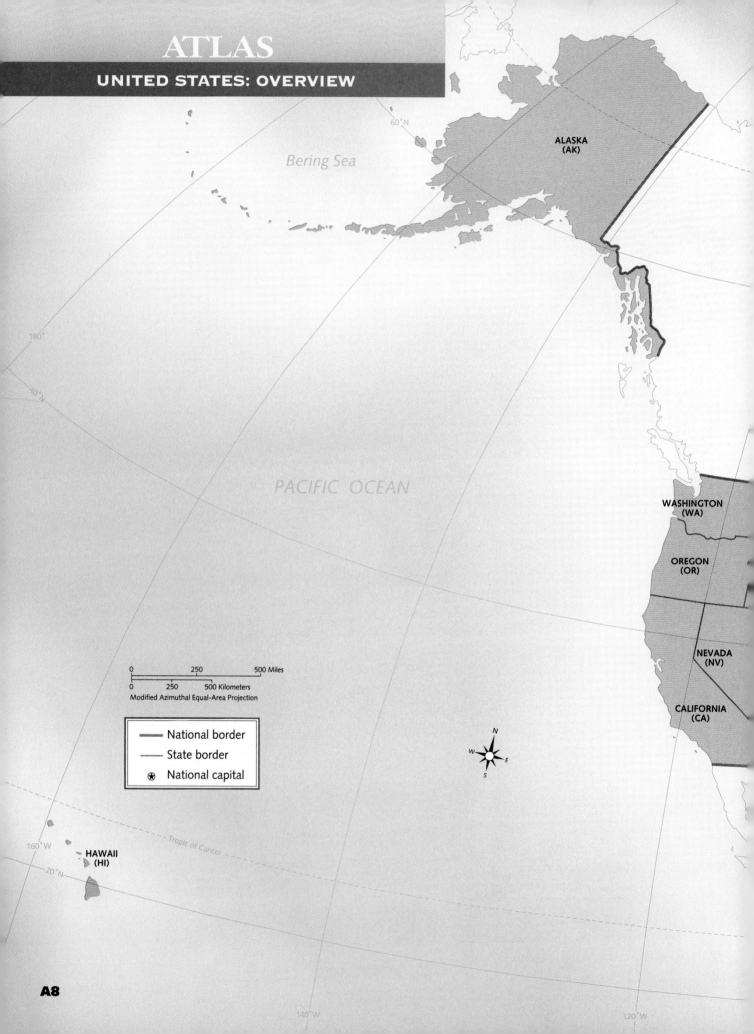

ALASKA
(AK)

Bering Sea

60°N

180°

40°N

PACIFIC OCEAN

WASHINGTON
(WA)

OREGON
(OR)

NEVADA
(NV)

CALIFORNIA
(CA)

0   250   500 Miles
0 250 500 Kilometers
Modified Azimuthal Equal-Area Projection

——— National border
——— State border
⊛ National capital

N
W   E
S

160°W

Tropic of Cancer

HAWAII
(HI)

20°N

140°W

120°W

CANADA

RUSSIA

ARCTIC OCEAN

70°N

170°E

ALASKA

Arctic Circle

120°W

CANADA

60°N

Fairbanks

*Bering
Sea*

Anchorage

180°

60°N

Juneau★

250   500 Miles

0   250   500 Kilometers

50°N

*PACIFIC
OCEAN*

170°W   160°W   150°W   140°W   130°W

120°W   110°W

Seattle
Tacoma
Olympia★   Spokane
WASHINGTON

Portland   *Columbia River*
★Salem

Eugene

OREGON

Great Falls

Helena★ **MONTANA**

Billings

IDAHO

★Boise

40°N

Snake River

Pocatello

WYOMING

Casper

NEVADA

Reno

Sacramento★   Carson City

San Francisco   Oakland
San Jose

*Great
Salt
Lake*

Ogden

Salt Lake City★

Provo

UTAH

Cheyen

Denv

Colorado River

Colora
Sprir

COLORADO

Puel

Fresno

CALIFORNIA

Las
Vegas

*PACIFIC
OCEAN*

Bakersfield

30°N

Flagstaff

Santa Fe

Los Angeles

San Bernardino

ARIZONA

Albuquerque

★Phoenix

NEW MEXICO

San Diego

Roswel

130°W

Tucson

	Northeast	⊛	National capital
	Southeast	★	State capital
	Middle West	•	Major city
	Southwest	—	National border
	West	—	State border

El Paso

Rio Grande

MEXICO

N
W ⊕ E
S

160°W   *PACIFIC
OCEAN* 155°W

Honolulu★

HAWAII

20°N

Hilo

0   125   250 Miles

0   125   250 Kilometers

0   250   500 Miles

0   250   500 Kilometers
Albers Equal-Area Projection

20°N

120°W

110°W

CANADA

MAINE
★ Augusta

VERMONT
Burlington • Portland
Montpelier **NEW**
HAMPSHIRE
NEW ★ Concord
YORK Manchester • Boston
Syracuse Worcester ★ **MASSACHUSETTS**
• Rochester Albany ● Providence
Hartford **RHODE ISLAND**
Buffalo **CONNECTICUT**
Bridgeport
Newark ● New York City

Trenton
PENNSYLVANIA ★ **NEW JERSEY**
Harrisburg Philadelphia
• Pittsburgh ● Wilmington
Baltimore **DELAWARE**
Annapolis ● Dover
Washington, **MARYLAND**
D.C.

NORTH DAKOTA Grand Forks
★ Bismarck Fargo •

Duluth

MINNESOTA

Sault Sainte Marie •

Lake Superior

MICHIGAN

Lake Huron

SOUTH DAKOTA
St. Paul
Rapid City Pierre ★ Minneapolis ★
Sioux Falls

WISCONSIN
Green Bay
Madison
Milwaukee
Rockford
Chicago

Grand Rapids
Lansing • Flint

Lake Michigan

Detroit

Lake Erie

Cleveland •
Toledo
Akron •

OHIO
Columbus ★
Wheeling
Dayton •
Cincinnati

WEST VIRGINIA
Charleston ●

NEBRASKA
Omaha •
Lincoln ★

Sioux City

IOWA
Cedar Rapids •
Davenport
Des Moines ★

ILLINOIS
Peoria •
Decatur •
Springfield ★

Gary

South Bend

INDIANA
Indianapolis ★

Louisville •

KENTUCKY
Frankfort ★
Lexington •

Evansville •

VIRGINIA
Richmond ★
Newport News
Norfolk
Roanoke •

KANSAS
Topeka ★
Kansas City
Wichita •

Missouri River

Jefferson City ★
MISSOURI
Springfield •

St. Louis

OKLAHOMA
Amarillo • Oklahoma City ★
Tulsa •

ARKANSAS
Fort Smith
Little Rock ★

Memphis •

TENNESSEE
Nashville ★
Chattanooga

Knoxville •

Tennessee River

Winston Salem •
Greensboro •
Raleigh ★
Charlotte •

NORTH CAROLINA

SOUTH CAROLINA
Columbia ★

Charleston

Lubbock •

Fort Worth
Abilene •
Odessa •
Dallas •

Red River

MISSISSIPPI
Meridian •
Jackson ★

Huntsville •
Birmingham •

ALABAMA
Montgomery ★

GEORGIA
Atlanta ★
Macon •
Columbus •

Savannah

Charleston •

TEXAS
Austin ★
San Antonio •

Houston •
Beaumont •

LOUISIANA
Shreveport •
Baton Rouge ★
New Orleans •

Biloxi •
Mobile •

Tallahassee ★

Jacksonville •

FLORIDA
Orlando •
St. Petersburg • Tampa •
Lake Okeechobee

West Palm Beach

Miami •

Laredo •
Corpus Christi •

Gulf of Mexico

ATLANTIC OCEAN

BAHAMAS

CUBA

Mississippi River
Missouri River
Platte River
Arkansas River

100°W   90°W   80°W   70°W
50°N
40°N
30°N
70°W
80°W
90°W
100°W

A11

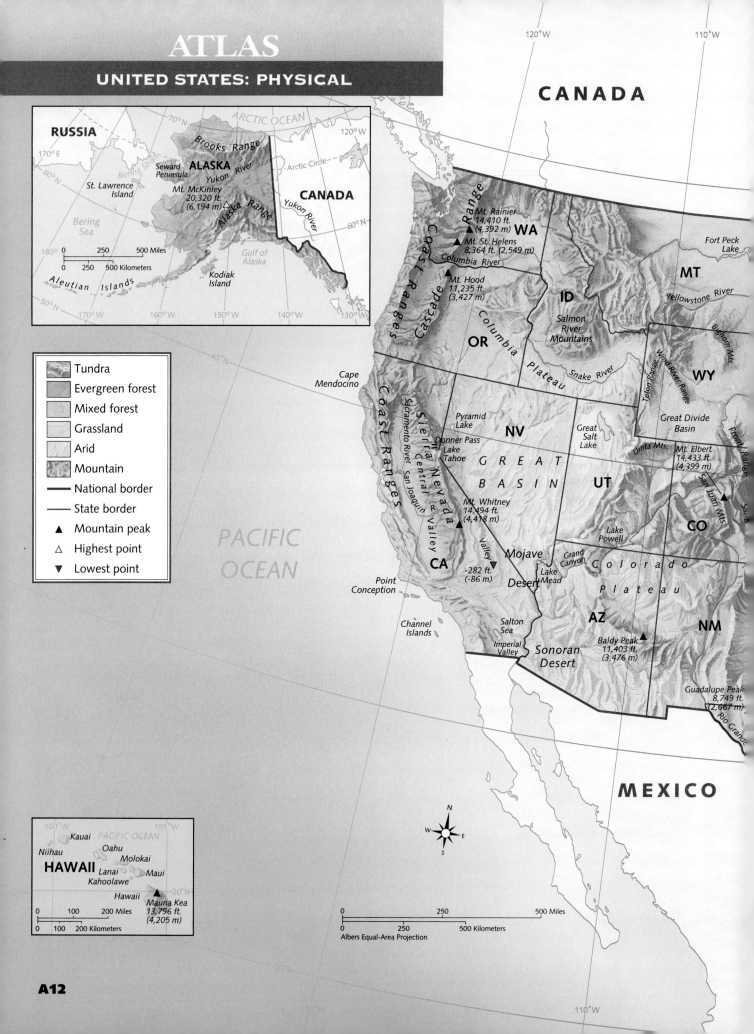

ATLAS

UNITED STATES: PHYSICAL

RUSSIA

ARCTIC OCEAN

Brooks Range

ALASKA

Seward Peninsula

Yukon River

Arctic Circle

70°N

120°W

CANADA

St. Lawrence Island

Mt. McKinley 20,320 ft. (6,194 m)

Alaska Range

Yukon River

60°N

Bering Sea

170°E

60°N

Gulf of Alaska

Aleutian Islands

Kodiak Island

0   250   500 Miles
0   250   500 Kilometers

180°   170°W   160°W   150°W   140°W   130°W   50°N

CANADA

120°W

110°W

Legend

- Tundra
- Evergreen forest
- Mixed forest
- Grassland
- Arid
- Mountain
- National border
- State border
- ▲ Mountain peak
- △ Highest point
- ▼ Lowest point

PACIFIC OCEAN

40°N

Cape Mendocino

Coast Ranges

Cascade Range

Columbia River

Mt. Rainier 14,410 ft. (4,392 m) ▲

Mt. St. Helens 8,364 ft. (2,549 m) ▲

WA

Fort Peck Lake

MT

Yellowstone River

Bighorn Mts.

Mt. Hood 11,235 ft. (3,427 m) ▲

Columbia Plateau

ID

Salmon River Mountains

Snake River

Teton Range

Wind River Range

WY

Great Divide Basin

Front Range

Pyramid Lake

Donner Pass

Lake Tahoe

Sierra Nevada

Sacramento River

Central Valley

San Joaquin R.

NV

G R E A T

B A S I N

Great Salt Lake

Uinta Mts.

Mt. Elbert 14,433 ft. (4,399 m) ▲

San Juan Mts.

Mt. Whitney 14,494 ft. (4,418 m) ▲

UT

Lake Powell

CO

CA

Valley

-282 ft. (-86 m) ▼

Mojave Desert

Grand Canyon

Lake Mead

Colorado Plateau

Point Conception

Channel Islands

Salton Sea

Imperial Valley

Sonoran Desert

AZ

Baldy Peak 11,403 ft. (3,476 m) ▲

NM

Guadalupe Peak 8,749 ft. (2,667 m)

Rio Grande

MEXICO

N
W   E
S

HAWAII

160°W   155°W   PACIFIC OCEAN

Kauai

Niihau

Oahu

Molokai

Lanai   Maui

Kahoolawe

Hawaii   Mauna Kea 13,796 ft. (4,205 m) ▲   20°N

0   100   200 Miles
0   100   200 Kilometers

0   250   500 Miles
0   250   500 Kilometers

Albers Equal-Area Projection

110°W

A12

CANADA

100°W   90°W   80°W   70°W

50°N

ME
▲ Mt. Katahdin
5,267 ft.
(1,605 m)

Lake of
the Woods

Isle
Royale

Lake
Superior

Keweenaw
Peninsula

St. Lawrence River

Lake
Champlain

VT
Green Mts.
White Mts.
▲ Mt. Washington
6,288 ft.
(1,917 m)

NH
Cape Ann
Cape
Cod

ND

Upper
Red Lake

Lower
Red Lake

Leech
Lake

Mille
Lacs
Lake

Mesabi
Range

Upper Peninsula

MN

WI

Wisconsin River

Lake
Winnebago

Lake Michigan

Upper Peninsula

Lower Peninsula

MI

Lake
St. Clair

Lake Huron

NY

Adirondack
Mountains

Finger
Lakes

Hudson R.

MA

Connecticut R.

CT

RI

Lake Ontario

Niagara
Falls

Lake Erie

PA

Long
Island

40°N

G
R
E
A
T

P
L
A
I
N
S

Lake
Oahe

SD

Black
Hills

Missouri River

IA

INTERIOR

PLAINS

NE

Sand Hills

North Platte R.

South Platte R.

Platte River

IL

Illinois River

Wabash River

IN

OH

Ohio River

WV

Allegheny Mts.

A
P
P
A
L
A
C
H
I
A
N

M
O
U
N
T
A
I
N
S

Potomac R.

MD

DE

Delaware
Bay

VA

Cape
Charles

Chesapeake
Bay

70°W

KS

Smoky Hills

Red Hills

MO

Missouri River

Lake of
the Ozarks

Harry S. Truman
Reservoir

Ozark Plateau

CENTRAL PLAINS

KY

Cumberland
Gap

Lake
Barkley

Cumberland R.

TN

▲ Mt. Mitchell
6,684 ft.
(2,037 m)

James R.

Roanoke R.

NC

Cape Fear River

P
I
E
D
M
O
N
T

Cape
Hatteras

OK

Canadian
River

Arkansas River

Ouachita
Mountains

AR

Red River

Mississippi River

Tennessee R.

Savannah River

SC

Oconee R.

Cape
Fear

Llano
Estacado

Pecos River

TX

Edwards
Plateau

Colorado River

Brazos River

Sabine River

Toledo
Bend
Reservoir

Sam
Rayburn
Reservoir

LA

Lake
Pontchartrain

Galveston
Bay

MS

Tombigbee R.

Alabama R.

AL

Chattahoochee R.

Stone
Mountain ▲

GA

Ocmulgee R.

Altamaha R.

Okefenokee
Swamp

C
O
A
S
T
A
L

P
L
A
I
N

St. Johns River

Cape
Canaveral

FL

ATLANTIC
OCEAN

Albemarle
Sound

BAHAMAS

Gulf of Mexico

Mobile
Bay

Mississippi
Delta

Tampa
Bay

Lake
Okeechobee

Everglades

Cape
Sable

Florida Keys

Straits of Florida

80°W

CUBA

100°W   90°W

30°N

ATLAS

INDIANA: CITIES AND HIGHWAYS

A14

Legend:
- State border
- ★ State capital
- • Other city
- Interstate highway
- U.S. highway
- State highway

Albers Equal-Area Projection

0   50   100 Miles
0   50   100 Kilometers

1. ~~capital~~

2. ~~Ohio Wabash 2 others~~

3. ~~Valparaiso~~

4. ~~Lake Michigan~~

5. ~~cities~~

6. ~~key~~

7. 4 border states

8. compass

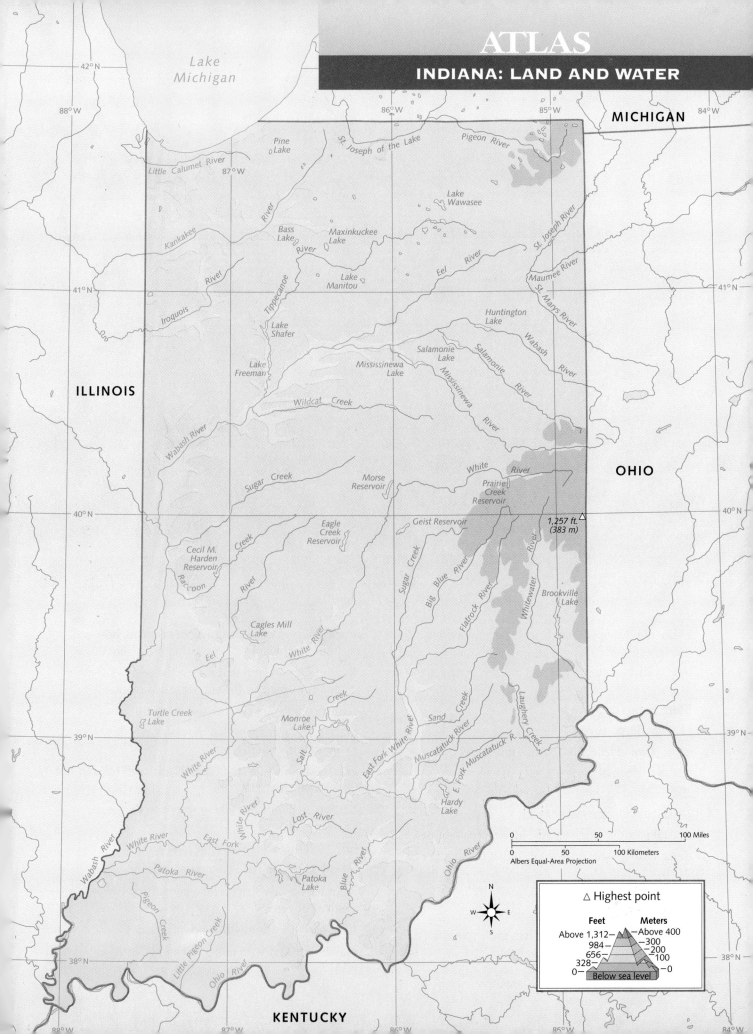

Lake Michigan

42° N

88° W

MICHIGAN

86° W

85° W

84° W

Pine Lake

Little Calumet River

87° W

St. Joseph of the Lake

Pigeon River

Lake Wawasee

Kankakee River

Bass Lake

Maxinkuckee Lake

Eel River

St. Joseph River

Maumee River

41° N

41° N

Tippecanoe River

Lake Manitou

Lake Shafer

Huntington Lake

St. Marys River

Wabash River

Iroquois River

Salamonie Lake

Salamonie River

ILLINOIS

Lake Freeman

Mississinewa Lake

Mississinewa River

Wildcat Creek

Wabash River

OHIO

Sugar Creek

White River

Morse Reservoir

Prairie Creek Reservoir

1,257 ft. △
(383 m)

40° N

Geist Reservoir

40° N

Eagle Creek Reservoir

Creek

Cecil M. Harden Reservoir

Sugar Creek

Big Blue River

Raccoon

River

Flatrock River

Whitewater River

Brookville Lake

Cagles Mill Lake

White River

Eel

Creek

Laughery Creek

Turtle Creek Lake

Monroe Lake

Sand Creek

39° N

White River

Salt Creek

East Fork White River

Muscatatuck River

E. Fork Muscatatuck R.

39° N

Hardy Lake

White River

East Fork

Lost River

Blue River

Ohio River

0   50   100 Miles

Wabash River

White River

Patoka River

0   50   100 Kilometers

Albers Equal-Area Projection

Patoka Lake

N
W   E
S

Pigeon Creek

Little Pigeon Creek

Ohio River

△ Highest point

Feet   Meters
Above 1,312 ──   ── Above 400
984 ──   ── 300
656 ──   ── 200
328 ──   ── 100
0 ──   ── 0
Below sea level

KENTUCKY

38° N

88° W

86° W

84° W

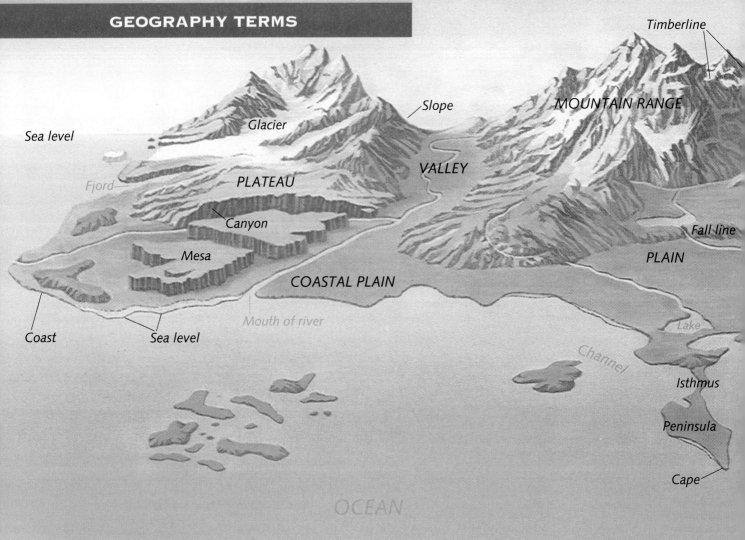

Timberline

Sea level

Slope

MOUNTAIN RANGE

Glacier

VALLEY

Fjord

PLATEAU

Canyon

Fall line

Mesa

PLAIN

COASTAL PLAIN

Coast

Mouth of river

Lake

Sea level

Channel

Isthmus

Peninsula

Cape

OCEAN

basin bowl-shaped area of land surrounded by higher land

bay body of water that is part of a sea or ocean and is partly enclosed by land

bluff high, steep face of rock or earth

canyon deep, narrow valley with steep sides

cape point of land that extends into water

channel deepest part of a body of water

cliff high, steep face of rock or earth

coast land along a sea or ocean

coastal plain area of flat land along a sea or ocean

delta triangle-shaped area of land at the mouth of a river

desert dry land with few plants

dune hill of sand piled up by the wind

fall line area along which rivers form waterfalls or rapids as the rivers drop to lower land

fjord deep, narrow part of a sea or ocean, between high, steep banks

floodplain flat land that is near the edges of a river and is formed by the silt deposited by floods

foothills hilly area at the base of a mountain

glacier large ice mass that moves slowly down a mountain or across land

gulf body of water that is partly enclosed by land but is larger than a bay

harbor area of water where ships can dock safely near land

hill land that rises above the land around it

island land that has water on all sides

isthmus narrow strip of land connecting two larger areas of land

lake body of water with land on all sides

marsh lowland with moist soil and tall grasses

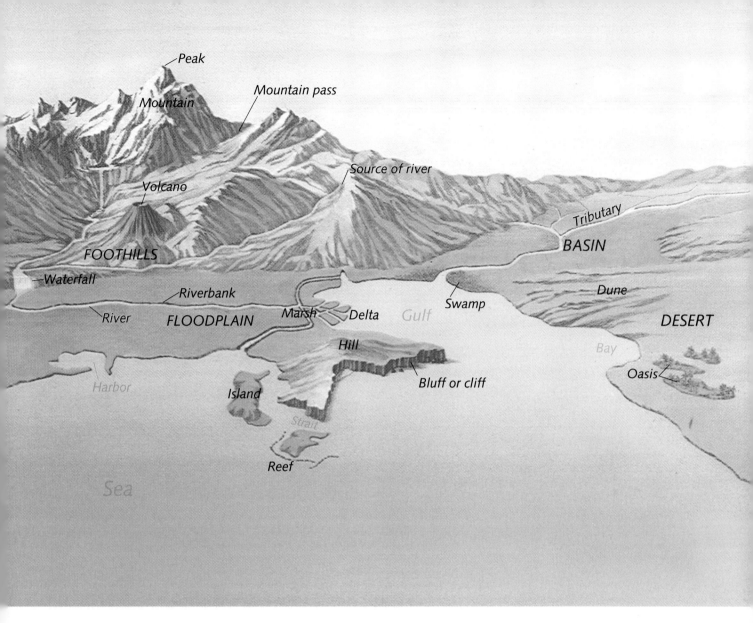

Labels on illustration: Peak · Mountain · Mountain pass · Source of river · Tributary · Volcano · BASIN · FOOTHILLS · Waterfall · Riverbank · Dune · Swamp · River · FLOODPLAIN · Marsh · Delta · Gulf · DESERT · Hill · Bay · Harbor · Island · Bluff or cliff · Oasis · Strait · Reef · Sea

mesa flat-topped mountain with steep sides

mountain highest kind of land

mountain pass gap between mountains

mountain range row of mountains

mouth of river place where a river empties into another body of water

oasis area of water and fertile land in a desert

ocean body of salt water larger than a sea

peak top of a mountain

peninsula land that is almost completely surrounded by water

plain flat land

plateau area of high, flat land with steep sides

reef ridge of sand, rock, or coral that lies at or near the surface of a sea or ocean

river large stream of water that flows across the land

riverbank land along a river

sea body of salt water smaller than an ocean

sea level the level that is even with the surface of an ocean or sea

slope side of a hill or mountain

source of river place where a river begins

strait narrow channel of water connecting two larger bodies of water

swamp area of low, wet land with trees

timberline line on a mountain above which it is too cold for trees to grow

tributary stream or river that empties into a larger river

valley low land between hills or mountains

volcano opening in the Earth, often raised, through which lava, rock, ashes, and gases are forced out

waterfall steep drop from a high place to a lower place in a stream or river

A17

Why Study INDIANA?

66 The origin of the term 'Hoosier' is not known with certainty. But it is certain that . . . Hoosiers bear the nickname proudly. 99

Meredith Nicholson,
Indiana writer,
1866–1947

THE POWERFUL IDEAS OF SOCIAL STUDIES

The members of Indiana's General Assembly are citizens chosen by citizens to make laws.

Indiana has people from many different backgrounds and cultures.

*F*or nearly 200 years the people of Indiana have been called Hoosiers. No one really knows what *Hoosier* first meant. Some say the word comes from pioneer days when people greeted one another along the trail with "Who's 'yere?" meaning "Who's there?" Others think it comes from *hoozer*, a word some Europeans used to describe the people who settled the hills of southern Indiana. To those Europeans, *hoo* meant "hill."

Whatever *Hoosier* once meant, today it means "a citizen of the state of Indiana." A **citizen** is a member of a country, a state, or a city or town. *Stories in Time* will help you learn what being a citizen of Indiana means.

To help you think, feel, and act as a citizen, *Stories in Time* begins every lesson with a question. The question connects you to one or more of five powerful ideas that citizens need to understand in order to make decisions. The powerful ideas help you organize your thinking, focus your reading, and see how the story in the lesson relates to your own life.

POWERFUL IDEA NUMBER *1*

COMMONALITY AND DIVERSITY

All people share the needs for basic things such as food, clothing, and shelter. The needs we share, or have in common, are examples of our commonality. At the same time, we all have different ways of thinking, feeling, and acting. That is our diversity.

CONFLICT AND COOPERATION

Because people do not all think alike, they sometimes have conflicts, or disagreements. But people can often solve their conflicts by cooperating, or working together.

CONTINUITY AND CHANGE

Some things have continuity—they stay the same—and other things change. Understanding both continuity and change can help you see how things in the world came to be as they are. You will learn that what happened in the past has helped shape your life. And you will see that understanding what happens today can help you make better decisions about the future.

INDIVIDUALISM AND INTERDEPENDENCE

Citizens can act by themselves to make a difference in the world. But much of the time, people do not act alone. They depend on others to help them. Such interdependence connects citizens with one another and affects their lives.

INTERACTION WITHIN DIFFERENT ENVIRONMENTS

People's actions affect other people. People also affect their **environment**—the place in which they live—and their environment affects them. This is true of their natural environment, their home environment, their school environment, and any other environments they may be a part of. Understanding such interactions will help you see why things happened in the past and why things happen today.

These students are showing interdependence by working together on a clean-up campaign.

 What are the five powerful ideas of social studies?

How To

Read Social Studies

Why Is This Skill Important?

Social studies is made up of stories about people and places. Sometimes you read these stories in library books. At other times you read them in textbooks like this one. Knowing how to read social studies in a textbook can make it easier to study and to learn. It will help you identify main ideas and important people, places, and events.

Understand the Process

Follow these steps to read any lesson in this book.

1. Preview the whole lesson.
   - Look at the title and headings to find out the topic of the lesson.
   - Look at the pictures, captions, and questions for clues to what is in the lesson.
   - Answer the Link to Our World question at the beginning of the lesson to find out what the lesson will teach.
   - Read the Focus on the Main Idea statement. It gives you the main idea that the lesson teaches.
   - Look at the Preview Vocabulary list to see what new terms will be introduced.
2. Read the lesson for information on the main idea. As you read, you will come to a number of questions. Each has this mark ✓ next to it. Be sure to find the answers to these questions before you continue reading the lesson.
3. When you finish the lesson, say in your own words what you have learned.
4. Look back over the lesson. Then answer the lesson review questions—from memory if possible. These questions will help you check your understanding, think critically, and show what you know.

Think and Apply

Use the four steps in Understand the Process each time you are asked to read a lesson in *Stories in Time.*

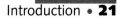

THE SUBJECTS OF SOCIAL STUDIES

*T*he main subjects of social studies are connected with one another to tell a story. Together they tell how people have lived over time and how people have made contributions as citizens.

GEOGRAPHY

Geography is the study of the Earth's surface and the way people live on it. Studying Indiana's geography will help you answer the following questions about places in your state. The five topics in the list of questions are so important that many people call them the five themes, or main topics, of geography.

QUESTIONS
- **Where is it?**
- **What is it like there?**
- **Who lives there, and how do they live there?**
- **How did they get there?**
- **How is this place like other places? How is it different?**

THEMES
1. **location**
2. **place**
3. **human-environment interactions**
4. **movement**
5. **regions**

The answers to these questions will tell you what you need to know in order to understand a setting.

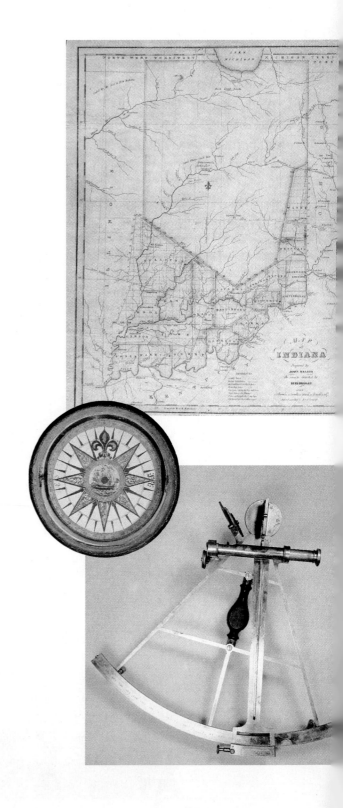

Some old tools of geography include this antique map (top), a bowl compass from 1750 (middle), and a sextant from 1785 (bottom) used for measuring distances.

HISTORY

History is the study of the past. It helps you see links between the past and the present. It also helps you understand how what happens today can affect the future. As you read about Indiana's past, ask yourself the questions below. They will help you think more like a historian, a person who studies the past.

- **What happened?**
- **When did it happen?**
- **Who took part in it?**
- **How and why did it happen?**

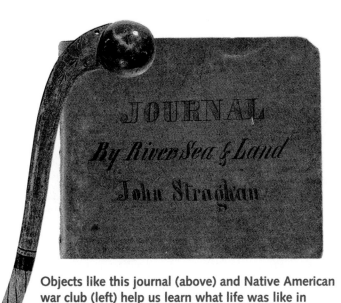

Objects like this journal (above) and Native American war club (left) help us learn what life was like in the past.

What do the illustrations on this 1857 three-dollar bill from Gosport, Indiana, tell you about the economy of Gosport at that time?

CIVICS AND GOVERNMENT

Civics and **government** is the study of citizenship and the ways in which citizens govern themselves. In *Stories in Time* you will learn about the rights of Indiana citizens and their responsibilities to their state and to their country. You will also learn how the Indiana government developed in the past and how it works today.

ECONOMICS

The **economy** of a state is the ways its people use resources and make choices to meet their needs. The study of the economy is called economics. You will read about the ways Hoosiers have made, bought, sold, and traded goods to get what they need or want. You will learn how the economy of Indiana came to be what it is today.

CULTURE

In this book you will learn about the people of the past who have affected the present. You will learn who those people were and what they said and did. You will explore their customs and beliefs and their ways of thinking and expressing ideas. All these things make up their **culture**. In *Stories in Time* you will discover the many cultures in Indiana's story, past and present.

 What are the main subjects of social studies?

How To

Read a Map

Why Is This Skill Important?

Knowing how to read maps is important for learning social studies and for taking action as a citizen. Maps tell you about the world around you through the five themes of geography: location, place, human-environment interactions, movement, and regions.

Understand the Process

Maps are drawings of places on the Earth. To help you read maps, mapmakers include certain parts on most maps. These are the title, the key, the compass rose, and the scale. Mapmakers often add a grid of numbered lines to help you locate places more easily.

1. The **map title** tells you the subject of the map. The title may also tell you what kind of map it is. Physical maps show landforms and bodies of water. Political maps show cities and state and national borders. Many of the maps in this book are historical maps that show Indiana as it was in the past.

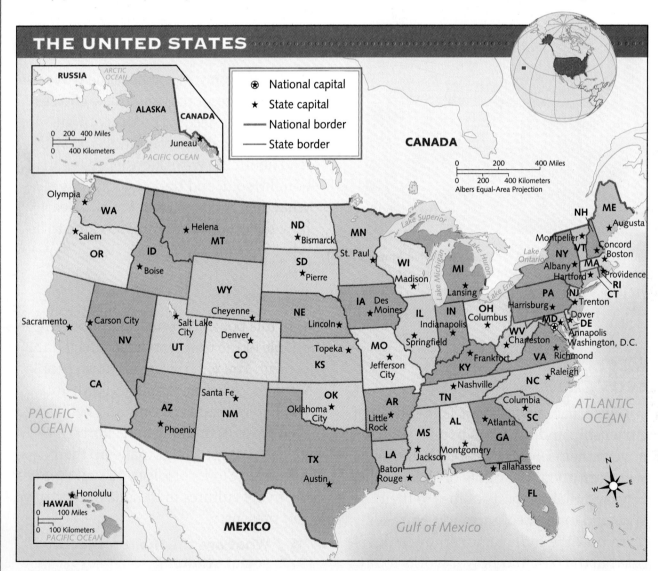

THE UNITED STATES

RUSSIA

ARCTIC OCEAN

ALASKA

CANADA

0   200   400 Miles
0   400 Kilometers

Juneau

PACIFIC OCEAN

⊛ National capital
★ State capital
— National border
— State border

CANADA

0   200   400 Miles
0   200   400 Kilometers
Albers Equal-Area Projection

Olympia
★ WA
★ Salem
OR
★ Boise
ID
★ Helena
MT
ND
★ Bismarck
MN
St. Paul ★
WI
Madison ★
Lake Superior
MI
Lansing ★
Lake Michigan
Lake Huron
Lake Ontario
Lake Erie
NH
ME
★ Augusta
Montpelier ★
VT
NY
★ Concord
Boston ★
MA
Albany ★
Hartford ★
Providence ★
RI
CT
PA
Harrisburg ★
NJ
★ Trenton

Sacramento ★
★ Carson City
NV
Salt Lake City ★
UT
Denver ★
CO
WY
Cheyenne ★
SD
★ Pierre
NE
Lincoln ★
IA
Des Moines ★
IL
Springfield ★
Indianapolis ★
IN
Columbus
OH
WV
Charleston ★
MD
Dover ★
DE
Annapolis ★
Washington, D.C.

PACIFIC OCEAN

CA

Santa Fe ★
NM
AZ
★ Phoenix
Topeka ★
KS
MO
Jefferson City ★
OK
Oklahoma City ★
AR
Little Rock ★
TN
★ Nashville
KY
Frankfort ★
VA
Richmond ★
Raleigh ★
NC
Columbia ★
SC
ATLANTIC OCEAN

★ Honolulu
HAWAII
0   100 Miles
0   100 Kilometers
PACIFIC OCEAN

TX
Austin ★

MS
Jackson ★
LA
Baton Rouge ★
AL
Montgomery ★
GA
Atlanta ★
Tallahassee ★
FL

N
W   E
S

MEXICO

Gulf of Mexico

2. The **map key**, which is sometimes called the map legend, explains what the symbols on the map stand for. The symbols may be colors, patterns, lines, or other special marks, such as circles or squares. The map key for the map below tells you that dots are used to show cities. A star stands for the state capital of Indiana, Indianapolis.

3. The **compass rose**, or direction marker, shows the main, or cardinal, directions—north, south, east, and west. It also helps you find the intermediate directions, which are between the cardinal directions. Intermediate directions are northeast, southeast, northwest, and southwest.

4. The **map scale** compares a distance on a map to a distance in the real world. A map scale helps you find the real distance between places on a map. Each map in this book has a scale that shows both miles and kilometers. A small map within a larger map is called an **inset map**. Inset maps have their own scales.

5. Many maps have numbered lines that cross to form a pattern called a **grid**. One set of lines crosses the map from right to left, or east to west. Another set crosses the map from top to bottom, or north to south. The location of a place can be described by using the numbers of two lines that cross.

Think and Apply

 Look at the maps on these pages. Identify the parts of the maps. With a partner, discuss the information you find.

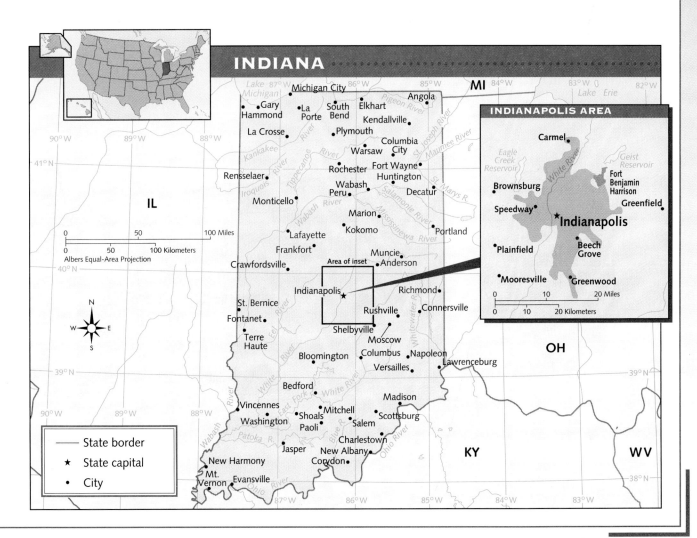

WHERE ON EARTH IS INDIANA?

*I*ndiana is one of twelve states that make up the Middle West region of the United States. The other states in this region are Ohio, Michigan, Wisconsin, Illinois, Minnesota, Iowa, Missouri, North Dakota, South Dakota, Nebraska, and Kansas.

The Middle West is one of five major regions that make up the United States. The other regions of the United States are the Northeast, the Southeast, the Southwest, and the West.

INDIANA WITHIN THE WESTERN HEMISPHERE

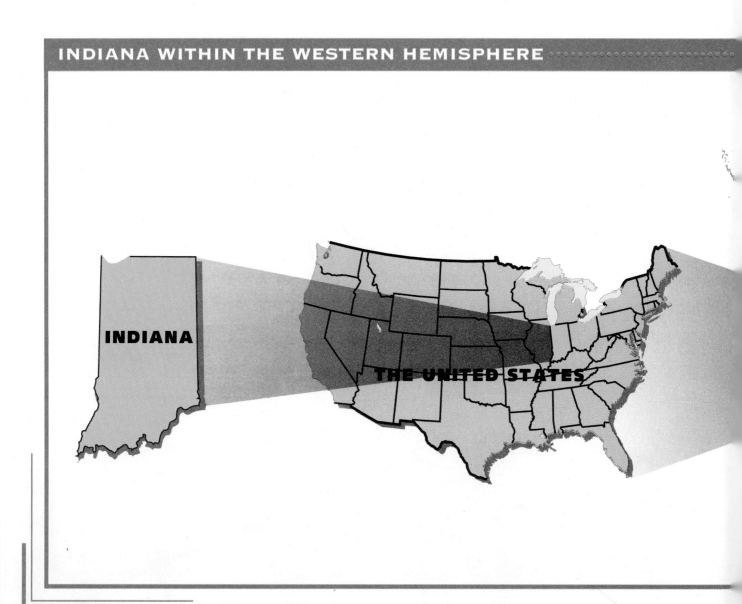

INDIANA

THE UNITED STATES

The United States is one of the countries on the main land area, or continent, of North America. Canada, the United States, and Mexico are the countries that make up the biggest part of North America.

North America is one of the seven continents on the Earth. North America and South America are the two continents completely in the Western Hemisphere.

The Western Hemisphere is the western half of the Earth. The Earth is a ball-like shape, or sphere, so half of it is called a hemisphere. *Hemi* means "half."

 **In what region of the United States is Indiana located?**

LEARNING FROM DIAGRAMS Indiana is a unique state in the United States. It is also a part of both the North American continent and the Western Hemisphere.

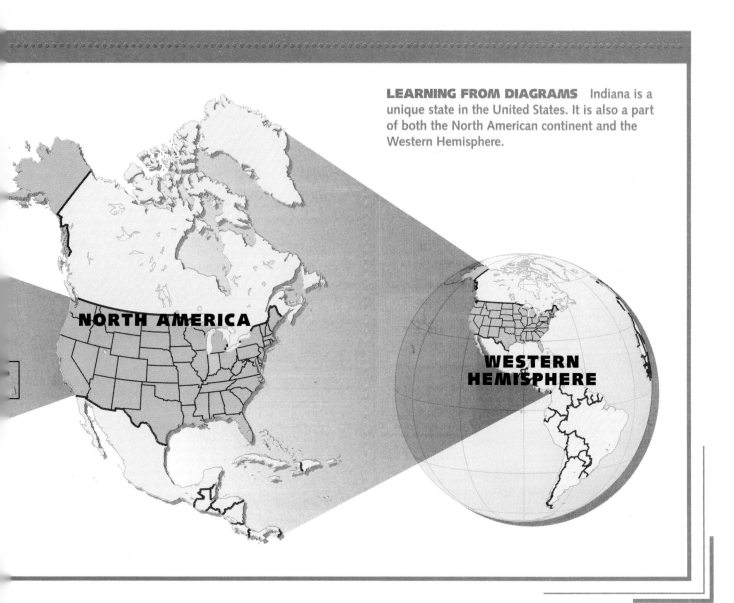

NORTH AMERICA

WESTERN HEMISPHERE

UNIT 1

THE *LAND AND EARLY PEOPLE OF INDIANA*

14,000
years ago

About 14,000
years ago
Glaciers cover
most of what is
now Indiana

12,000
years ago

About 12,000
years ago
As glaciers begin
to melt, people
follow herds of
giant animals
into the area

10,000
years ago

About
10,000
years ago
Giant animals
die out

8,000
years ago

The story of Indiana is a story of land *and* people. For thousands of years land has been the reason people came to Indiana. People have always depended on the land, and sometimes they have fought over it. So the history of Indiana's people begins with its land and natural geography—its landforms and soil, its rivers and lakes, its climate, and its plant and animal life.

← Cataract Falls, Lieber State Recreation Area

| 6,000 years ago | 4,000 years ago | 2,000 years ago | Present |

About 2,000 years ago
Mound Builders settle in what is now Indiana

About 400 years ago
New groups of Native Americans arrive

About 300 years ago
Europeans reach what is now Indiana

Canoeing the Wabash
with Grandpa

by Paul Johnson

Paul Johnson was ten years old on July 2, 1990, when he and his grandfather set out on an adventure. They took a canoe trip down the Wabash River, all the way across the state of Indiana. On their journey the two explorers learned much about the state's natural beauty and its rich history.

We dropped the canoe off alongside the river and drove back to a farm house. Grandpa asked the farmer if we could walk across his field to where the Wabash started. I never knew a river started from a creek, but the Wabash starts in the farmer's field. It's so small there that we could step across it. Grandpa said we were going to travel the entire length of the Wabash River, so we'd walk the first part (25 miles) until it got deep enough to canoe. Grandma and Dad took the car home, and Grandpa and I started walking along the creek through the fields and woods.

Grandpa told me there used to be Indians where we were hiking, so I kept looking for arrowheads. In the afternoon we came to a lake, and Grandpa let me fish while he cooked supper. After supper, we hiked till dark and then camped on the edge of a farmer's field. Grandpa and I put the tent up. Because we'd hiked 15 miles that day, I went right to sleep.

When I woke up, it was just getting light. Grandpa had the fire going and had made hot chocolate for me. We started out just after the sun came up. The corn and the wheat along the edge of the river were higher than my head. We saw a groundhog in the field, redwing blackbirds in the trees, and lots of deer tracks along the river. In the afternoon we got to Fort Recovery and met Grandma and Dad with our supplies for the canoe trip.

We loaded up the canoe and started out. The water was pretty low, so we hit bottom a lot and had to get out and pull the canoe over the rocks. We finally got to where the water was a little deeper, and we could paddle for an hour or two before we'd hit a shallow spot. There were lots of ducks on the river. The mother duck would splash around and make lots of noise while her four or five baby ducks would sneak along the shore and hide. We saw big, gray cranes in the river, and I saw two deer on the shore.

Grandpa told me stories of how a long time ago the French traders used to canoe down the Wabash River from the Great Lakes to trade with the Indians. He said they carried blankets and knives and guns to trade for the beaver and otter skins the Indians had. One night we camped where a French trading post used to be. Grandpa said there used to be wolves and mountain lions there and the early pioneers had to keep the campfire burning all night to keep the wolves away. He told me that tonight was my turn to keep the fire going all night, and he'd do it the next night.

After 16 days Paul and his grandpa reached the end of the Wabash River, where it flows into the Ohio River. They had traveled more than 475 miles (764 km) and had a great adventure together. Now it is time for you to begin your own adventure into the story of Indiana's geography and the people who lived here long ago.

CHAPTER 1

INDIANA'S GEOGRAPHY

> 66 By the day I trotted from one object which attracted me to another, singing a little song of made-up phrases about everything I saw while I waded catching fish, chasing butterflies over clover fields, or following a bird with a hair in its beak. 99
>
> Geneva "Gene" Stratton-Porter, Indiana writer, 1868–1924, describing Wabash County when she was ten years old

THE SHAPE OF THE LAND

LESSON 1

Link to Our World

Why does the land where you live look the way it does?

Focus on the Main Idea
Read to find out what makes each of the three natural regions of Indiana different.

Preview Vocabulary
glacier   sand dune
natural region   till
moraine   sea level
marsh

Indiana was a special place for Geneva Stratton-Porter, best known as Gene. As a girl she formed a lively interest in nature and her state's natural geography. Later, as a writer, she described in her books the beauty of her home state's rolling hills and broad plains. But the land that is now Indiana has not always looked the way it does today. Forces in nature have changed it over time.

ICE SHAPED THE LAND

By about 14,000 years ago, huge **glaciers**, or masses of ice, had crept down from the north. The glaciers moved slowly, usually less than a foot a day, carving away hills and digging deep holes. About 10,500 years ago, the huge glaciers melted, filling the holes to form lakes. Five of the largest are the Great Lakes—Superior, Huron, Michigan, Erie, and Ontario.

The glaciers formed two of the three main natural regions that are in Indiana. A **natural region** is a part of the Earth that has one major kind of natural feature, such as mountains, hills, or plains. The glaciers flattened the land to form the Great Lakes Plain and the Central Till Plain, but they did not reach the Southern Hills and Lowlands region.

Glaciers once covered much of what is now Indiana.

✓ **What force long ago formed two of Indiana's natural regions?**

Indiana Dunes State Park on the shores of Lake Michigan has an area of more than 2,180 acres.

Close to Lake Michigan great wind-blown **sand dunes** rise behind the beaches of the lakeshore. Writer Edwin Way Teale called them "hills of gold shining in the sun." These hills build up from sand that the wind sweeps from the beaches. Over the years the Indiana Dunes shift and change size and shape because of the steady wind. This happens so slowly that you cannot actually see the dunes move. As the dunes have shifted, ancient forests that were buried thousands of years ago have been uncovered.

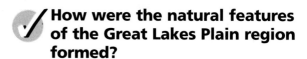 **How were the natural features of the Great Lakes Plain region formed?**

THE GREAT LAKES PLAIN

The northern one-third of what is now Indiana is part of a broad lowland plain worn flat by the glaciers. The plain lies along much of the Great Lakes shoreline and is called the Great Lakes Plain. Many small lakes and low, rocky hills are the main natural features of the Great Lakes Plain region. The hills, called **moraines** (muh•RAYNZ), are formed of the stony soil carried by glaciers and left behind when they melt.

Because of its many lakes, Indiana's Great Lakes Plain region is sometimes called the Northern Lake Country. The region also has large **marshes**, lowland areas with wet soil and tall grasses.

THE CENTRAL TILL PLAIN

Most of central Indiana was flattened by the glaciers. There they left behind a thick, smooth layer of soil. This thick layer of soil is called **till**. It gives this natural region of Indiana its name—the Central Till Plain.

Here and there in the Central Till Plain, low hills and shallow valleys break the region's flatness. One of these hills in Franklin Township in Wayne County is

The rich soil of the Central Till Plain region allows farmers to grow crops such as corn, soybeans, and grain. Many farms are located in central Indiana.

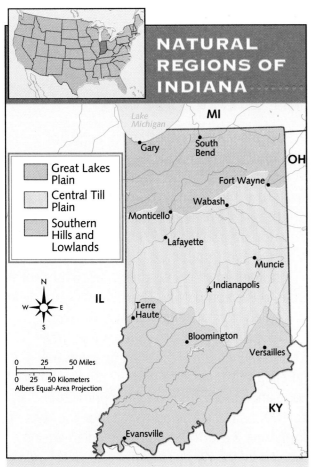

NATURAL REGIONS OF INDIANA

Great Lakes Plain

Central Till Plain

Southern Hills and Lowlands

N
W E
S

0   25   50 Miles
0   25   50 Kilometers
Albers Equal-Area Projection

REGIONS Indiana has three natural regions.

■ Which two regions seem the most alike?

the highest point in the state—1,257 feet (383 m) above sea level. The height of landforms is measured from sea level. Land at **sea level** is the same height as the surface of the oceans.

What does the land of the Central Till Plain look like?

THE SOUTHERN HILLS AND LOWLANDS

The Southern Hills and Lowlands of south-central Indiana is the only region the ancient glaciers did not reach. It kept its hills when the rest of the state was flattened.

The region has several groups of rounded hills with stretches of lowlands

in between. Indiana's lowest point— 320 feet (98 m) above sea level—is in the Southern Hills and Lowlands region. This point is located along the Ohio River in Posey County near where the states of Indiana, Illinois, and Kentucky meet.

Deep inside some of the region's hills are many caves, or caverns. There are more than 700 caves in Indiana. The best known are the Bluespring, Marengo, and Wyandotte caves.

Why are the natural features of the Southern Hills and Lowlands different from those of the state's other regions?

LESSON 1 REVIEW

Check Understanding

1. **Recall the Facts**   What are the three natural regions of Indiana?
2. **Focus on the Main Idea**   How is each natural region in Indiana different from the others?

Think Critically

3. **Link to You**   Which natural region of Indiana do you live in? Describe the land where you live.
4. **Think More About It**   How would Indiana be different if the glaciers had moved through all of the state?

Show What You Know

Map Activity   Use clay to make a landform map of Indiana. Model the land features of each of the three regions. Look at the map on this page to help you complete your clay map. Display your clay map in the classroom.

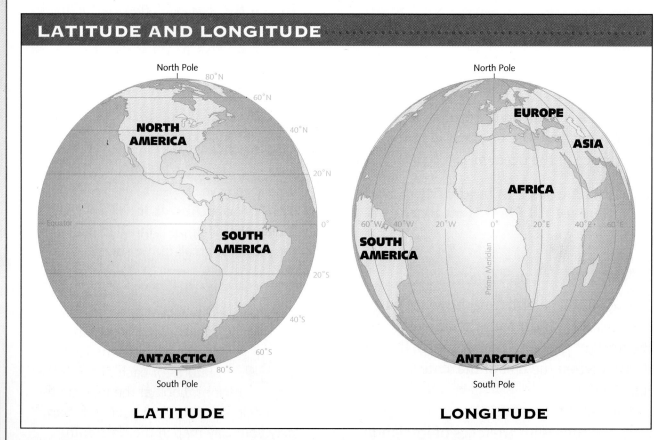

Use Latitude and Longitude

Why Is This Skill Important?

Has anyone ever asked you where your city or town is? One correct answer would be to say it is in Indiana. But there is a more exact way to tell where a place is.

Latitude and Longitude

To help you find places, mapmakers draw grid lines on maps and globes. One grid line is the **equator**, an imaginary line that runs east and west around the middle of the Earth. The equator is a line of **latitude**. Other lines of latitude run east and west around the globe both north and south of the equator.

The equator divides the Earth into two halves—a northern half and a southern half. These halves are called **hemispheres**. Places north of the equator are in the Northern Hemisphere. Places south of the equator are in the Southern Hemisphere.

Lines of latitude are labeled in degrees (°), from 0° at the equator to 90° at the North and South poles. The lines of latitude north of the equator are also labeled *N* for *North*. The lines south of the equator are labeled *S* for *South*.

Another set of lines is drawn from the North Pole to the South Pole. These north-south lines are called lines of **longitude**, or meridians.

The **prime meridian**, which passes near London, England, is the starting point for labeling the lines of longitude. Lines of longitude are labeled from 0° at the prime meridian to 180°, halfway around the globe. The lines of longitude west of the prime meridian are also labeled *W* for *West*. The lines east of the prime meridian are labeled *E* for *East*.

LATITUDE AND LONGITUDE

LATITUDE

LONGITUDE

INDIANA LATITUDE AND LONGITUDE

(Map showing Indiana with neighboring states Illinois, Michigan, Ohio, and Kentucky. Cities labeled include Gary, South Bend, Fort Wayne, Kokomo, Lafayette, Portland, Noblesville, Richmond, Indianapolis, Terre Haute, Moscow, Midland, Versailles, Lyons, Salem, Vincennes, Corydon, Evansville. Latitude lines: 38°N, 39°N, 40°N, 41°N. Longitude lines: 89°W, 88°W, 87°W, 86°W, 85°W, 84°W. Scale: 0–40–80 Miles; 0–40–80 Kilometers. Albers Equal-Area Projection.)

Understand the Process

When lines of latitude and longitude are drawn on a map or globe, they form a pattern called a grid. These lines make it easy to find **location**, or where a place is. You can give the location of a place by naming the line of latitude and the line of longitude that are closest to that place.

- Which line of latitude is closest to the southern border of Indiana?
- Between which lines of longitude is Indiana located?
- Find Fort Wayne on the map of Indiana. Near which line of latitude is Fort Wayne? Near which line of longitude is it? To tell Fort Wayne's location, name its latitude first and then its longitude. Fort Wayne is near 41°N latitude and 85°W longitude.
- Look at the map of Indiana again. Find Noblesville. Which line of latitude is closest to it? Its line of latitude is near 40°N. Which line of longitude is closest? Noblesville is near 86°W longitude. Noblesville's location is near 40°N latitude and 86°W longitude.
- Which lines of latitude and longitude describe the location of Lyons?

Think and Apply

Use latitude and longitude to tell where you or someone else lives in Indiana. Write a note to a friend that describes how you found your location on the map.

RIVERS AND LAKES

Link to Our World

What rivers and lakes are near where you live?

Focus on the Main Idea
Read to find out about Indiana's important rivers and lakes.

Preview Vocabulary
source	river system
mouth	dam
tributary	reservoir
fork	

Although Indiana is far from any ocean, water is important to the people who live in the state. Indiana's rivers and lakes supply fresh water to farms, factories, and homes. The state's many bodies of water also provide recreation for the people of Indiana. Fishing, swimming, and boating are all popular forms of water recreation. You will learn later in this book that bodies of water—both natural and human-made—have been important to trade and settlement in Indiana's history.

THE WABASH RIVER SYSTEM

There are more than 30 rivers in Indiana, but the Wabash River is one of the best known. It is also the state's longest river. From its **source**, or beginning, in western Ohio, the Wabash flows 475 miles (764 km) west and then south across most of Indiana. Along the way, it carves a path through Indiana's Central Till Plain.

Near Terre Haute the Wabash River forms the border between Indiana and Illinois. At its mouth it flows into the Ohio River. The **mouth** of a river is the place where it flows into a larger body of water. The Wabash and the Ohio rivers join where the states of Illinois, Indiana, and Kentucky meet.

On the Wabash River's journey through the state, it is joined by a number of smaller rivers, or tributaries (TRIH•byuh•tair•eez). A **tributary** is a river or creek that

The Wabash River as seen from Harmonie State Park

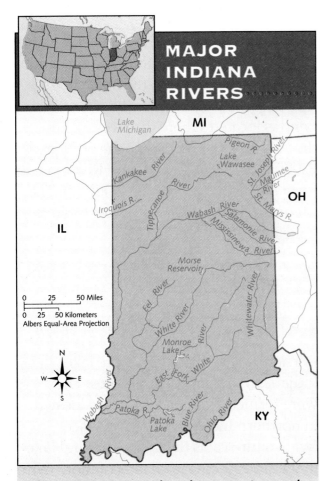

MAJOR INDIANA RIVERS

LOCATION Indiana has many rivers and lakes.

■ What river helps form the border between Indiana and Kentucky?

land around it. The Wabash River and its tributaries drain about two-thirds of Indiana and a large part of Illinois.

✓ **What is the longest river in Indiana?**

OTHER INDIANA RIVERS

While the Wabash River is the longest in Indiana, other rivers are also important. The Ohio River forms Indiana's southern border. The largest city in southern Indiana, Evansville, is located along the Ohio River.

No part of the Ohio River flows across Indiana, but there are several large rivers in southern Indiana that flow into the Ohio. Two of these rivers are the Wabash

The Ohio River has long been used to transport people and goods. It flows through six states from its source to its mouth.

flows into a larger river or creek. In northern and central Indiana, the Mississinewa (mih•suh•SIN•uh•wah), the Salamonie (SAL•uh•moh•nee), and the Tippecanoe (tih•pee•kuh•NOO) rivers join the Wabash River as tributaries.

Farther south, the White River flows into the Wabash. The White River has two **forks**, or branches. Its West Fork flows southwest across the state, passing through Indianapolis. The East Fork of the White River winds through the hills and lowlands of southern Indiana.

Together the Wabash River and its many tributaries make up the largest **river system** in the state. A river system drains, or carries water away from, the

River in the southwestern part of the state and the Whitewater River in the southeastern part of the state.

The Ohio River serves as the state's main water link with much of the rest of the United States. The river begins at Pittsburgh, Pennsylvania, on the western slope of the Appalachian Mountains. It then flows 981 miles (1,579 km) to the Mississippi River at Cairo, Illinois. The Ohio is one of the most important rivers in the United States. It was the nation's first highway, the main route for settlers traveling west.

In northwestern Indiana the Kankakee (kang•kuh•KEE) River flows west from near the city of South Bend to the Illinois River in the state of Illinois. Like the Ohio River, the Illinois River is a tributary of the Mississippi River.

Rivers in northeastern Indiana flow into the Great Lakes. From its source in the state of Michigan, the St. Joseph of the Lake River flows south into Indiana and then turns, or bends, to the north to flow into Lake Michigan. The city of South Bend is located where the river makes the "bend." At Fort Wayne the St. Marys River and a second St. Joseph River join to form the Maumee (maw•MEE) River. The Maumee flows northeast across Ohio to Lake Erie.

 **What rivers in Indiana flow into the Great Lakes?**

LAKES AND RESERVOIRS

There are more than 36 large lakes in Indiana. Many are natural lakes. They were formed by glaciers and are located in northern Indiana. Lake Wawasee (wah•wuh•SEE) is the largest natural lake in the state. It covers an area of more than 3,400 acres.

Clifty Falls in Clifty Falls State Park, New Madison, drops 70 feet (about 21 m).
Clifty Canyon is so deep that sunlight reaches the bottom only at noon.

Where?

Indiana's Lost River

A lost river is one that flows mostly underground. It is "lost" because in some places you cannot see it from the surface. The river disappears into sinkholes, or hollow places underground. One of the longest lost rivers in the United States is in Indiana's Southern Hills and Lowlands region. It begins above the surface and then vanishes from sight. The lost river in Bluespring Caverns near Bedford can carry boats for more than a mile on its underground waters.

Indiana also has some lakes that were made by people. Walls, or **dams**, were built across many rivers and creeks to help control flooding. A dam can protect against flooding by not letting too much water flow through the river at one time.

When a dam is built across a river or creek, it causes water to back up. The land behind the dam is flooded, and a lake is formed. A lake made by people in this way is called a **reservoir** (REH•zuh•vwar).

Most of Indiana's reservoirs are in southern Indiana, where flooding can be a problem. The largest reservoir is Lake Monroe. It was made by building a dam across Salt Creek near Harrodsburg. The water in Monroe Reservoir covers an area more than three times the size of Lake Wawasee.

✓ **What is the difference between a natural lake and a reservoir?**

LESSON 2 REVIEW

Check Understanding

1. **Recall the Facts** What river and its tributaries form the largest river system in Indiana?
2. **Focus on the Main Idea** What bodies of water are important to the people of Indiana?

Think Critically

3. **Link to You** What rivers, creeks, or lakes are near where you live?
4. **Think More About It** Many of Indiana's largest cities are located near bodies of water. Why do you think they are located there?

Show What You Know

 **Riddle Activity** Prepare five riddles that can be answered by naming a different river or lake in Indiana. One example might be, "I am an Indiana river named for a color, and I branch into two utensils." Challenge a partner to solve your riddles.

WEATHER AND CLIMATE

Link to Our World

What gives the place where you live climate features all its own?

Focus on the Main Idea
Read to find out why different parts of Indiana have different climate features.

Preview Vocabulary

weather	drought
climate	lake effect
temperature	humid
precipitation	tornado

Hoosier poet James Whitcomb Riley described the local weather in Indianapolis in a poem that he wrote in the late 1800s.

"They's been a heap o' rain, but the
    sun's out to-day,
And the clouds of the wet spell is all
    cleared away,
And the woods is all the greener, and
    the grass is greener still;
It may rain again to-morry, but I don't
    think it will. "

How would you describe today's weather where you live? **Weather** in a place can be described by several features—temperature (TEM•per•cher), precipitation (prih•sih•puh•TAY•shuhn), and wind. The kind of weather a place has most often, year after year, makes up its **climate**.

TEMPERATURE

Temperature is the measure of how warm or cold a place is. Often the temperature of a place depends on its location.

Like much of the northern part of the United States, Indiana is about halfway between the equator and the North Pole. This means that the average temperatures in Indiana fall between the year-round heat of the equator and the year-round cold of the North Pole.

Indiana summers are warm. Daytime temperatures in most parts of the state may range from 86°F to 90°F

As this thermometer shows, Indiana winters can be very cold!

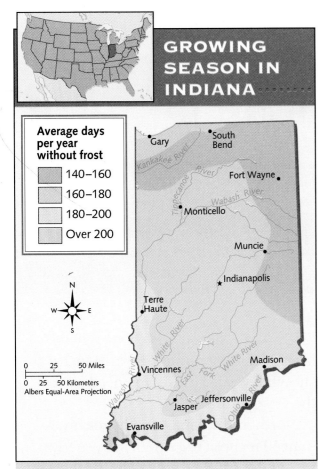

GROWING SEASON IN INDIANA

Average days per year without frost

- 140–160
- 160–180
- 180–200
- Over 200

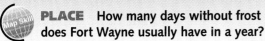

Gary
South Bend
Kankakee River
Tippecanoe River
Fort Wayne
Wabash River
Monticello
Muncie
Indianapolis
Terre Haute
White River
White River
East Fork
Madison
Vincennes
Wabash River
Ohio River
Jeffersonville
Jasper
Evansville

N W E S

0 25 50 Miles
0 25 50 Kilometers
Albers Equal-Area Projection

PLACE How many days without frost does Fort Wayne usually have in a year?

(30°C to 32°C). On some summer days, but not many, temperatures rise above 100°F (38°C). The highest temperature ever recorded in Indiana was 116°F (47°C) at Collegeville on July 14, 1936.

Winter is cold in Indiana. Temperatures average about 40°F to 44°F (4°C to 7°C) in the daytime. At night they average between 22°F and 26°F (-6°C and -3°C). Some winter day temperatures remain below 32°F (0°C), the temperature at which water freezes. On some winter days, but not many, temperatures in Indiana drop below 0°F (-18°C). The lowest temperature ever

When?

Growing Season

The growing season is the time of year when the weather is warm enough for plants to grow. Corn needs four to five warm months to grow, from planting until harvest. The growing season is measured from the time of the last freeze to the time of the first freeze. In Indiana the growing season is different in the north and in the south. Northern Indiana's growing season is about 150 days. The growing season is about 200 days in the southern part of the state.

recorded in Indiana was 35 degrees below zero, or -35°F (-37°C), on February 2, 1951, at Greensburg.

✓ How does Indiana's location affect its climate?

PRECIPITATION

Precipitation is another important part of climate. **Precipitation** can be rain, sleet, hail, or snow. Yearly precipitation is measured as rainfall, even though some of it is not rain. Most of Indiana receives about

Indiana must use snowplows in the winter to keep roads clear of snow.

43

This flood in Waverly, on the banks of the White River southwest of Indianapolis, shows what can happen in towns built along rivers.

40 inches (102 cm) of rainfall a year. An inch of snow is not the same amount of water as an inch of rainwater. Ten inches (25 cm) of snow equals about 1 inch (about 3 cm) of rainfall. So a 10-inch snowfall would make up only 1 inch of the yearly rainfall.

Northern Indiana usually gets more than 40 inches (102 cm) of snow a year. In the winter of 1929, however, 107 inches (272 cm) of snow fell at LaPorte, in north-western Indiana. That set a record in the state for the most snow in a year.

Southern Indiana receives much less snow—only about 10 inches (25 cm) a year. The south, though, receives more rain than the north. Average precipitation in the south is 44 inches (112 cm) a year. In the south, especially along the Ohio River, floods can be a problem in the spring. That is when water from melting snow is added to water from rain.

Even with all of its rainfall, now and then the southern part of the state has dry periods. A long period with very little or no rain is called a **drought**. Droughts can cause serious problems. If the weather gets too dry, crops can dry up and the soil can blow away.

LEARNING FROM GRAPHS The amount of precipitation Indiana receives varies across the state. ■ Which month shows the largest amount of average precipitation?

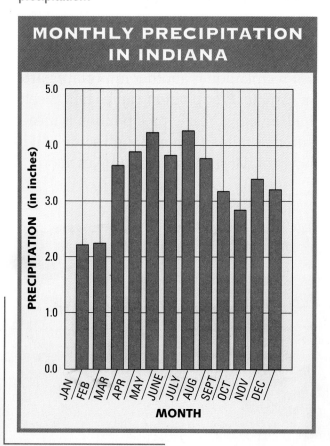

MONTHLY PRECIPITATION IN INDIANA

PRECIPITATION (in inches) / MONTH

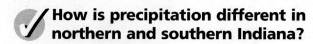

How is precipitation different in northern and southern Indiana?

WIND

Northern Indiana gets more snow than southern Indiana because of its location near Lake Michigan. In the winter, cold, dry winds blow down from the north. As the cold, dry air passes over Lake Michigan, it picks up moisture, or water. When this air moves over the land, it drops the moisture in the form of snow. This effect of Lake Michigan on the area's weather is called the **lake effect**.

In the summer, winds in Indiana most often come from the south. The warm air carries a lot of moisture picked up from the Gulf of Mexico. It makes the Indiana summers humid. **Humid** air has a lot of moisture in it.

Like most of the states in the Middle West region of the United States, Indiana gets strong, and often sudden, storms. These storms bring thunder, lightning, heavy rains, and high winds. Especially dangerous are tornadoes. A **tornado** is a funnel-shaped storm of swirling winds. The narrowest part of a tornado sweeps close to the ground. When it touches the ground, its strong winds often blow apart buildings and turn over cars and trucks.

The winds of a tornado are the strongest on Earth. Winds around the center of a tornado can reach speeds of more than 200 miles (320 km) per hour.

 How do winds blowing over water affect the climate of Indiana?

L ESSON 3 REVIEW

Check Understanding

1. **Recall the Facts** How are climate and weather different?
2. **Focus on the Main Idea** Why do different parts of Indiana have different climate features?

Think Critically

3. **Think More About It** How do you think climate affects the way people live?
4. **Cause and Effect** How does Lake Michigan affect the climate of Indiana?

Show What You Know

Creative Writing Activity Write a short poem or paragraph describing some part of Indiana's climate— temperature, precipitation, or wind. In your writing, describe how that part of the climate makes you feel.

The Storm

by Marc Harshman   illustrated by Mark Mohr

Jonathan lives on a farm that is not far from Indianapolis. When he was younger, an accident caused him to lose the use of his legs, so he uses a wheelchair to move around. Arriving home from school one day in the spring, Jonathan is greeted by his mother. She has to go out, and she asks Jonathan to put the horses in the barn. Read now what happens when a storm comes up.

Back in the barn he turned on Dad's milking radio:

"A line of thunderstorms approaching east-central Indiana could have severe hail and lightning and a tornado watch has been issued for Wayne, Randolph, Jay, and Delaware counties."

He'd heard this before. A "watch" meant there was a chance, nothing more—it seemed there were dozens every spring. Only the warnings got his attention. This did mean, though, that there was a good chance of a storm and Jonathan liked any kind of storm.

He put his hands to the rubber rims and pushed himself out the west doors. There were ripples in the grass and the skies had clouded. It was peaceful. Since his accident he felt more alert somehow. He liked watching those ripples in the grass, the tumbling of the clouds overhead, the way the fluffy tops of the sycamores by the creek bent and tossed in the rising wind.

But. That rising wind. He wasn't sure he liked the low wail that began moving through the farmyard, nor the green-yellow tint of the sky. They were signs the old-timers said meant "twister."

"Better get busy and see to closing things up," he told himself. "Who knows?"

The radio was still running the same advisory: "wind . . . hail . . . tornado watch . . ."

He called to the horses, reached up from his chair and undid the latch, backing away as the gate swung open. Buster nuzzled his ear as he wheeled along beside them into the barn. Once inside he gave them each a scoop of oats. Usually he liked to linger here, thinking and talking, but as he felt the barn creak and moan under the wind, he turned himself back out to take another look.

linger
stay on

He could hear now a continuous rumble of thunder and to the southwest the sky had turned a deep, deep blue. Here and there it was fractured by lightning. For a moment the wind stopped. The cackling of the hens, the snorting of the hogs, the chittering of the birds—all went silent. Then a sharp whistling rose up from somewhere. There was a worried nicker from Henry.

Jonathan looked again at the sky. And there he saw it, saw the strange, black thumb press itself down out of the bulging mass of clouds and stretch into a narrow tongue just licking over the surface of the ground.

Tornado!

It was so incredible that for a moment he simply stared. From the rise of the farmyard he watched the snakelike funnel slowly twist across the distant fields and broaden into a larger blackness. Before his eyes it became a black wall headed straight for the farm. Fear replaced amazement. He hurried back across the lot. The

nicker
sound a horse makes

wind was shrieking now. But before he could get to the house, he heard horses.

Looking back, there were Buster and Henry tearing madly around the inner lot. How could they have gotten out? He didn't know. And not just Buster, but Henry, pride and joy of his father's. Jonathan couldn't think if he had time or not, if it was safe or not.

He raced toward them, his arms aching with the effort. His hands burned against the friction of the rubber wheels. He didn't think he could push any harder, but the horses had to be saved. He had to save them for Dad.

First he had to get Buster calmed. If he could get him calmed, Henry would follow. He held out his sugar cubes. After circling and snorting around him, Buster came, and with Jonathan's hand on his neck, allowed himself to be calmed enough so that Jonathan could snap on a lead rope. He then did the same with Henry. On their leads they followed him back [into the barn].

The barn shook. Like a freight train the twister kept coming. The screaming wail of it was inside as well as outside, was inside him. And though he was drenched in sweat, he was freezing with goose bumps, too. Each second he expected to be his last.

chaff
grain husks

Shading his eyes from the swirling chaff, he tried to squint through the slats of the siding to see. But it was darker than night, the electric gone now. There was just himself and the

animals and the pounding of the storm, so deep, so strong, it felt as if the earth itself was shaking. The dried chaff and straw choked him and he gave up trying to keep his eyes open.

Cra-aaack! Whuumph! Suddenly hay swooshed down all over them. Keeping hold of both leads in one hand, Jonathan tried to move his chair out from under the beam that seemed to hang just over them. Finally he got to where he could see it resting on the cross bars above the stall. It could have killed them.

To work their way out he had to pull the hay loose from his wheelchair and then tug on the leads, tug and coax. It was then that he realized the thumping had stopped, the wind lessened and been joined by the pleasanter sound of rain. "We're saved," he shouted to Buster and Henry. "We're saved!"

Although the tornado caused damage to trees and buildings on the farm, Jonathan and the horses were safe because of his quick thinking. But Jonathan was also lucky. A barn is no real protection in the direct path of a tornado. Dealing with a tornado, you cannot count on luck.

Literature Review

1. How did Jonathan know a tornado was possible?
2. What would you do if a tornado came near your home or school?
3. Use the information in the story to list ways to tell when a tornado might come.

Solve a Problem

Why Is This Skill Important?

Have you ever faced a problem as serious as Jonathan's? People face all kinds of problems every day. Learning how to solve small ones now can help you solve bigger problems later on in your life.

Remember What You Have Read

Think about how Jonathan solved the problem of the horses being outside with the tornado coming. He had to find a way to get both the horses and himself inside. Do you remember what he did?

Understand the Process

Here is a way to understand what Jonathan did. You can follow these steps to solve most problems on your own.

1. State the problem. In Jonathan's case, the problem was that a tornado was coming, and the horses were outside.

2. Divide the problem into smaller parts. Jonathan's problem can be broken down into two smaller parts—how to get the horses calmed down, and how to protect them and himself from the tornado.

3. Work to solve the problem one part at a time. Jonathan first calmed the horses by giving them sugar cubes.

4. Check to see if what you are doing is working. Jonathan could tell that the horses had calmed down, because they stopped running.

5. Work on the other parts of the problem. Jonathan led the horses into the barn.

Think and Apply

Think about the problem of a tornado passing near your home. With a family member, prepare a plan that you can use to stay safe. Compare your plan with those of your classmates.

LESSON 5

NATURAL RESOURCES

Link to Our World

How do people use the natural resources found in your part of the state?

Focus on the Main Idea
Read to find out how people in Indiana use the state's many natural resources.

Preview Vocabulary
natural resource   broadleaf
fertile   needleleaf
mineral   habitat
bituminous   prairie
pollute
limestone

An early European explorer in what is now Indiana described the land as not only beautiful but also rich. The explorer said that "one can find there, in abundance with very little trouble, everything necessary" for people to live. The explorer was describing Indiana's important natural resources. A **natural resource** is something found in nature that people can use. Soil, minerals, trees, and animals are all natural resources.

SOIL

The soil left behind by the glaciers is one of Indiana's most valuable natural resources. Because the soil is so **fertile**, or good for growing crops, more than two-thirds of the state is farmland. A writer traveling through Indiana once described the soil as "fat as a hog and so fertile you felt that if you stuck a fork in the earth the juice would spurt. . . ."

Indiana's farmland is mostly in the central and northern parts of the state. In the fertile soil there, farmers grow a variety of crops, such as corn, wheat, soybeans, tomatoes, potatoes, onions, and oats. Corn and soybeans are Indiana's most important farm products.

Two corn seedlings. Corn is one of Indiana's most important crops.

Corn and soybeans are mostly used as feed for cattle and hogs. They have other uses, too. They are made into products that people eat. Corn can also be used as a source of fuel.

Indiana produces more popcorn (unpopped) than any other state in the United States. It grows about 148 million pounds in a year—one-fourth of the nation's total! In 1952 Hoosier Orville Redenbacher started one of the biggest popcorn companies in the country.

✓ **What are the two most important farm products grown in Indiana soil?**

Freshly popped Indiana popcorn

MINERALS

A **mineral** is a natural resource found in the ground. Indiana's most important mineral resources are coal and limestone.

In southwestern Indiana a large deposit of coal lies close to the surface. The kind of coal found there is called **bituminous** (buh•TYOO•muh•nuhs) coal, or soft coal. Today bituminous coal is most often used to provide power, rather than to heat homes, as was common in the past. Power plants in Indiana burn coal to

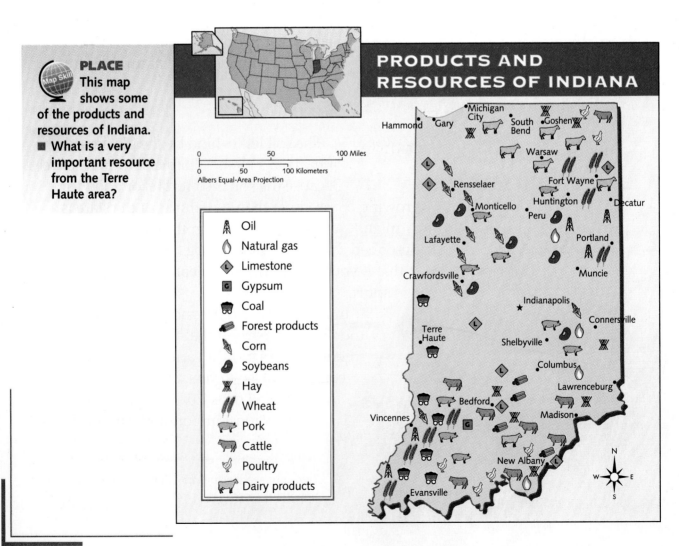

PLACE This map shows some of the products and resources of Indiana.

■ What is a very important resource from the Terre Haute area?

PRODUCTS AND RESOURCES OF INDIANA

0   50   100 Miles
0   50   100 Kilometers
Albers Equal-Area Projection

Legend:
- 🛢 Oil
- 💧 Natural gas
- ◇ Limestone
- G Gypsum
- Coal
- Forest products
- Corn
- Soybeans
- Hay
- Wheat
- Pork
- Cattle
- Poultry
- Dairy products

Michigan City, Hammond, Gary, South Bend, Goshen, Warsaw, Fort Wayne, Rensselaer, Monticello, Huntington, Decatur, Peru, Lafayette, Portland, Crawfordsville, Muncie, Indianapolis, Connersville, Terre Haute, Shelbyville, Columbus, Lawrenceburg, Bedford, Madison, Vincennes, New Albany, Evansville

make electricity. The heat from the burning coal turns water into steam. The steam turns turbines, which look like huge pinwheels. These turbines are connected to other machines, which make electricity, that then travels through wires to all parts of the state.

Unfortunately, Indiana's coal contains a high content of sulfur. Sulfur **pollutes**, or spoils, the air when it is burned. For this reason, many coal mines in Indiana are now being closed. Scientists are searching for ways to take the sulfur from the coal when it is burned.

The other important mineral found in Indiana is limestone, the state stone. **Limestone** is a hard rock used for making buildings. It was formed long, long ago when a great sea covered much of North America. Over thousands of years, as tiny sea animals died, their skeletons piled up at the bottom of the sea. In time the weight of the water pressed the skeletons into layers of rock now called limestone.

Several famous buildings in the United States have been made of Indiana limestone. Some of these are the Empire State Building in New York; the Pentagon near Washington, D.C.; and the state capitol buildings in West Virginia, Nebraska, Tennessee, and Indiana. Many Indiana county courthouses are made of limestone, too. Indiana supplies two-thirds of all the limestone used in the United States.

Other minerals found in Indiana are oil, natural gas, and gypsum. Gypsum is a kind of rock that is like limestone. When it is crushed into a powder, gypsum can be used to make many products—from plaster to toothpaste!

 What are Indiana's two most important mineral resources?

What?

Indiana Limestone

Limestone became popular as a building material after the great Chicago fire of 1871. The fire destroyed more than 17,000 buildings in less than 24 hours. When the people of Chicago rebuilt their city, they decided to use a material that would not burn. They chose limestone. Much of it came from the limestone quarries of southern Indiana. Since then Indiana limestone has been used to make many famous buildings all over the United States—state capitols and churches as well as university and government buildings.

TREES

Forests cover about one-sixth of the state today. But at one time forests covered almost all of Indiana. One early traveler told of spending "day after day among trees of a hundred feet high, without a glimpse of the surrounding country."

Most trees in Indiana's forests are broadleaf trees. A **broadleaf** tree has wide, flat leaves that fall off each year before the winter. Before they fall, the green leaves change color. When autumn comes, Indiana's forests become brilliant with shades of orange, yellow, and red. The colorful leaves of ash, beech, black walnut, shagbark hickory, red oak, maple, poplar, and other broadleaf trees are a sign of the season.

Indiana's state tree is the yellow poplar or tulip tree (left). A broadleaf (below) shows bright colors in the fall.

Indiana's largest forest areas are in the Southern Hills and Lowlands region of the state. There the Hoosier National Forest covers more than 193,000 acres.

✓ **What two kinds of trees make up the Indiana forests?**

ANIMALS

Animals were an important natural resource when people first arrived in the Indiana area thousands of years ago. People used animals for food and for making clothing and tools, just as we do today.

Where people have not built homes and businesses, many animals have their **habitats**, or places where they find food and shelter. In Indiana the two most common kinds of habitats are wetlands and forests.

Marshes are in northern Indiana and in areas around rivers and lakes. Beavers, muskrats, river otters, and many waterbirds, such as sandhill cranes and

The forests in Indiana also have some needleleaf trees. All **needleleaf** trees have thin, sharp leaves like needles. These leaves stay green all year. That is why some people call them evergreens. Red cedar and pine are two kinds of needleleaf, or evergreen, trees.

Some trees in forests are cut down for lumber. Most lumber is used for buildings and for furniture. The wood from trees is also used to make other products, such as wood chips for gardens and pulp for paper.

Indiana is home to many kinds of birds. The red cardinal was chosen as Indiana's state bird in 1933.

The peony became Indiana's state flower in 1957. It blooms in shades of many colors.

LESSON 5 REVIEW

Check Understanding

1. **Recall the Facts** What made the soil of Indiana so fertile?
2. **Focus on the Main Idea** How do people in Indiana use the state's many natural resources?

Think Critically

3. **Link to You** What are some of the natural resources found where you live?
4. **Think More About It** In what ways do you think early people used Indiana's natural resources?

Show What You Know

Poster Activity Create a poster about one of Indiana's natural resources. Describe its uses and its importance to people or the environment. Include pictures and a short slogan. Share your poster in a classroom display.

wood ducks, live in these wetlands. Forests are the habitats of squirrels, rabbits, deer, and game birds such as quail, ruffed grouse, and wild turkeys. Other Indiana birds include sparrows, larks, blue jays, orioles, swallows, wrens, and cardinals. The red cardinal is the state bird.

Animal habitats are easily damaged or destroyed. Two hundred years ago, herds of buffalo roamed the grasslands, or **prairies**, of western Indiana. Huge flocks of passenger pigeons and Carolina parakeets darkened the sky as they flew overhead. These and other animals have died out. Some were hunted until there were no more. Others were crowded out when people built settlements and farms in their habitats.

Hoosiers are working to protect Indiana's wetlands. The wetlands provide homes for many animals, such as these river otters.

✓ **What are the two most common animal habitats in Indiana?**

REVIEW

CONNECT MAIN IDEAS

Use this organizer to show that you understand how the chapter's main ideas are connected. First, copy the organizer onto a separate sheet of paper. Then complete it by writing two sentences to summarize each lesson.

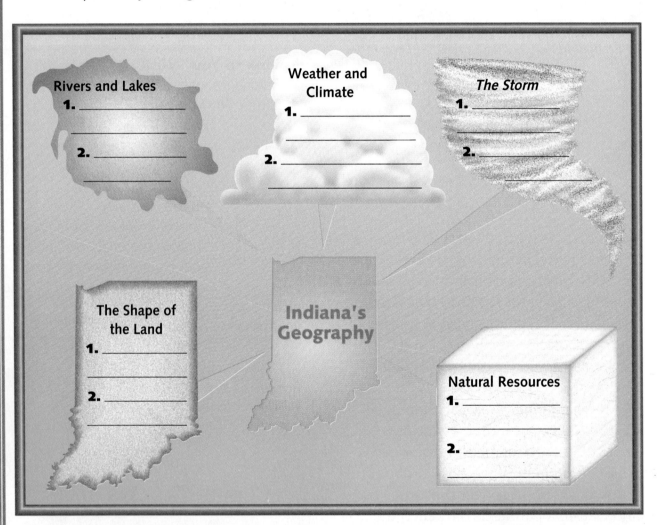

Rivers and Lakes
1. _____
_____
2. _____
_____

Weather and Climate
1. _____
_____
2. _____
_____

The Storm
1. _____
_____
2. _____
_____

The Shape of the Land
1. _____
2. _____

Indiana's Geography

Natural Resources
1. _____
_____
2. _____
_____

WRITE MORE ABOUT IT

1. Write a Descriptive Paragraph
Describe what you might see, hear, feel, and smell on a walk through a forest, field, marsh, or other natural region near where you live.

2. Design a Bumper Sticker Think of a saying about a natural feature, animal, tree, or mineral resource that is found in Indiana. Then write your saying on a strip of paper to make a bumper sticker. Illustrate your work.

USE VOCABULARY

Use each vocabulary word in a sentence that helps explain its meaning.

1. glacier
2. moraine
3. sand dune
4. tributary
5. river system
6. mineral
7. bituminous
8. tornado
9. precipitation
10. drought

CHECK UNDERSTANDING

1. What are the three natural regions of Indiana?

2. What is a till plain?

3. What is the longest river that flows through Indiana? Into what other important river does it flow?

4. What have some people in Indiana done to control flooding by rivers?

5. What is the difference between a natural lake and a reservoir?

6. How does Lake Michigan affect climate in Indiana?

7. What is one of Indiana's most valuable natural resources?

8. What are Indiana's two most important farm crops?

9. What is limestone? How was it formed?

THINK CRITICALLY

1. **Explore Viewpoints** Why might some people not want to put a dam across a river or creek?

2. **Link to You** Have you ever been on one of Indiana's rivers or lakes? What did you see there? If you have not been on a river or lake, what do you think you might see or do there?

3. **Think More About It** How are wind, temperature, and precipitation related to climate?

4. **Cause and Effect** How does Indiana's location affect its climate?

5. **Personally Speaking** How do you think Indiana might look 100 years from now? Explain your answer.

6. **Think More About It** Why do you think the animals that live in wetlands are different from those that live in forests?

APPLY SKILLS

How to Use Latitude and Longitude Look at the map of Indiana on page 37. What is the longitude of the point farthest east and the point farthest west in Indiana? What line of latitude runs nearest to the middle of Indiana?

How to Solve a Problem Develop a plan that will help you prepare for a possible blizzard, or major snowstorm. Share your plan with a family member.

READ MORE ABOUT IT

The Year of No More Corn by Helen Ketteman with pictures by Robert Andrew Parker. Orchard. This tall tale book describes Indiana's climate and farm products.

Weather by Martyn Bramwell. Franklin Watts. This book describes the many different characteristics of weather.

THE EARLY PEOPLE OF *I*NDIANA

> ❝ Our Cause is Just. . . . Our Country will be grateful. ❞
>
> George Rogers Clark to Patrick Henry of Virginia, in a letter dated February 3, 1779

George Rogers Clark fought in the American Revolution. His actions in what is now Indiana made him a hero in the state.

THE EARLIEST PEOPLE

Link to Our World

How do people today change as the world around them changes?

Focus on the Main Idea
Read to find out how life changed for the earliest people of Indiana as their land and climate changed.

Preview Vocabulary
band	culture
cooperate	earthworks
extinct	trade
scarce	
tribe	
specialize	

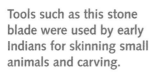

Tools such as this stone blade were used by early Indians for skinning small animals and carving.

Many thousands of years ago some of the world's ocean water was locked in glacier ice. At that time the level of the oceans was lower than it is today. A narrow piece of land connected the continents of Asia and North America. People from Asia may have traveled into North America along this land route. For thousands of years these people's children and their children's children moved to places all over the North American continent. They may have reached present-day Indiana as long as 12,000 years ago.

THE LAND AND PEOPLE LONG AGO

When the earliest people arrived in what is now Indiana, the glacier ice still covered much of the land except for the Southern Hills and Lowlands region. That land was covered with forests. The rich plant life provided food for many large animals. Some of these animals weighed thousands of pounds. Giant deer and huge mastodons and mammoths roamed the forests and plains. Mastodons and mammoths were huge elephant-like animals. Many were as tall as 14 feet (4 m) and had tusks 14 to 16 feet (4 to 5 m) long.

The earliest people who came to Indiana were most likely hunters looking for food. They traveled in **bands**, or small groups of families, that lived and worked together. Because they were always on the move, they did not build lasting shelters.

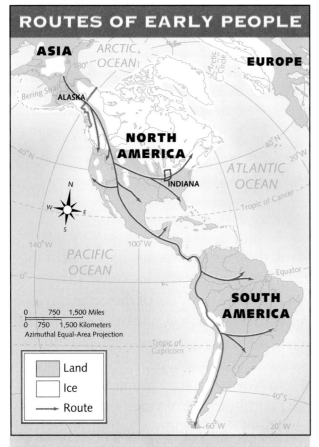

ROUTES OF EARLY PEOPLE

MOVEMENT This map shows the routes early people may have followed from Asia to the Americas.
■ Why do you suppose early people took the routes they did?

Instead, they used natural rock shelters they found, or they made their own shelters from animal skins. At night the people camped near rivers or creeks. During the day they followed and hunted the giant animals.

Imagine how hard it was for these people to hunt. Their main weapon was a wooden spear with a tip made of rock. To kill an animal the size of a mammoth, they had to **cooperate**, or work together as a team. The animals were too large to be killed by one person alone.

From one mammoth a band could get enough meat to last for months. The people used the hide to make clothing and shelters. The bones were made into tools and weapons.

What animals did early people hunt in what is now Indiana?

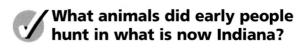

Large animals like these mastodons were resources for early people.

FOOD GATHERERS

Over hundreds of years the environment of the Indiana area slowly changed. The climate became warmer and drier. The glaciers began to melt. Many of the plants that the giant animals ate could no longer grow. By about 10,000 years ago, the mastodons and other giant animals began to die out, or become **extinct**.

Some people moved away as the environment changed. Other people stayed but changed their ways of life. Since there were no giant animals to hunt for food, clothing, and shelter, they had to fish and to hunt smaller animals. The people also began to rely more on plants for food.

Some of the earliest people lived in places where food was **scarce**, or hard to find. In time they learned where certain plants grew best. They also learned at what times of the year nuts, berries, and other plant parts would become ripe enough to eat. The people traveled each season to places where they could gather food and hunt.

 How did early people change their way of life when the giant animals they hunted died out?

EARLY FARMERS

Between 7,000 and 4,700 years ago, some people in North America began to farm. They found that if they planted seeds, they could grow food instead of having to find it.

Early corn was much smaller than corn grown today.

Not all people became farmers, however, because not every place was good for farming. The first farms in what is now Indiana were along the Ohio River and its tributaries. These places had plenty of water, and the soil was fertile.

The early farmers grew mainly beans, squash, and maize, a kind of corn.

The earliest farmers still gathered food, hunted, and fished, too. Many no longer moved from place to place, however. They stayed in one place, cleared land for planting, and built shelters together to make settlements, or communities. With more food, people lived longer and the number of people in each settlement grew. Some people formed **tribes**, or groups of many bands that share land and have the same way of life.

In some farming tribes people began to **specialize**. They worked at one job they could do well. Some people in a tribe specialized in making pots or weaving. Others farmed or hunted. This separation of jobs is called division of labor. It helped the tribe meet the needs of its people more easily.

Each tribe soon developed its own ways of dressing, speaking, and behaving and its own beliefs. These things make up a **culture**. A tribe's culture helped unite the people within the tribe. Its culture also set the tribe apart from others.

How did farming change the way some early people lived?

THE MOUND BUILDERS

About 3,000 years ago some tribes in North America began building huge mounds, or piles, of earth. They built these **earthworks** first as burial places and later as platforms for temples and for the homes of their leaders. Some of these earthworks were only 4 feet (about 1 m) high. Others stood 70 feet (21 m) tall and covered an area bigger than a football field! All the different groups of people who built these earthworks are today known as Mound Builders.

Between 2,000 and 500 years ago, groups of Mound Builders lived in settlements in present-day Indiana, Illinois, Ohio, Michigan, and other nearby states. Each settlement grew crops, which provided enough food for as many as 1,000 people. Some of the people built sturdy houses out of wood and earth. Others made houses out of mud. For protection most Mound Builder groups built walls of wooden posts and clay around their settlements.

To get things they could not grow or make themselves, the Mound Builders set up vast trade systems using the rivers to transport goods. **Trade** is the exchange of goods. The Mound Builders traded tools and carvings with people living as far away as the Gulf of Mexico and the Rocky Mountains. In return the Mound Builders received items not found in Indiana, such as sharks' teeth, which might have been used for tools or jewelry.

The largest Mound Builder settlement in North America was at Cahokia in Illinois. The largest settlement in the Indiana area is today called Angel Mounds. It was part of a

Where?

Indiana Mounds

At Mounds State Park near Anderson, you can see earthworks built more than 2,000 years ago. The largest is called the Great Mound. At Angel Mounds State Historic Site near Evansville, the earthworks were built about 1,000 years later than those at Mounds State Park. They were made by a different group of Mound Builders. Both places are open to the public. At either one you can learn about the early people who lived in what is now Indiana.

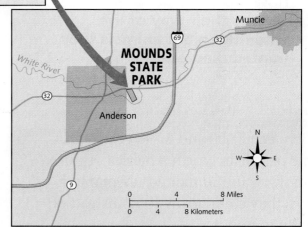

This community building at Angel Mounds was rebuilt by scientists to show how it looked during the time of the Mound Builders.

Mound Builder town located near present-day Evansville. About 1,000 people lived at Angel Mounds between 1,000 and 500 years ago. Then, for reasons no one knows, these people stopped trading and stopped building mounds. They may have died of diseases or moved away because of a drought or some other change in climate. The Mound Builders left behind their great earthworks, many of which were filled with baskets, pottery, art, and other reminders of a highly developed culture in our state's past.

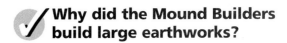 **Why did the Mound Builders build large earthworks?**

LESSON 1 REVIEW

Check Understanding

1. **Recall the Facts** Why did mammoths and other giant animals become extinct?
2. **Focus on the Main Idea** How did life change for the earliest people of Indiana when their environment changed?

Think Critically

3. **Personally Speaking** Would you rather have lived as a hunter and gatherer, a farmer, or a trader? Explain your answer.

4. **Cause and Effect** How did farming affect the other kinds of work people did?

Show What You Know

 **Art Activity** Suppose you have written a book called *The Mound Builders of Indiana*. Draw a cover for your book. Show a scene of Mound Builder life. Add your book cover to a bulletin board display in your classroom.

Work Together in Groups

Why Is This Skill Important?

In learning social studies you will often find it helpful to work with a partner or in a group. Many projects you will do in your social studies class would be difficult for one person to do alone. When you work together, each of you can work on just part of the project. However, for a group project to succeed, each member needs to cooperate with the others. Knowing how to work together is an important skill not only for students but for all citizens.

Understand the Process

Suppose your group is asked to do a project, such as presenting a short play about everyday life among Indians in Indiana long ago. You and the other group members might find it helpful to follow a set of steps like this.

1. Organize and plan together.
   - Set your goal as a group.
   - Share your ideas.
   - Cooperate with others to plan your work.
   - Make sure everyone has a job to do.

2. Act on your plan together.
   - Take responsibility for your job.
   - Help one another.
   - If there are disagreements, take time to talk about them.
   - Show your group's finished work to the class.

3. Talk about your work.
   - Discuss what you learned by working together.
   - Think about ways you and your classmates can work together on future projects.

An important part of survival for early people was knowing how to work together. The Mound Builders worked together to build huge mounds, raise crops, and hunt for game.

Think and Apply

How could you apply these steps to the project about Indian life? Apply them as you take part in all the group activities in *Stories in Time.*

INDIAN NEWCOMERS

Link to Our World

In what way is Indiana today a place of many cultures?

Focus on the Main Idea
Read to compare the cultures of Native Americans who came to what is now Indiana.

Preview Vocabulary
headwaters
portage
government
council
military
civil

The canoe was important to Native Americans and Europeans for moving goods and people.

By the 1600s Mound Builders no longer lived in what is now Indiana. Various other groups of Native Americans, or American Indians, moved into the area. Together these groups of Native Americans were called the Indians of the Eastern Woodlands. The Woodlands was made up of most of the land west of the Atlantic Ocean and east of the Mississippi River. It got its name from the thick forests that covered the land.

Many of the people living in the Eastern Woodlands shared some ways of life. They hunted and farmed to get food. They used animal skins to make clothing, and they used wood and tree bark to make shelters. They used canoes to travel the rivers and lakes. Like the Mound Builders before them, the people of the Eastern Woodlands moved to the Indiana area to provide food, clothing, and shelter for themselves and their families.

THE MIAMI PEOPLE

Among the first people from the Eastern Woodlands to move into what is now Indiana were the Miamis. The first band of Miamis settled at the **headwaters**, or upper part, of the Maumee River, where the city of Fort Wayne is now located. There they built a settlement that they called Kekionga (kee•kee•ohn•GUH).

The people of Kekionga lived in shelters that each housed one family. The Miamis made their cabins by covering a frame of bent poles with tree bark or mats made of woven grass.

In the open fields near Kekionga, the women grew beans, squash, pumpkins, melons, and the group's most important crop—corn. Corn was such an important food crop for the Miamis that they had a harvest festival each year in honor of the Corn Spirit, one of their important gods.

In the forests and at the waters near Kekionga, the men hunted deer, rabbit, and beaver. From these animals they got meat, skins, and furs. For the Miamis, a successful hunt meant that they would have enough to eat throughout the winter.

Kekionga was located along an important portage (POHR•tij) between the Maumee and Wabash rivers. A **portage** is an overland route between two bodies of water. The portage made it possible for the Miamis to hunt over a larger area and to build new settlements throughout the Wabash River valley. Over time the Miami people became the largest group of Native Americans in what is now central Indiana.

✓ **What were the sources of food for the Miamis?**

LEARNING FROM DIAGRAMS
■ Why do you suppose the meeting house was designed the way it was?

Mats of tree bark or woven grass

Opening for smoke

Frame poles

A WIGWAM

A MIAMI VILLAGE

Meeting house

Drying rack

Corn or other crop

GOVERNMENT AMONG THE MIAMIS

Whenever people live in large groups, they have a government. **Government** is a system for deciding what is best for the group, including ways to protect the group from others and ways to settle disagreements within the group. A government has rules and leaders. There are many kinds of governments.

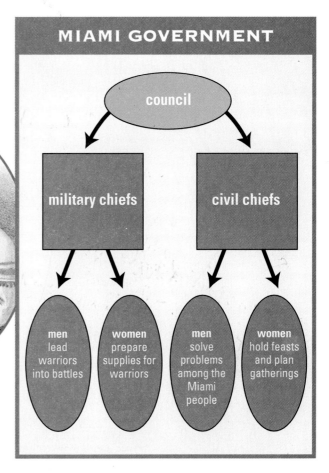

The Miami people elected chiefs to lead them. There were chiefs for each band and for the tribe as a whole. Each level of Miami government included a **council**, or group of advisers. The council was made up of the older men and women of each group. They helped the chiefs make decisions.

Each chief among the Miamis had a specialized job. Some chiefs had jobs related to war. These **military** chiefs and their councils decided when wars would be fought. Each group of Miamis had two military chiefs—a man and a woman. The man led the warriors in battle. The woman made sure that the warriors had the supplies they needed to fight.

Other chiefs in each group of Miamis had jobs related to nonmilitary matters. These **civil**, or citizen, chiefs made decisions in peacetime. The men solved problems among the Miami people. The women were in charge of festivals and of organizing workers in each group.

What kinds of chiefs did the Miami people have?

MIAMI GOVERNMENT

council

military chiefs

civil chiefs

men
lead warriors into battles

women
prepare supplies for warriors

men
solve problems among the Miami people

women
hold feasts and plan gatherings

LEARNING FROM DIAGRAMS Miami government was divided into civil and military branches.
■ Which branch would settle a disagreement between two tribe members?

NEWCOMERS FROM THE EAST AND NORTH

After the Miamis settled much of the Wabash River valley, more tribes from the Eastern Woodlands came to live in the Indiana area. During the 1600s and 1700s, the Lenapes (better known as the Delawares), the Shawnees, and others settled south of the Miamis. They had come from places to the east.

Many of these groups had been forced to move west when Europeans began settling the lands along the Atlantic coast. The Europeans built their settlements on land where the Indians had farmed and hunted for hundreds of years. The

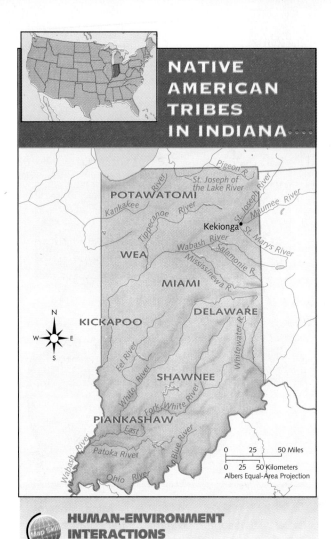

NATIVE AMERICAN TRIBES IN INDIANA

POTAWATOMI

Kekionga

WEA

MIAMI

KICKAPOO

DELAWARE

SHAWNEE

PIANKASHAW

Pigeon R.
St. Joseph of the Lake River
Kankakee River
Tippecanoe River
St. Joseph River
Maumee River
Wabash River
St. Mary's River
Salamonie R.
Mississinewa R.
Eel River
White River
Whitewater R.
Fork White River
East
Blue River
Wabash River
Patoka River
Ohio River

0   25   50 Miles
0   25   50 Kilometers
Albers Equal-Area Projection

HUMAN-ENVIRONMENT INTERACTIONS
■ Which Native American groups settled in what is now Indiana?

Indians moved west of the European settlements but were forced to keep moving by other Indian groups who did not want to give up their land to the newcomers. In the 1600s and 1700s, the Iroquois fought with the Delawares and other Indian groups, forcing them westward into the Indiana area. The Iroquois of the Eastern Woodlands were a powerful group of tribes from what is now New York State.

During this time the Kickapoos and other Miami bands, including the Piankashaws (py•ANG•kuh•shawz) and Weas (WAY•uhz), also began moving into the Indiana area. They came from the Great Lakes region and settled mostly in

what is now western Indiana. Like the tribes from the east, the Indian groups from the Great Lakes had been forced from their lands by Indian wars and the coming of the Europeans.

The last Indians of the Eastern Woodlands to come to the Indiana area were the Potawatomis (paht•uh•WAHT•uh•meez). Most of the Potawatomis had lived near the northern shores of Lake Michigan and in other areas around the Great Lakes. By the late 1700s, however, groups of Potawatomis had built settlements along the St. Joseph of the Lake River and in other parts of northwestern Indiana.

✓ **What groups of Native Americans moved to the Indiana area in the 1600s and 1700s?**

LESSON 2 REVIEW

Check Understanding

1. **Recall the Facts**   Why did many Native American groups come to Indiana?
2. **Focus on the Main Idea**   What did the different Indian groups of the Eastern Woodlands have in common?

Think Critically

3. **Past to Present**   How was Miami government similar to government in the United States today?
4. **Explore Viewpoints**   How do you think the Miamis felt about newcomers moving into the Indiana area?

Show What You Know

Art Activity   Draw a picture of everyday life in Kekionga or another Indian settlement. Compare your picture with that of a partner.

How To

Read a Time Line

Why Is This Skill Important?

It is sometimes hard to understand how events relate to one another in time. A **time line** is a graph that shows the order in which events took place and the amount of time that passed between them. To understand the history of Indiana, you need to know when important events happened.

Understand the Process

The time line on this page shows when events happened in the early history of Indiana. The marks on the line show points in time. Like a map, a time line has a scale. But the scale on a time line shows units of time, not units of distance. On the time line below, the space between two marks stands for a unit of one **century**, or 100 years. Just as days and years are units of time, so is a century. The dates near the left end of the time line came first. The dates near the right end of the time line came later.

The first part of the time line describes the end of the time of the Mound Builders in what is now the state of Indiana. This was sometime in the fifteenth century, or between the years 1401 and 1500. Look to the right to see what happened next. In the sixteenth century, or between the years 1501 and 1600, few Native American groups lived in Indiana, although some Native Americans moved through looking for food. What happened next? Between which years did the events take place? In which century was that?

Think and Apply

Make a time line that shows the twentieth and twenty-first centuries. Label the centuries and every five years from the year you were born. Mark the year you will graduate from high school and other important years for you in both centuries. Add pictures to your time line, and then display it on a bulletin board in your classroom or elsewhere in your school.

TIME LINE OF NATIVE AMERICAN SETTLEMENT IN INDIANA

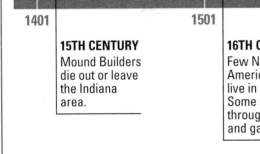

1401

15TH CENTURY
Mound Builders die out or leave the Indiana area.

1501

16TH CENTURY
Few Native American groups live in Indiana. Some move through to hunt and gather food.

1601

17TH CENTURY
Miamis settle near the Maumee River and build the settlement of Kekionga. Other tribes of the Eastern Woodlands follow.

1701

18TH CENTURY
Potawatomis move into the Indiana area from the Great Lakes area. They are the last Indians of the Eastern Woodlands to settle in Indiana.

LESSON 3

FRENCH EXPLORERS AND TRADERS

Link to Our World

Why might people today start new settlements?

Focus on the Main Idea
Read to find out why the French started settlements in the Indiana area.

Preview Vocabulary
colony
voyageur
permanent
right
status symbol

The French often traded metal arrowheads to Native Americans for beaver fur.

For thousands of years Native Americans were the only people in North and South America. Then, starting with Christopher Columbus in 1492, European explorers, traders, and settlers began to arrive. These Europeans came from countries such as Spain, Portugal, France, and Britain. Like the Native Americans, the Europeans wanted to use the many natural resources of the Americas. For the Native Americans, life would never again be the same after the arrival of the Europeans.

THE COMING OF THE FRENCH

The French landed on the east coast of present-day Canada in the middle 1500s. They set up fishing camps but soon learned that they could make more money by trading with the Native Americans to get furs. The French fur trade grew rapidly. Soon more fur traders came, as well as explorers and soldiers.

Among the first Europeans to arrive in what is now Indiana was the French explorer René-Robert Cavelier (ka•vuhl•YAY). He was known as Sieur de La Salle, or "Sir" La Salle (luh•SAL). La Salle came from the French colony of New France, which is now part of Canada. A **colony** is a place set up and ruled by a faraway country.

La Salle began exploring the lands west of New France for three reasons. He wanted to find a water route through North America to the Pacific Ocean. He wanted to claim land for France. And he wanted to expand the French fur trade. To meet his goals, La Salle made three trips into the western lands. One trip began in 1679.

By late in the year, La Salle and his crew of 26 explorers had reached the south-eastern shore of Lake Michigan. From there they paddled in eight canoes up the St. Joseph of the Lake River into what is now Indiana. On a cold, snowy December day, they camped at the bend in the southern part of the river, near the present-day city called South Bend.

La Salle learned from his Indian guide, White Beaver, that a portage connected the St. Joseph River to the headwaters of the Kankakee River. The Kankakee, La Salle believed, would lead him to larger rivers and possibly to the Pacific Ocean. With White Beaver's help, La Salle found the portage.

From the Kankakee River, the French explorers paddled into the Illinois River. Near present-day Peoria, Illinois, La Salle built a fort. He then returned to New France for supplies.

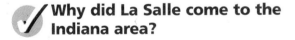 **Why did La Salle come to the Indiana area?**

THE MEETING AT THE COUNCIL OAK

La Salle returned to the Indiana area in 1681. There he found great unrest among the Indians. The Miami people were at war with their neighbors to the west, the Illinois. The Delawares and Shawnees were also at war. They were fighting with Iroquois warriors who were making raids into the Ohio River valley from the east.

The explorations of La Salle increased French land claims in North America.

La Salle met with chiefs of the Miami tribe at a village near the Kankakee portage. He urged the Miamis to make peace with the Illinois. He warned them that the greater threat came from the Iroquois, who were being helped by the British. La Salle offered aid from France, Britain's enemy, in fighting off the Iroquois.

The next day the chiefs met under a great oak tree they called the Council Oak. They decided to accept La Salle's offer and said,

66 We make you the master of our beaver and our lands, of our minds and our bodies. 99

Having won the friendship of the Miamis, La Salle and his crew continued their trip. They followed the Kankakee River to the Illinois River, reaching it on February 6, 1682. Two months later they reached the mouth of the Mississippi River, where the river flows into the Gulf of Mexico. With shouts of "Long live the king!" La Salle claimed for France the entire Mississippi River valley, including all the land drained by its tributaries. He named it Louisiana to honor the French king Louis XIV. Indiana was a part of this land.

 What decision did the Miami leaders make at the Council Oak?

THE FUR TRADE

La Salle died in 1687. The French, however, continued to explore the land he had claimed and to expand the fur trade. By the early 1700s many French fur traders were at work throughout the region.

What?

Beaver Hats

A beaver hat was a status symbol for many European people. If you were important or wanted people to think you were important, you had to wear a beaver hat. Beaver fur for making hats was valued so much in Europe that by the 1500s the beaver had become scarce there. About this time Europeans found out that North America was a good source of beaver fur. So the fur trade in North America grew and grew.

The Indians had raccoon, fox, and beaver furs to trade. Beaver fur was especially valuable. It brought a high price when sold in Europe. For all the different kinds of fur, the French traders offered goods such as tools, knives, guns,

Voyageurs took furs from Indiana to Canada and brought other items back to trade. Native Americans were eager to trade furs for European goods like the copper kettle shown below.

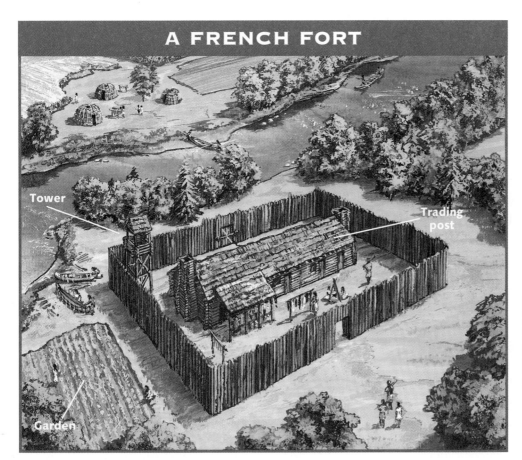

A FRENCH FORT

Tower

Trading post

Garden

LEARNING FROM DIAGRAMS The French started building trading posts in Indiana in 1717.

■ What do you suppose was the purpose of the tower in the back of the fort?

blankets, shirts, mirrors, glass beads, and metal pots.

As soon as the fur traders had gathered a large number of furs, they hired **voyageurs** (voy•uh•ZHERZ) to take the furs to Montreal, the largest settlement in New France. *Voyageur* is a French word meaning "traveler." In Montreal the voyageurs put the furs on ships sailing to Europe. On their return to the Indiana area, the voyageurs brought back more goods for the traders.

 How did the fur trade work?

FRENCH FORTS AND TRADING POSTS

To make trading easier, the French built trading posts where the Indians could bring their furs and trade them for goods.

In some ways the trading posts were like stores of today. Soldiers protected the trading posts and the French claim to the land by keeping other Europeans away.

The first French trading post in Indiana was Fort Ouiatenon (wee•AHT•uh•nohn), near present-day Lafayette. The French built it in 1717 near a Wea village. The main job of the soldiers at Fort Ouiatenon was to keep the peace with the Illinois Indians. The French also kept the British from trading with the Indians.

In 1721 the French built another trading post and fort, near the Miami settlement of Kekionga. Fort Miami, close to the present-day city of Fort Wayne, was very important to the French. Its location at the portage between the Maumee and Wabash rivers helped the French control the Wabash River valley.

By 1732 the French had built a third trading post and fort, on the lower Wabash closer to the Ohio River. They also built a settlement there, which the traders named Vincennes (vin•SENZ) after the French captain in command of the fort. With a population of more than 300 traders and their families, Vincennes was Indiana's first **permanent**, or lasting, European settlement. It became the present-day city of Vincennes.

 **Why did the French build trading posts?**

THE GENTLE INVASION

The coming of the French to the Indiana area is sometimes called "the gentle invasion." Historians gave it this name because the French and the Indians were friendly to each other. Perhaps this is because the French did not try to force the Indians off their land. They respected the Indians' **rights**, or legal claims, to the land. The French also treated the Indians as equal trading partners.

The Indians felt that the French were more helpful than harmful. The Indians liked European goods and valued them as status symbols. A **status symbol** is an object that is a sign of wealth or importance. Many Indians felt they could not do without these goods.

The gentle invasion brought many changes to Native American cultures. Because of trade, many of the objects the Indians used every day were replaced with European goods. The Indians now used cloth instead of animal skins for clothing. They used metal pots instead of handmade clay pots. They hunted with guns, which replaced the bows and arrows.

The coming of the Europeans also had bad effects on the Indians. As more and more European settlers moved into Indiana, many Native Americans died in wars or were forced to move away. Death also came in another form. With the Europeans came diseases, such as measles and smallpox, that killed many thousands of people.

 **How did Europeans change Indian cultures and ways of life?**

LESSON 3 REVIEW

Check Understanding

1. **Recall the Facts** What were the names of the first three French settlements in Indiana?
2. **Focus on the Main Idea** Why did the French start settlements in the Indiana area?

Think Critically

3. **Link to You** What items would you trade today, if you were setting up a trading post in your community?
4. **Think More About It** Was the gentle invasion completely gentle? Explain.
5. **Personally Speaking** Would you like to have been an explorer traveling with La Salle? Why or why not?

Show What You Know

 **Advertising Activity**
Imagine that you are a French or Indian trader. Create an advertisement to make people want to trade with you instead of with someone else. Show your advertisement in a classroom display.

HowTo

Follow Routes on a Historical Map

Why Is This Skill Important?

How do you get from your home to school? You follow a route. A **route** is a path that a person takes to get from one place to another. Some maps show the routes of explorers.

Understand the Process

This map shows the routes La Salle took on three different trips. Read the map key to learn which trip each symbol stands for.

- The red line shows La Salle's route on his trip in 1670.
- The blue line shows La Salle's route in 1679.
- What does the green line show?

Now trace each route with your finger. Use the map to answer these questions.

1. On which trip did La Salle travel on the Ohio River?
2. On which trip did he find the Kankakee River?
3. Down which river did La Salle travel to reach the Gulf of Mexico?

Think and Apply

Write a paragraph describing the route you follow to get from home to school. Have a partner read your paragraph and then draw a map that shows your route.

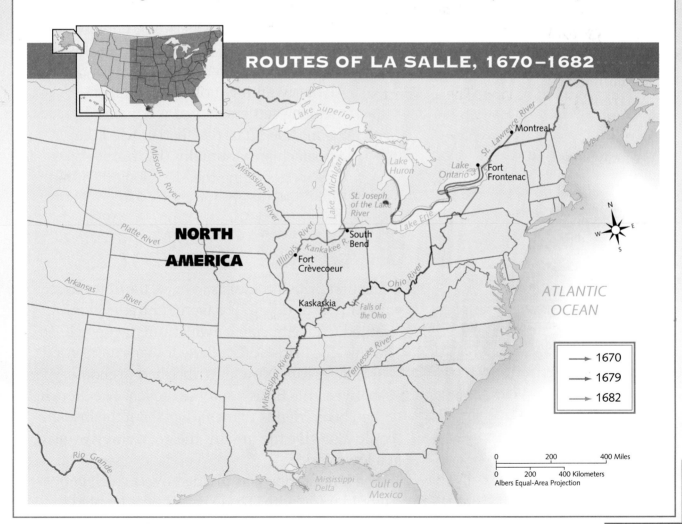

ROUTES OF LA SALLE, 1670–1682

THE BRITISH IN INDIANA

Link to Our World

Why do countries and groups of people have conflicts today?

Focus on the Main Idea
Read to find out why the French, British, and Native American peoples fought one another in the 1700s.

Preview Vocabulary
colonist
treaty
ally
unite
proclamation

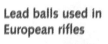

Lead balls used in European rifles

In 1607 the British built their first permanent settlement in North America, at Jamestown, Virginia. In the years that followed, thousands of settlers came to live in the 13 colonies that the British set up along the Atlantic coast. The people who lived in the colonies were called **colonists**.

Unlike the French, most of the British colonists in North America did not live by trading with the Native Americans. Instead, they cleared and fenced the land for farming. Always wanting more land, English-speaking settlers moved westward. By the middle 1700s they had crossed the Appalachian Mountains. By the late 1700s they were settling the area along the Ohio River in southern Indiana.

TAKING SIDES

The first British colonists to enter the Ohio River valley in the middle 1700s were fur traders who wanted to take business away from the French. To do this, the British offered the Indians more goods for fewer furs. Now the tribes had to choose between the British and the French. The French had been friends to the Indians. But the British could also give the Indians the goods they wanted, at a lower price.

The Miami tribe was divided over which people they should trade with. Those bands who wanted to

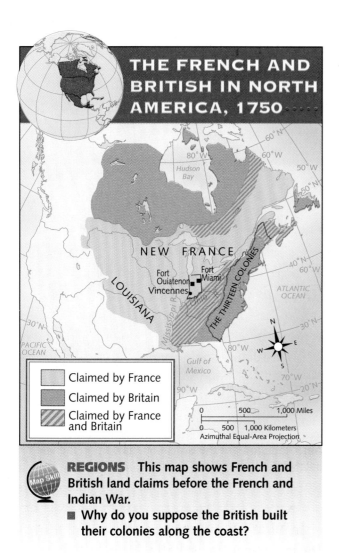

THE FRENCH AND BRITISH IN NORTH AMERICA, 1750

Hudson Bay

NEW FRANCE

Fort Ouiatenon
Vincennes

Fort Miami

LOUISIANA

THE THIRTEEN COLONIES

ATLANTIC OCEAN

PACIFIC OCEAN

Gulf of Mexico

Claimed by France
Claimed by Britain
Claimed by France and Britain

0   500   1,000 Miles
0   500   1,000 Kilometers
Azimuthal Equal-Area Projection

REGIONS This map shows French and British land claims before the French and Indian War.

■ Why do you suppose the British built their colonies along the coast?

trade with the British were led by Chief Demoiselle (de•moh•SEL). In 1748 Demoiselle's followers, along with groups of Delawares and Shawnees, signed a treaty with the British so they "might be admitted into the Friendship and Alliance of the King of Great Britain." A **treaty** is an agreement among nations.

In time the French lost more of their Indian **allies**, or friends, to the British through treaties and trade. To make matters worse, some of the Miami leaders who sided with the French died of smallpox. The French now feared having their trading posts destroyed and their

citizens killed. Worst of all, they feared losing the fur trade. They blamed the British.

 Why did Indian groups have to take sides between the French and the British?

THE FRENCH AND INDIAN WAR

The bad feelings between the British and the French soon turned into a war. Indians fought on both sides in this war, but more fought on the side of the French. Because of this, the war came to be known in North America as the French and Indian War. The fighting began in 1754 near what is now the city of Pittsburgh in western Pennsylvania.

Most of the fighting was in the lands west of the Appalachian Mountains and in Canada. The British colonists could not win the war with just the help of their Indian allies. So the British government sent its army to help the colonists. In what is now Indiana, British soldiers captured France's Fort Miami and Fort Ouiatenon, taking control of the Wabash River valley. Now the British were able to force the French out of Indiana and take over their fur trade.

The French and Indian War ended in 1763 when the French and the British signed the Treaty of Paris. The French agreed to give the British both Canada and the French lands between the Appalachian Mountains and the Mississippi River. The Treaty of Paris meant that Britain would rule what is now Indiana.

 What was the result of the French and Indian War?

PONTIAC'S WAR

An Ottawa chief named Pontiac (PAHN•tee•ak) took the side of the French in the French and Indian War. Like most other Native Americans, Pontiac wanted to trade with the French rather than the British. He also did not want British settlers to keep clearing Indian hunting lands for farming. To stop the loss of Indian lands, Pontiac **united**, or brought together, the tribes of the Great Lakes area and of the Ohio and Mississippi river valleys against the British.

In this picture, Chief Pontiac urges other Native Americans to fight the British by "taking up the war hatchet."

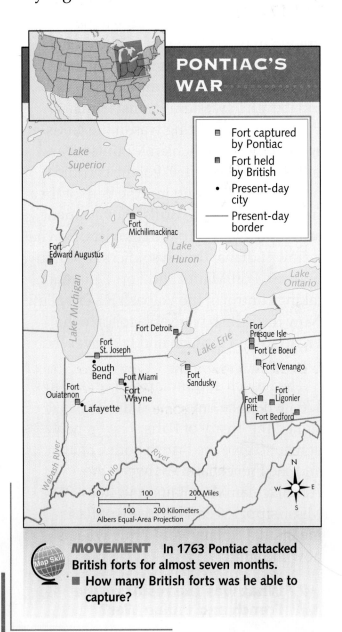

PONTIAC'S WAR

- ■ Fort captured by Pontiac
- ■ Fort held by British
- • Present-day city
- — Present-day border

Lake Superior

Fort Michilimackinac

Fort Edward Augustus

Lake Huron

Lake Michigan

Lake Ontario

Fort Detroit

Lake Erie

Fort St. Joseph

South Bend

Fort Presque Isle

Fort Le Boeuf

Fort Venango

Fort Ouiatenon

Fort Miami

Fort Wayne

Fort Sandusky

Fort Pitt

Fort Ligonier

Fort Bedford

Lafayette

Wabash River

Ohio River

0   100   200 Miles
0   100   200 Kilometers
Albers Equal-Area Projection

N W E S

MOVEMENT In 1763 Pontiac attacked British forts for almost seven months. ■ How many British forts was he able to capture?

In May 1763, Pontiac and his united Indian army started attacking British forts. Within a few weeks almost every fort in what is now western Pennsylvania, Ohio, Michigan, and Indiana was destroyed. Among them were Fort Miami and Fort Ouiatenon.

Pontiac's army depended on the French for guns and for other supplies, but by October 1763 the French had ended their war with Britain. As winter came, many Indian warriors returned to their homes. Without the French supplies and the Indian warriors, Pontiac had to give up control of the British forts. By winter the British again had control of the forts and had forced most of the French settlers to leave.

✓ **What was the cause of Pontiac's war?**

THE PROCLAMATION OF 1763

With most of the French driven out of the lands west of the Appalachian Mountains, many settlers in the 13 British colonies wanted to move there. Some had already crossed the mountains and started farms. To stop this westward movement, the British king, George III, issued the Proclamation of 1763. A **proclamation** is an order from a leader to the citizens.

The Proclamation of 1763 said that no colonist could move to land west of the Appalachian Mountains. George III said these lands were to be used only by the Indians. He ordered this to please his Indian allies. He also wanted to make it easier for the British government to control the fur trade by keeping the colonists out of the way.

Indian leaders knew that the colonists had already forced Indians to move westward from the eastern side of the Appalachians. So the Indians were pleased that the British king wanted to keep the colonists off their land.

✔ **What was the Proclamation of 1763?**

THE PROCLAMATION LINE OF 1763

Hudson Bay

60°W   50°W

50°N

St. Lawrence R.

Lake Superior

Lake Huron

Lake Michigan

Lake Ontario

Lake Erie

ATLANTIC OCEAN

40°N

THE THIRTEEN COLONIES

Mississippi River

Ohio River

LOUISIANA

0   250   500 Miles
0   250   500 Kilometers
Azimuthal Equal-Area Projection

80°W   30°N

FLORIDA

Gulf of Mexico

90°W

Spanish
British
British (reserved for Indians)
Proclamation Line of 1763

HUMAN-ENVIRONMENT INTERACTIONS
■ Which country claimed Florida in 1763?

LESSON 4 REVIEW

Check Understanding

1. **Recall the Facts**   Which groups of people were on the two sides in the French and Indian War?
2. **Focus on the Main Idea**   Why did the French, British, and Native American peoples fight one another in the 1700s?

Think Critically

3. **Think More About It**   What problems do you think the Proclamation of 1763 might have caused?
4. **Explore Viewpoint**   Why do you think some Native Americans liked the French? Why do you think some liked the British?

Show What You Know

Debate Activity   Work in one of three groups that stand for the Indians, the French, and the British in 1760. Each group should think of why it should control Indiana's lands. List the reasons on a class chart with three columns, and discuss which reasons are best.

LESSON 5

THE AMERICANS FIGHT FOR FREEDOM

Link to Our World

How can one person affect history?

Focus on the Main Idea
Read to find out how George Rogers Clark affected the history of Indiana.

Preview Vocabulary

tax	surrender
revolution	territory
pioneer	
frontier	
flatboat	
stockade	

An early settler's ax

When the British controlled the lands west of the Appalachian Mountains, there was much trouble in the region. American colonists moved into what they called "the West," even though the Proclamation of 1763 did not allow it. Native Americans who lived on that land fought the colonists and sometimes fought one another.

THE AMERICAN REVOLUTION

Back in the 13 colonies along the Atlantic coast, the American colonists were angry about the British king's proclamation. They grew even angrier when they found out that the British government expected them to pay the costs of the French and Indian War. To collect the money, the British government made the American colonists pay new taxes. A **tax** is the money a government collects to pay for the government services that it provides.

Some colonists argued that the government in Britain did not have the right to tax colonists living in North America. Those colonists decided it would be best for them to break away from British rule. They wanted to start their own country and make their own laws. The British and the colonists could not agree, and they began fighting.

In this painting by John Trumbull, members of the Second Continental Congress sign the Declaration of Independence.

The fight with the British was called the American Revolution, and it began in 1775. A **revolution** is a sudden, violent change in government and in people's lives. Although the American Revolution started in 1775, the Americans did not say they had formed a new country until July 4, 1776. They did this in the Declaration of Independence, which stated that the colonies were now the United States of America.

 Why did the American colonists choose to fight a war with the British?

THE WAR IN THE WEST

At the beginning of the American Revolution, all the fighting took place in the 13 colonies along the Atlantic coast. Meanwhile, in the lands west of the Appalachian Mountains, the American settlers worried about what would happen to them. They thought that if the British were not driven out of the West, the British would probably keep those lands even if the Americans won the war. But there was another reason for the Americans to worry—and that was Henry Hamilton.

Henry Hamilton commanded the British forts in the West from his post at Fort Detroit. He knew that if the war spread to the West, the British would need Indian help to defeat the Americans. Hamilton met with the leaders of the Miamis, Shawnees, and other Indian groups. He told them that without their support the British might lose the war. If the British lost the war, he warned, the Americans would force the Indians off their land. Hamilton offered the Indians tools, knives, and guns if they would kill American settlers.

From 1775 on, the American settlers throughout the West had to fight off many Indian attacks in what is now Indiana and nearby states. Although the colony of Virginia claimed much of this land, its leaders at first did not help the American

George Rogers Clark
1752–1818

George Rogers Clark was born and raised in the colony of Virginia, but he left at the age of 19. He went to work in the lands west of the Appalachian Mountains as a surveyor. A surveyor measures the land so maps can be drawn. While Clark was in the West, he explored the forests and hunted. He knew the land was rich in natural resources, and he wanted Americans to be able to settle there. He himself built a home and farm near the Ohio River in what is now Kentucky.

settlers there. Then in 1777 George Rogers Clark went to see Governor Patrick Henry and other Virginia leaders. He told them, "If a country is not worth protecting, it is not worth claiming."

Clark had been a **pioneer** in the West, one of the first settlers in what is now Kentucky. He knew why the Americans in the West feared Henry Hamilton and the British. Clark, who was just 25 years old, asked Governor Henry to let him lead a small army on a secret mission against Hamilton and the British. The governor agreed that the western lands were worth protecting. He gave Clark permission and helped him get money to pay for soldiers and supplies.

✓ **Why did the Americans fear Henry Hamilton?**

CLARK'S ARMY

By 1778 George Rogers Clark had raised enough money to pay for a small army of about 150 farmers from the Virginia frontier. The **frontier** was the western edge of European settlement. The frontier farmers had no uniforms, only their deerskin shirts and trousers. They carried hunting rifles as weapons.

From Virginia, Clark led his soldiers to Fort Pitt in what is now western Pennsylvania. They boarded flatboats there and traveled down the Ohio River to the Falls of the Ohio, an area of rapids,

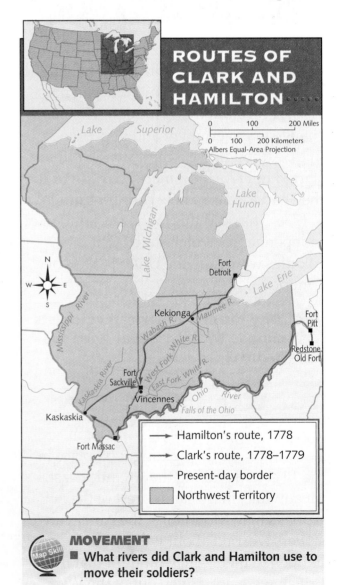

ROUTES OF CLARK AND HAMILTON

0   100   200 Miles
0   100   200 Kilometers
Albers Equal-Area Projection

Lake Superior
Lake Huron
Lake Michigan
Lake Erie
Fort Detroit
Kekionga
Maumee R.
Wabash R.
Fort Pitt
Redstone Old Fort
Mississippi River
West Fork White R.
East Fork White R.
Kaskaskia River
Fort Sackville
Vincennes
Ohio River
Falls of the Ohio
Kaskaskia
Fort Massac

→ Hamilton's route, 1778
→ Clark's route, 1778–1779
— Present-day border
▨ Northwest Territory

MOVEMENT
■ What rivers did Clark and Hamilton use to move their soldiers?

or fast-moving water, near where Louisville, Kentucky, and Jeffersonville, Indiana, are now located. A **flatboat** is a large wooden boat with a flat bottom and square ends. At the Falls of the Ohio, 40 or more Kentucky frontier farmers joined Clark and his Virginians.

On June 26, 1778, Clark's small army continued down the Ohio River. They traveled up the Mississippi River as far as the Kaskaskia (ka•SKAS•kee•uh) River before setting off on foot. Their goal was to attack the British who held the French fort at Kaskaskia. It was located on the Mississippi River in what is now southern Illinois. Shortly after midnight on July 4, 1778, Clark's soldiers sneaked inside the stockade of the fort and captured it. A **stockade** is a wall of strong posts built for protection.

With the help of French people living at Kaskaskia, Clark and his soldiers went on to capture nearby Cahokia on the Mississippi River. Within six weeks they also took Vincennes on the Wabash River and claimed the West for the Americans.

Hearing about Clark's victories, the British commander Henry Hamilton feared that the Americans might next attack his headquarters at Fort Detroit. Hamilton decided it was necessary

This sword was given to George Rogers Clark in 1812 to honor the march to Vincennes.

to take action. Without delay the British commander led an army of over 500 soldiers, more than half of whom were Indians, to recapture Vincennes.

Hamilton's soldiers traveled in canoes up the Maumee River from Lake Erie. They crossed the portage at Kekionga and paddled down the Wabash River.

On December 17, 1778, Hamilton's army attacked the fort at Vincennes and easily defeated the small group of American soldiers Clark had left there to guard it. The British renamed it Fort Sackville to honor Lord Sackville, a friend of the British king.

✓ **Why did George Rogers Clark attack forts in the West?**

CLARK'S LONG MARCH

At Kaskaskia, George Rogers Clark learned that Vincennes had been captured by the British. He wanted to take it back, but he did not have enough soldiers for a regular battle. He decided, instead, on a surprise attack in the middle of winter.

On February 6, 1779, Clark and his soldiers at Kaskaskia set out for Vincennes, 180 miles (290 km) away. The weather was rainy and cold, and most of the land was flooded or frozen. During the day Clark and his soldiers pushed through the forests in deep water. "We plunged into the water sometimes to the neck," one soldier wrote in a diary. At night they slept in trees or in the shallowest water they could find.

After splashing through the flooded southern Illinois forests for more than two weeks, many of Clark's soldiers wanted to go home. They were hungry, cold, wet, and discouraged. They did not want to go on until their drummer raised their spirits. He used his drum as a raft to cross the high water.

Here is how Carl Carmer describes what the drummer did in his book *The Boy Drummer of Vincennes.*

> **66**I almost drowned
> When I went under
> But the drum was a raft
> And I climbed aboard.
> Then I let her pound
> Like all-fired thunder!
> While the general laughed
> And the men all roared

I sat aft
And played "The Boatman's Daughter".
Toddle on your toddy-pots,
Totter through the water.**99**

The hungry, cold, and wet soldiers finally reached dry land on February 23, 1779. Vincennes was just 2 miles (about 3 km) away.

 Why did George Rogers Clark and his soldiers go on their long march?

VICTORY AT FORT SACKVILLE

From their camp outside of Vincennes, the American soldiers planned their attack on Fort Sackville. George Rogers Clark knew that Henry Hamilton and the British soldiers did not expect them. After all, who would have thought any army was daring enough to go through the flooded Illinois forests in the middle of winter?

As night fell on February 24, 1779, Clark and his soldiers began to make their way to Fort Sackville. At dawn the next day, Clark ordered some of his soldiers to go behind a small hill near the fort. There they marched back and forth waving big flags. The British inside the fort could see only the tops of the flags. To them it looked as if a huge American army was about to attack.

The British fired their guns, but Clark's frontier soldiers were better shots. By the end of the day on February 25, 1779, Henry Hamilton knew he was beaten. He sent Clark a message saying he would **surrender**, or give up, the fort. Some Hoosiers today celebrate George Rogers Clark Day on February 25 in honor of his victory at Fort Sackville.

This painting showing Clark's march is part of a mural in the George Rogers Clark Memorial in Vincennes.

Clark demanded the surrender of Fort Sackville (left) in a letter (above) written to Hamilton.

Clark's victory helped strengthen American claims to the vast region west of the Appalachian Mountains. Later, part of this region north of the Ohio River became known as the Northwest Territory. A **territory** is land that is owned by a country but is not part of any state. When the American Revolution ended in 1783, the United States had gained the lands from the Appalachians to the Mississippi River, a region that included the Northwest Territory.

 How did the Americans win Fort Sackville from the British?

LESSON 5 REVIEW

Check Understanding

1. **Recall the Facts** When did the American Revolution begin and end?
2. **Focus on the Main Idea** How did George Rogers Clark affect the history of Indiana?

Think Critically

3. **Think More About It** What kind of leader was George Rogers Clark?
4. **Personally Speaking** What do you think might have happened if George Rogers Clark had not made his daring attack on Fort Sackville?

Show What You Know

 Simulation Activity With a partner, role-play an imaginary conversation between George Rogers Clark and Henry Hamilton before the British surrender of Fort Sackville. Then role-play a conversation after the surrender. Plan how the two conversations should be different.

REVIEW

CONNECT MAIN IDEAS

Use this organizer to show that you understand how the chapter's main ideas are connected. Copy the organizer onto a separate sheet of paper. Then complete it by writing an answer to each question.

The Early People of Indiana

Lesson 1

Who came to Indiana?
_____

Why did they come?
_____

Where did they go?
_____

What did they do?
_____

Lesson 2

Who came to Indiana?
_____

Why did they come?
_____

Where did they go?
_____

What did they do?
_____

Lesson 3

Who came to Indiana?
_____

Why did they come?
_____

Where did they go?
_____

What did they do?
_____

Lesson 4

Who came to Indiana?
_____

Why did they come?
_____

Where did they go?
_____

What did they do?
_____

Lesson 5

Who came to Indiana?
_____

Why did they come?
_____

Where did they go?
_____

What did they do?
_____

WRITE MORE ABOUT IT

1. **Write a Story** Imagine that you are a Native American who has just met a European trader traveling across Indiana. Write a story that you could tell your children. Describe some of the ways the European people and their goods are different from people and goods you have seen before.

2. **Write a Report** Write a short report that discusses the culture of the Mound Builders.

3. **Write a Journal Entry** Imagine that you are with George Rogers Clark on his march from Kaskaskia to Vincennes. Write a journal entry about what one day was like during his march.

USE VOCABULARY

For each pair of vocabulary words, write a sentence or two explaining how the words are related.

1. scarce, extinct
2. band, tribe
3. council, government
4. colony, frontier
5. ally, unite

CHECK UNDERSTANDING

1. Why did early people in North America first move to the area that is now Indiana?
2. In what ways were the different tribes of Indians of the Eastern Woodlands alike?
3. How did the Miami Indians govern themselves?
4. Who was the first European explorer known to have reached what is now Indiana?
5. How did the French remain on friendly terms with the Indians?
6. How did Britain come to rule lands west of the Appalachian Mountains after 1763?
7. Why did American colonists choose to fight the British?
8. Why did George Rogers Clark attack British forts?

THINK CRITICALLY

1. **Think More About It** Why was river travel important to both Native Americans and European explorers and settlers?

2. **Past to Present** The Miami Indians had many kinds of chiefs. Do citizens in the United States today have leaders at different levels and for different purposes? Explain your answer.

3. **Personally Speaking** Who do you think gained more from the fur trade, the French or the Indians? Explain your answer.

4. **Link to You** What kind of person was George Rogers Clark? Would you like to have been one of his soldiers? Why or why not?

APPLY SKILLS

How to Work Together in Groups
Make a list of steps to follow when working with a group of your classmates.

How to Read a Time Line Draw a time line to show the twentieth century through the twenty-fifth century. In what century is the year 2150? What is the last year of the twenty-fifth century?

How to Follow Routes on a Historical Map Look in newspapers or old magazines for a map that shows routes. Cut out the map and tape it to a sheet of paper. Below the map, describe the routes shown. What places are along the routes?

READ MORE ABOUT IT

Mounds of Earth and Shell by Bonnie Shemie. Tundra Books. This book describes the earthworks and structures that Native Americans built in Indiana and nearby areas.

George Rogers Clark: War in the West by Susan and John Lee. Childrens Press. The authors tell the story of Clark's life.

License (Plate) to Save the Environment

Look at the Indiana license plates on cars you see. Some of the license plates are sky blue with a picture of an eagle flying in front of a golden sun. The eagle and the word *environment* tell you that these license plates are special. The money paid for them is used to buy land for all Hoosiers to use.

The money from the sale of these license plates goes to the Indiana Heritage Trust, or IHT. The IHT was started in 1992 by Evan Bayh, who was Indiana's governor at the time. He wanted the IHT to buy "some of the state's most beautiful natural areas and manage them responsibly for Hoosiers who enjoy outdoor activities, now and in the future."

The IHT has collected more than four million dollars from the sale of license plates. The money has been given to the Indiana Department of Natural Resources and to local community groups. They have bought more than 7,000 acres of land now being used as parks, wildlife areas, and hiking trails in all parts of the state. Their efforts have helped Indiana keep its beautiful environment.

INDIANA
H B 00
ENVIRONMENT

THINK AND APPLY

Imagine that you and a partner work for the state of Indiana. It is your job to come up with ideas to help people take better care of the environment. With your partner, prepare a list of what people in the state can do today to make sure that the state's environment remains beautiful and can be enjoyed by Hoosiers in the future.

BUILDING CITIZENSHIP

STORY CLOTH

A story cloth uses pictures instead of words to tell a story. Follow the pictures shown in this story cloth to help you review what you read about in Unit 1.

Summarize the Main Ideas

1. Many thousands of years ago, glaciers covered much of what is now Indiana. Early people followed herds of giant animals to hunt them for food, clothing, and shelter.

2. Early farmers and settlers grew crops in the fertile soil.

3. Some of the largest early settlements were built by the Mound Builders. Later, Indians of the Eastern Woodlands moved into what is now Indiana.

4. The French explored the Indiana area and traded with the Indians living there. The French built trading posts and a permanent settlement at Vincennes.

5. The British took the area from the French by winning the French and Indian War. The British wanted to keep colonists out of the area, leaving the land to the Indians.

6. In the American Revolution, George Rogers Clark defeated the British at Fort Sackville, giving control of the Indiana area to the new country—the United States of America.

Draw Another Scene   Choose one group of people described in Unit 1 but not shown in this story cloth. Draw a picture that shows a scene of daily life for the group you chose. Tell where your scene should be placed in the story cloth.

UNIT 1
REVIEW

COOPERATIVE LEARNING WORKSHOP

Remember

- Share your ideas.
- Cooperate with others to plan your work.
- Take responsibility for your work.
- Show your group's work to the class.
- Discuss what you learned by working together.

Activity 1
Build a Diorama

To show the environment of one of Indiana's three natural regions, build a diorama inside a shoebox. The scene you and your classmates will make should show the region in a way that shows how it is different from Indiana's other two natural regions. Add your diorama to a classroom display.

Activity 2
Draw Scenes of Daily Living

To show how people interact with their environment in different ways, draw scenes from daily life at two different times in Indiana history. You might draw scenes of early hunters and gatherers, early farmers, or Mound Builders, as well as scenes of Miami, French, British, or American settlers. Include your scenes in a classroom display.

Activity 3
Design a Hero's Medal

Working with your classmates, draw a design for a medal honoring George Rogers Clark and his soldiers. The design might include a scene from their march, their victory at Fort Sackville, or another event. Include a slogan or motto that you think would be appropriate.

Activity 4
Perform a Simulation

Working with your classmates, role-play a scene about a fur trade. Show what you would trade and how you think it was done. How do you think your simulation might be different depending on whether you play the role of a French, British, or Native American trader?

USE VOCABULARY

From the first column, choose a word that is related to a word in the second column. Tell how the words in each pair are related.

1. tribe
2. tributary
3. government
4. climate

a. council
b. precipitation
c. river system
d. culture

CHECK UNDERSTANDING

1. Which natural region of Indiana was never covered by the great glaciers?

2. Which Indiana river system is the largest?

3. What are three of Indiana's most important natural resources?

4. How did the lives of early hunters change after the giant animals died out?

5. When did Indians of the Eastern Woodlands begin to settle in what is now Indiana?

6. What was the first permanent French settlement in the Indiana area?

7. How did the British gain control of the lands west of the Appalachian Mountains?

8. What did the Proclamation of 1763 try to do?

THINK CRITICALLY

1. **Link to You** How do land and water features affect how and where people live today?

2. **Past to Present** George Rogers Clark believed in the fight for freedom. How do you think people in the United States today feel about fighting for freedom?

3. **Personally Speaking** Do you think rivers are as important to people today as they were to the early people of Indiana?

4. **Cause and Effect** How did the arrival of Europeans change life for the Native Americans?

APPLY GEOGRAPHY SKILLS

How to Follow Routes on a Historical Map On March 18, 1925, one of the worst tornadoes in United States history ripped through Missouri, Illinois, and Indiana. It was called the Tri-State Tornado because it traveled through three states. Use the map below to answer the questions.

1. Where did the tornado start and end?

2. What Indiana towns were damaged?

THE TRI-STATE TORNADO, 1925

UNIT 2

PIONEER DAYS

"BOONVILLE BEGINNINGS"

1780

1783
American
Revolution
ends

1790

1794
Battle of Fallen
Timbers

Fort Wayne is built

1800

1800
Harrison
becomes
governor of
Indiana
Territory

1809
The Ten O'Clock
Line becomes a
new border

1810

1811
Battle of
Tippecanoe

1814
Community of
Harmonie is founded

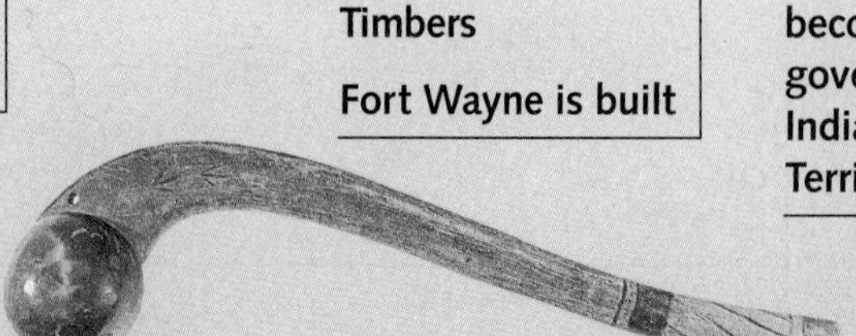

After winning its independence, the United States formed its own government. This government gave people great freedom. While the nation's leaders were setting up this new government in the East, many people were looking toward the western frontier. These people, called pioneers, settled the lands west of the Appalachian Mountains.

Life was hard for the pioneers, but they faced problems and dangers with courage. They often had to find new ways of doing things and invent what they needed. Their pioneer spirit made Indiana strong.

← "Boonville Beginnings," a 1941 mural by Ida Ableman

1820

1830

1840

1850

1816
Indiana becomes
a state

1825
Indianapolis becomes
the capital of Indiana

Robert Owen starts
the community of
New Harmony

1847
Indiana's first
railroad line
connects Madison
with Indianapolis

1853
Wabash and Erie
Canal opens

THE FLOATING HOUSE

by Scott Russell Sanders
illustrated by Helen Cogancherry

It is 1815, and the McClure family is floating down the Ohio River on a flatboat. The flat-bottomed boat is loaded with the family's wagon, farm tools, and household goods as well as its horse, cow, pig, and mule. With a pioneering spirit of adventure, the McClures have set out to start a new life on the western frontier.

Every afternoon before sunset, the McClures tied up on the bank, along with four or five other boats. The children pulled in trotlines to see what fish they had caught, and they gathered driftwood for fires. They refilled water barrels from the river, but let the mud settle out before drinking. The mothers traded food and lantern oil and stories. The fathers hunted deer and turkey for supper, then took turns all night standing guard.

> **trotline** fishing line with several hooks attached

sandbox box in which a fire was made for cooking

Before falling asleep, Mary and Jonathan watched embers glowing in the sandbox on deck. They smelled sawdust from the poplar and walnut lumber their father had used in building the boat, and the tar he had used for caulking the joints. They smelled tallow from the candles their mother had made. They listened to owls hoot and wolves howl. Even on windless nights, they heard limbs crashing in the woods. And always, beneath every other sound, they heard the lap and stir of the river.

The farther they journeyed, the wilder the land appeared. There were clearings for homesteads, and occasional towns, but mostly the shores were thick with trees, still brown and bare from the hard winter. Grapevines looped from trunk to trunk, and nests clotted the branches. Eagles and hawks circled overhead.

Bears swam across the current, snorting, black eyes gleaming. And once the whole river was blocked by a churning carpet of squirrels.

As the flatboat glided along, people called from shore, "Hello, the boat!"

"Hello, the shore!" the children called back. "What place is this?"

Steubenville, the people might answer, or Wheeling, Marietta, Point Pleasant, Gallipolis, Maysville. So many mysterious names! Jonathan and Mary had never before set foot outside of Pennsylvania, and here within a month they would see Ohio and western Virginia, Kentucky, and Indiana. Why, Indiana wasn't even a state yet, it was so thinly settled.

And that was where they were headed, to a settlement named Jeffersonville, across the river from Louisville, at the falls of the Ohio.

"How will we know the place?" the children asked.

"You'll hear the roar of the rapids," their mother said.

"How long until we get there?" they kept asking.

A good while, their father answered; then he said a week; then only a few days.

The children listened for a waterfall. They studied every island, every bluff, every field planted with spindly orchards, every log cabin surrounded by stumps.

Would the house they build in Indiana look like one of those lonesome cabins?

Just when it seemed they had reached the edge of the world, they came to Cincinnati, a city as large as Pittsburgh, all chimneys and church spires. The wharves were crowded with ships. The streets rang with hammers, clattered with carts, huffed and puffed with steam engines.

They floated on, past settlements with names like Lawrenceburgh and Madison. At last, one day about noon, Mary and Jonathan heard a low rumble, like the sound of an empty barrel rolling on the floor. They stared ahead and saw the water foaming white. "Rocks!" they shouted.

"Those must be the falls," their father said.

"And that must be Louisville," their mother said, pointing to a sizable town on the left bank.

"So that must be Jeffersonville," their father said, steering the boat toward a village on the right bank.

No sooner had the McClures tied up at the dock than dogs came running to sniff them and children came running to meet them and folks of all ages came to help unload the flatboat.

From the government office, the McClures bought a parcel of land overlooking the falls. Before dark, with more help from these new neighbors, they dismantled the boat, hauled the lumber to their farm, and began building a house with the very same wood.

FROM TERRITORY TO STATEHOOD

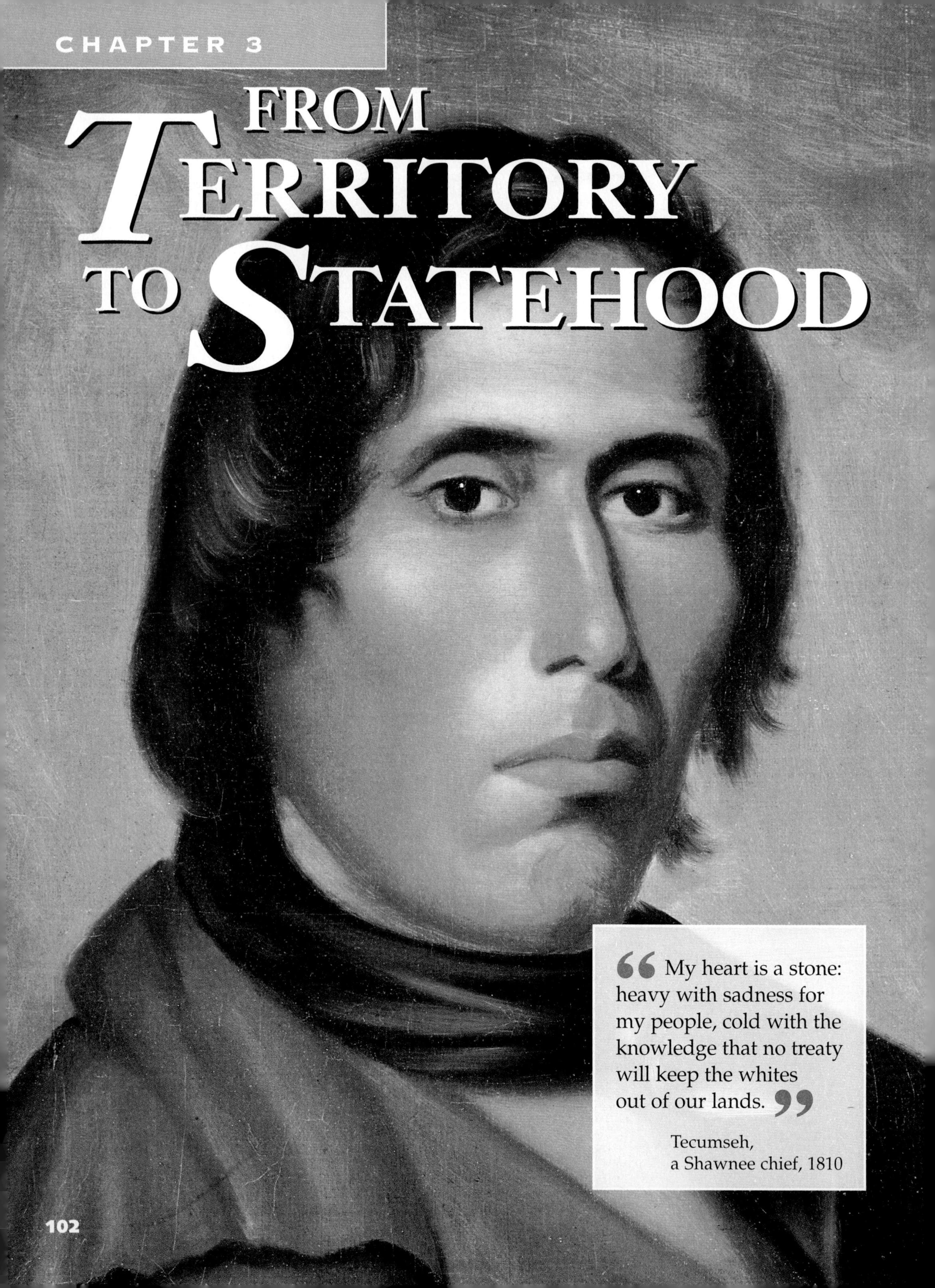

> 66 My heart is a stone: heavy with sadness for my people, cold with the knowledge that no treaty will keep the whites out of our lands. 99
>
> Tecumseh,
> a Shawnee chief, 1810

THE NORTHWEST TERRITORY

Link to Our World

How do government leaders today solve problems?

Focus on the Main Idea
Read to find out how government leaders solved problems in the western land.

Preview Vocabulary

ordinance	conflict
township	confederation
section	retreat
deed	turning point
Congress	
slave	

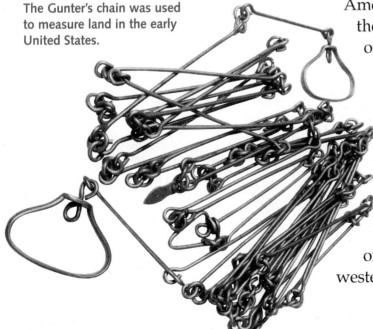

The Gunter's chain was used to measure land in the early United States.

After the American Revolution ended, the leaders of the new state of Virginia decided to reward George Rogers Clark and his soldiers for their bravery. Virginia gave them a stretch of land along the north bank of the Ohio River, near the Falls of the Ohio. On that western land Clark and his soldiers started farms and built a new town, called Clarksville. It was the first American settlement in what is now Indiana.

Some people thought that the western land was not Virginia's to give. Leaders in New York said the land belonged to their state. Virginia and New York settled their disagreement by turning the land over to the new United States government. The Native Americans living there, however, thought the land was something no one should own.

ORGANIZING THE WESTERN LAND

Government leaders wanted to sell the western land to raise money to run the new government. In 1785 the United States government passed an **ordinance**, or law, to begin dividing up the western land for sale and settlement.

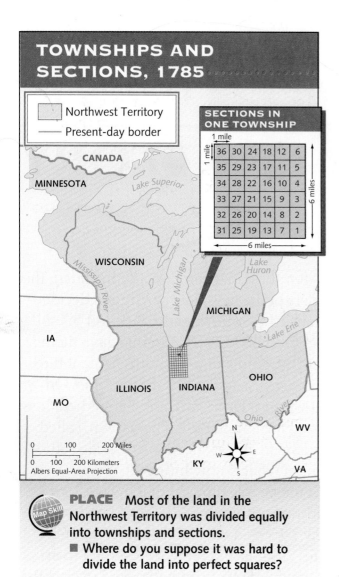

TOWNSHIPS AND SECTIONS, 1785

Northwest Territory
Present-day border

SECTIONS IN ONE TOWNSHIP

36	30	24	18	12	6
35	29	23	17	11	5
34	28	22	16	10	4
33	27	21	15	9	3
32	26	20	14	8	2
31	25	19	13	7	1

1 mile
6 miles
6 miles

CANADA
MINNESOTA
Lake Superior
WISCONSIN
Mississippi River
Lake Michigan
Lake Huron
MICHIGAN
Lake Erie
IA
ILLINOIS
INDIANA
OHIO
MO
Ohio River
WV
KY
VA

0   100   200 Miles
0   100   200 Kilometers
Albers Equal-Area Projection

PLACE Most of the land in the Northwest Territory was divided equally into townships and sections.
■ Where do you suppose it was hard to divide the land into perfect squares?

The Land Ordinance of 1785 told how the land was to be divided and sold. The land was to be divided into **townships**, pieces of land 6 miles (about 10 km) square. Each township was then to be divided into 36 parts called **sections**, each 1 mile (about 2 km) square. The sections were to be numbered 1 to 36. Each section in a township was to be divided further and sold for no less than $1 an acre.

This method for dividing and describing land is still used today. Township names and section numbers are listed on property deeds. A **deed** is a document that describes a piece of land and tells who owns it.

Government leaders knew that education would be important in providing opportunities for all citizens. So the Land Ordinance stated that the money from section number 16 in every township was to be used for public schools.

✓ What did the Land Ordinance of 1785 do?

SETTING UP A GOVERNMENT

In 1787 the United States government passed the Northwest Ordinance, another important law for the western land. In this ordinance the land that was west of the Appalachian Mountains and north of the Ohio River was named the Northwest Territory. The territory was to be ruled by a governor who would be chosen by the President of the United States and approved by the Congress. **Congress** is the part of the United States government that makes the nation's laws. As soon as 5,000 free adult men were living in the territory, they would be allowed to set up their own territorial government.

The Northwest Ordinance also told how areas of the Northwest Territory could become states. To become a state, an area had to have at least 60,000 free adults. The people in a new state would be "on an equal footing with the original states in all respects whatsoever." That is, they would have the same rights and freedoms as people in the original, or first, 13 states.

Unlike people in the original states, however, the people of the Northwest Territory were not allowed to keep slaves. A **slave** is a person who is owned as the property of another person.

The Northwest Ordinance made it clear that the United States planned to grow larger by making new states out of the western land. However, the country's plans for growth would put in danger both the Native Americans and the American settlers living there.

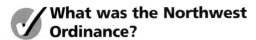 **What was the Northwest Ordinance?**

CONFLICT IN THE NORTHWEST TERRITORY

On October 5, 1787, Major General Arthur St. Clair became the first governor of the Northwest Territory. As governor, the biggest problem he faced was **conflict**, or fights and disagreements. Both the British and the Indians continued to attack American settlers moving into the Northwest Territory.

After the American Revolution the British had kept some of their forts near the Great Lakes. They did so to protect their fur trade with the Indians in the region. The British encouraged their Indian trading partners to form a confederation to fight the Americans. A **confederation** is a large group made up of several smaller groups that have the same goals and want to work together. The Delawares, Miamis, Potawatomis, and Shawnees were among the Indian tribes that joined this confederation. Its military chief was the Miami leader Michikinikwa (muh•chee•kee•NEE•kwah), which means "Little Turtle."

From his settlement at Kekionga, Chief Little Turtle commanded a large army of confederation warriors. Nearby, in late 1791, Little Turtle's warriors defeated an American army of more than 3,000

Little Turtle (left) and Anthony Wayne (below, at center), both strong leaders, wanted to control the Northwest Territory for their own people.

Although the Native Americans lost the Battle of Fallen Timbers, more United States soldiers than Indians were killed or injured.

soldiers led by Major General Arthur St. Clair. Angry that the Americans had lost, President George Washington chose a new general, Major General Anthony Wayne. His soldiers called him "Mad Anthony" because he was daring and brave.

Wayne set out for the Northwest Territory in the fall of 1793 with an army of about 1,000 soldiers. The Americans traveled into what is now western Ohio, where they built Fort Greenville. That same winter the British built a new fort in the Northwest Territory. The fort was located near the mouth of the Maumee River in northwestern Ohio. It was given the name of an old French fort, Fort Miami.

Many of the tribes of the Indian confederation were happy to see the new British fort. They thought the British would help them fight the Americans. But Little Turtle worried that the American army would be too strong for the Indians. He knew that Anthony Wayne was a good leader. "This chief," Little Turtle said of

Anthony Wayne, "always sleeps with one eye open." Little Turtle wanted the confederation tribes to make peace, but the other chiefs would not agree to this.

 **Why did Indians and American settlers fight each other in the Northwest Territory?**

THE BATTLE OF FALLEN TIMBERS

In the spring of 1794, several thousand Indian warriors under the leader Blue Jacket prepared to fight the Americans near Fort Miami. Anthony Wayne and his soldiers set out from Fort Greenville, but Blue Jacket did not wait for Wayne's army to attack. He decided instead to attack the American soldiers at a place in Ohio where a tornado had blown down many trees. Blue Jacket thought the fallen trees would make it hard for the American soldiers to fight there.

On August 20, 1794, the two armies met at "the place of the fallen timbers." The trees, however, were not a problem for the American soldiers, who won the battle in under two hours.

When the Indians **retreated**, or turned back from battle, many of them went to Fort Miami. But they were sent away from the fort because the British did not want to get into a war with the United States.

After the Battle of Fallen Timbers, Anthony Wayne and his soldiers marched back along the Maumee River to its headwaters. At the Maumee-Wabash portage, where the French had built their first trading post in Indiana, the Americans built Fort Wayne.

Why did Blue Jacket decide on Fallen Timbers for the attack?

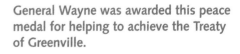
General Wayne was awarded this peace medal for helping to achieve the Treaty of Greenville.

THE TREATY OF GREENVILLE

The Battle of Fallen Timbers was a turning point for both the Native Americans and the United States government in the Northwest Territory. A **turning point** is an event that causes an important change to take place. Losing the battle ended the Indians' hopes of ever stopping the Americans from settling the northwest frontier. Winning the battle helped the Americans take firm control of that land.

Little Turtle and the other chiefs from the Delaware, Shawnee, and Wyandot tribes agreed to make peace with the

The Treaty of Greenville was signed on August 3, 1795, almost exactly a year after the Battle of Fallen Timbers.

Americans. In 1795 they met with Anthony Wayne at Fort Greenville in Ohio. After much talk, both sides came to an agreement called the Treaty of Greenville.

In the treaty the Americans agreed to let the Indians live in the western part of the Northwest Territory. In return, the Indians agreed to let the Americans settle in the eastern part, in what now makes up much of Ohio and some of southeastern Indiana. The Americans also agreed to pay the Indians for the land.

After signing the Treaty of Greenville, Little Turtle said, "I have been the last to sign it and I will be the last to break it." The agreement brought to the Northwest Territory a period of peace that lasted for 15 years.

 What did the Treaty of Greenville do for the Northwest Territory?

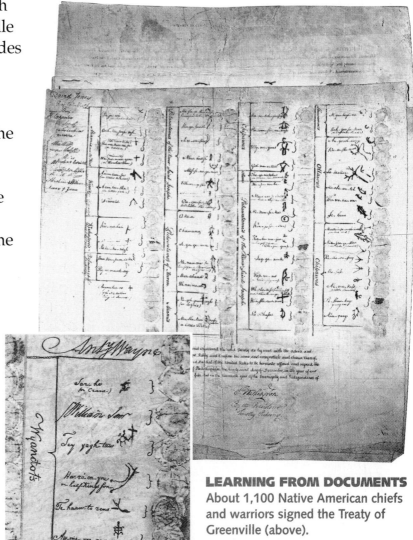

LEARNING FROM DOCUMENTS
About 1,100 Native American chiefs and warriors signed the Treaty of Greenville (above).
■ What American's signature appears on the close-up at left?

LESSON 1 REVIEW

Check Understanding

1. **Recall the Facts** What law set up a government for the Northwest Territory?
2. **Focus on the Main Idea** How did government leaders work to bring about an orderly settlement of the West?

Think Critically

3. **Think More About It** What might have happened if the Indians had won the Battle of Fallen Timbers?

4. **Personally Speaking** How would you have felt if you were a Native American and settlers began moving onto your land?

Show What You Know

Simulation Activity With a partner, imagine that you are at the Fort Greenville meeting in 1795. Role-play a conversation between Little Turtle and Anthony Wayne. Share your conversation with the class.

CONFLICT CONTINUES IN THE NORTHWEST TERRITORY

Link to Our World

How can different points of view cause problems for people today?

Focus on the Main Idea
Read to find out how different points of view caused problems between the Native Americans and the American settlers.

Preview Vocabulary
census
boundary line

In 1800 the United States Congress passed a law that divided the Northwest Territory into two parts. One part became the Ohio Territory. The other became the Indiana Territory. The Indiana Territory stretched from Indiana's present-day eastern border to the Mississippi River. President John Adams chose William Henry Harrison as the first governor of this vast land. The old French settlement of Vincennes became the Indiana Territory's capital.

THE INDIANA TERRITORY CHANGES

During the 13 years that Harrison was governor, the borders of the Indiana Territory changed. In 1805 Congress made the Michigan Territory from the northern part of the Indiana Territory. In 1809 the western part became the Illinois Territory. These divisions gave the Indiana Territory almost the same borders the state has today.

Although the Indiana Territory became smaller in size, the number of people who were living there grew. The 1800 **census**, or official government count of people, showed that only 5,641 American settlers lived in the territory. By 1810, however, the number had grown to more than 20,000. By 1815, just five years later, that 20,000 had tripled—to more than 60,000!

Most of the American settlers lived in a small part of the Indiana Territory near the Ohio River. The rest of the territory was Indian land, as agreed to in the Treaty of

William Henry Harrison, first governor of the Indiana Territory

Greenville. As governor of the territory, William Henry Harrison was in charge of buying Indian land for American settlement. Harrison made new treaties with the tribes. In each treaty a tribe agreed to sell some land, often for very little money.

In 1809 William Henry Harrison met with Little Turtle and the chiefs of several other tribes to sign the Treaty of Fort Wayne. Under the terms of this treaty, the tribes agreed to sell more than 2.9 million acres of land to the United States government for about three cents an acre. The treaty described a new **boundary line**, or border, separating United States land from Indian land. This border was called the Ten O'Clock Line because it was said to follow the same line as a shadow cast by stakes stuck in the ground at ten

o'clock in the morning on the day the treaty was signed.

The tribes that did not sign the treaty were angry that so much of their land was being turned over to the United States government. "Sell a country!" cried the Shawnee chief Tecumseh (tuh•KUM•suh). "Why not sell the air, the clouds, and the great sea, as well as the earth?" He decided to do something about it.

 **What was the Ten O'Clock Line?**

TECUMSEH AND THE PROPHET

Like Pontiac and Little Turtle before him, Tecumseh wanted the Indian people to form a confederation. He and his brother traveled from tribe to tribe, telling

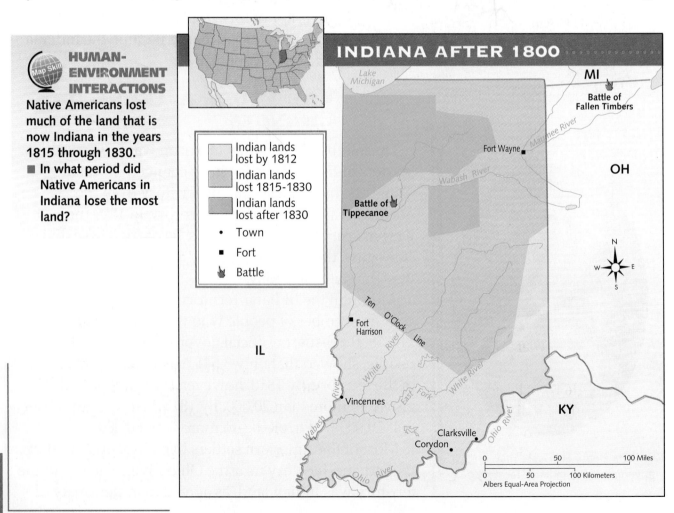

Map Skill HUMAN-ENVIRONMENT INTERACTIONS
Native Americans lost much of the land that is now Indiana in the years 1815 through 1830.
■ In what period did Native Americans in Indiana lose the most land?

INDIANA AFTER 1800

Legend:
- Indian lands lost by 1812
- Indian lands lost 1815-1830
- Indian lands lost after 1830
- • Town
- ■ Fort
- 🖐 Battle

Lake Michigan
MI
Battle of Fallen Timbers
Maumee River
Fort Wayne
Wabash River
OH
Battle of Tippecanoe
Ten O'Clock Line
Fort Harrison
White River
IL
East Fork
White River
Vincennes
Ohio River
KY
Clarksville
Corydon
Wabash River
Ohio River

N W E S

0   50   100 Miles
0   50   100 Kilometers
Albers Equal-Area Projection

Prophetstown

Prophetstown was located on the Wabash River, near where Lafayette is today. The Indian town was laid out along regular street lines. In addition to log houses in which people lived, it contained two public buildings as well as a guest house. After the Battle of Tippecanoe in 1811, the Indians left Prophetstown, and the American soldiers burned it. In 1812

Tecumseh's followers tried to rebuild, but that same year the town was destroyed a second time by American soldiers.

the people that together they could stop American settlement. He said,

66 A single twig breaks, but the bundle of twigs is strong. Some day I will embrace our brother tribes and draw them into a bundle, and together we will win our country back. 99

Tecumseh's brother was a well-known religious leader named Tenskwatawa (ten•SKWAHT•uh•wah). Because many Shawnees believed that Tenskwatawa could see into the future, they called him "the Prophet."

In 1808 Tecumseh and the Prophet moved from their Ohio lands and built a town they called Prophetstown, just below the mouth of the Tippecanoe River. It served as the capital of Tecumseh's Indian confederation and as a training center for more than 1,000 warriors. The warriors at Prophetstown were eager to fight the Americans. However, Tecumseh hoped to settle the disagreements between the Indians and the American settlers in a peaceful way.

After the Treaty of Fort Wayne was signed, Tecumseh asked to meet with William Henry Harrison. The two men met in Vincennes in August 1810 to discuss their disagreements.

Tecumseh told Harrison that no chief or group of chiefs had the right to sell land, because it did not belong to any individual or tribe. It belonged to *all* Native Americans. To show Harrison how the Indians felt about being crowded off their lands, Tecumseh crowded Harrison off a bench on which they were both sitting. This angered Harrison, who is said to have raised his sword. Tecumseh is then said to have raised his tomahawk, warning Harrison that his people would fight to save their land.

The bad feelings between Harrison and Tecumseh were like the feelings between most American settlers and Native Americans at that time. The meeting between Tecumseh and Harrison lasted several days, but it did not settle their disagreements.

✔ **Why did Tecumseh and William Henry Harrison meet at Vincennes?**

BATTLE OF TIPPECANOE

Fearing there would be more Indian attacks on American settlers, William Henry Harrison began gathering an army. In 1811 Harrison ordered a fort built on the east bank of the Wabash River near what is now Terre Haute. The American soldiers trained at Fort Harrison, as it was called, during the summer of 1811.

Knowing this, Tecumseh worked to get more tribes to join his confederation. He visited the tribes living south of the Ohio River. Before he left, he told the Prophet to keep the peace until he returned. With Tecumseh gone, William Henry Harrison decided to lead his army from Fort Harrison to Prophetstown.

On November 7, 1811, more than 1,000 American soldiers camped just outside the town. Thinking the Americans were going to attack, the Prophet ordered his warriors to attack first. Harrison's soldiers fought back, forcing the

The Prophet called himself Tenskwatawa, which means "the open door." Why do you suppose he used this name?

After the Battle of Tippecanoe, many Native Americans lost faith in Tecumseh, the Prophet, and the idea of an Indian confederation.

Indians to retreat. This was the Battle of Tippecanoe.

After the battle, Harrison had his soldiers destroy Prophetstown. Some of Tecumseh's warriors then went all through the territory, attacking American settlers. Others went with Tecumseh to Canada, where the Indian leader asked the British for their help.

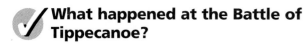 **What happened at the Battle of Tippecanoe?**

THE WAR OF 1812

Many Americans believed that the British had been helping the Indians all along. They said the British were giving the Indians guns and other supplies.

American settlers in the Northwest Territory urged the United States government to take over Canada and force the British to leave North America. At this same time, the British were also attacking American trading ships. For that reason, the United States declared war on Britain. This was the War of 1812. In it Tecumseh and his warriors fought for the British.

The War of 1812 lasted more than two years. An important turning point came in 1813. That fall a ship of the United States Navy, under the command of Oliver Hazard Perry, won a battle against British ships on Lake Erie. After the victory Perry sent a message to William Henry Harrison, who was now the general of the army in the Great Lakes

MAJOR BATTLES OF THE WAR OF 1812

CANADA (GREAT BRITAIN)

Lake Superior

Fort Mackinac 1812

INDIANA TERR.

ILLINOIS TERR.

MICHIGAN TERR.

MISSOURI TERRITORY

Frenchtown 1813

Fort Dearborn (Chicago) 1812

INDIANA TERR.

Put-in-Bay 1813

York (Toronto) 1813

The Thames 1813

Lake Ontario

Plattsburg 1814

ME (Part of MA)

VT NH

NY

MA

CT RI

PA

NJ

Fort McHenry (Baltimore) 1814

DE

MD

Washington, D.C. 1814

OH

KY

VA

TN

NC

SC

GA

MISSISSIPPI TERRITORY

Horseshoe Bend 1814

LA

New Orleans 1815

FLORIDA (SPAIN)

Gulf of Mexico

ATLANTIC OCEAN

N S E W

0 200 400 Miles
0 200 400 Kilometers
Albers Equal-Area Projection

American victory
British victory

 LOCATION When the War of 1812 ended in December 1814, many British and American soldiers did not know it.
■ What major battle took place after the War of 1812 officially ended?

"Our lives are in the hands of the Great Spirit. We are determined to defend our lands, and if it be his will we wish to leave our bones upon them." With Tecumseh's death, the Indian confederation lost its greatest leader. Without Tecumseh's strong leadership, the confederation broke up. The War of 1812 ended in 1814.

✓ **Why was Perry's victory on Lake Erie a turning point in the War of 1812?**

LESSON 2 REVIEW

Check Understanding

1. **Recall the Facts** Which cause of the War of 1812 was the most important to the American settlers in the Northwest Territory?
2. **Focus on the Main Idea** How did different points of view cause problems between the Native Americans and the American settlers?

Think Critically

3. **Explore Viewpoints** What was Tecumseh's view of the treaties between the United States and the Native Americans? What was Harrison's view?
4. **Think More About It** Why did the British help the Indians? What did the British have to gain?

Show What You Know

Plan-a-Marker Activity
Imagine that you and a partner are members of a historical society. You have been asked to plan a historical marker for the Battle of Tippecanoe. Write a message of about 40 words that might appear on your marker. Share your message with the class.

region. The message said, "We have met the enemy and they are ours."

Perry's victory weakened the British control of the Great Lakes. Because of this, the Americans were able to cross Lake Erie by boat and attack the British at Fort Detroit. By the time the Americans arrived, however, the British were retreating up the Thames (TEMZ) River. The Americans followed, and in less than a week the two armies were fighting.

In the Battle of the Thames, Harrison's army killed or captured most of the British soldiers and their Indian allies. Among those who died in the battle was Tecumseh. Before the battle Tecumseh had told his warriors and the British soldiers,

Identify Cause and Effect

Why Is This Skill Important?

Suppose you are waiting for your ride to school. You discover that you have forgotten your homework. You run back to get it, and you miss your ride.

Something that makes something else happen is a **cause.** What happens is the **effect.** Running back to get your homework is the cause of your missing your ride. Missing your ride is the effect of running back to get your homework.

Life is full of causes and effects. Because history is about life in the past, history books are filled with stories of causes and effects!

Remember What You Have Read

In the last lesson you read the following sentences.

> With Tecumseh's death, the Indian confederation lost its greatest leader. Without Tecumseh's strong leadership, the confederation broke up.

Now you can think about the causes and effects these sentences describe.

Understand the Process

Look for word clues to help you identify causes and effects. The cause here is Tecumseh's death. What is the effect of Tecumseh's death?

Sometimes things that happen in history have more than one cause. The chart shows several events that led to the War of 1812. Each one was a cause of the war. From the chart you will see that sometimes the effect of one thing that happens becomes the cause of the next thing that happens.

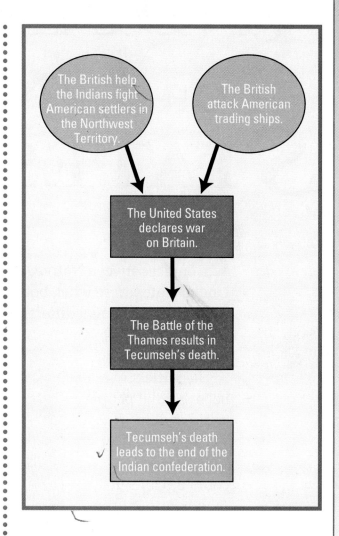

Think and Apply

Think about the causes and effects of things that happen in people's lives. What might be some causes of a family's moving away from a community? What might be some effects for the family that is moving? What might be some effects for the community the family is leaving or for the community it is moving to?

INDIAN LAND OR UNITED STATES LAND?

Conflict between Native Americans and settlers from the United States arose when both groups wanted the same land. The two groups, who had different viewpoints on land ownership, tried to solve their conflict by fighting.

The settlers believed that people could own land. They could buy or sell it, just as they could buy or sell other kinds of property. The Native Americans did not believe this was possible. They thought that the land belonged to everyone together.

Tecumseh and William Henry Harrison were leaders of the two sides in this conflict, which was often bitter. They met face-to-face in 1810 and again in 1811. At each meeting both leaders expressed their beliefs strongly. Read the following parts of a speech made by Tecumseh to Harrison at Vincennes in 1810 and a letter written by Harrison to Tecumseh in 1811.

Tecumseh's speech to Harrison,
August 20, 1810

66 Since the peace [at
Greenville] was made you
have killed some [Indians].
. . . you have taken our lands
from us and I do not see how
we can remain at peace with
you if you continue to do so. . . .
. . . you wish to prevent the
Indians to do as we wish them to
unite and let them consider their land as
the common property of the whole. . . .

You are continually driving the red people when at last
you will drive them into the great lake where they can't
either stand or work. . . .

If you continue to purchase [land] of them [Indian
chiefs] it will produce war among the different tribes and
at last I do not know what will be the consequence to the
white people. 99

Harrison's letter to Tecumseh, June 24, 1811

66 Listen to me, I speak to you about matters of
importance, both to the white people and yourselves;
open your ears, therefore, and attend to what I shall say . . .
. . . our citizens are alarmed, and my warriors are
preparing themselves; not to strike you, but to defend
themselves and their women and children. . . .
. . . what can be the inducement
[something that persuades] for
you to undertake an enterprise
[action] where there is so little
probability of success; do you
really think that a handful of
men that you have about
you are able to contend with
the power of the Seventeen
Fires [states of the United
States]. 99

COMPARE
VIEWPOINTS

1. What was Tecumseh's viewpoint in the disagreement? How do you know?

2. What was William Henry Harrison's viewpoint? How do you know?

3. Why do you think each leader held his particular viewpoint?

THINK
–AND–
APPLY

People often have different viewpoints on things because of their backgrounds, their jobs, or the places where they live. Choose a current issue in Indiana about which people in your community have different ideas. Talk with someone about his or her feelings. Find out why that person thinks the way he or she does. Also talk with someone who feels a different way about the idea.

BUILDING CITIZENSHIP

Note: A series of periods (. . .) called an ellipsis is used when words are left out of quotations. Brackets [ ] around a word show a word that has been added to a quotation to make its meaning clear.

LESSON 3

THE NINETEENTH STATE

Link to Our World

How do people today organize new groups?

Focus on the Main Idea
Read to find out how the people of Indiana worked to set up their new state.

Preview Vocabulary
represent
enabling act
constitution
delegate
convention
site

Jonathan Jennings was the first governor of the state of Indiana.

By the end of the War of 1812, Indiana's leaders were preparing the territory to become a state. A census taken in 1814 showed that more than 63,000 free adults were living in the Indiana Territory. According to the Northwest Ordinance, Indiana could now become a state.

JONATHAN JENNINGS

Jonathan Jennings led Indiana into statehood. He was born in New Jersey, but he grew up in Pennsylvania. He moved to the Indiana Territory as a young adult and worked as a lawyer in Vincennes before moving to Charlestown in 1809.

Jennings wanted to **represent**, or speak for, the people of the Indiana Territory as a member of the United States Congress. To get people to vote for him, Jennings traveled all over the territory during election time. He gave speeches in town halls and in churches, and he often visited voters in their homes. People got to know and like the popular and hardworking young man. They elected him to Congress as their representative in 1809. And they kept electing him again and again, in 1811, 1813, and 1815.

Jonathan Jennings told Congress that the people of Indiana wanted the territory to become a state. As a state, Indiana could have more representatives in Congress. When the territory had enough people, Jennings asked Congress to pass an enabling act

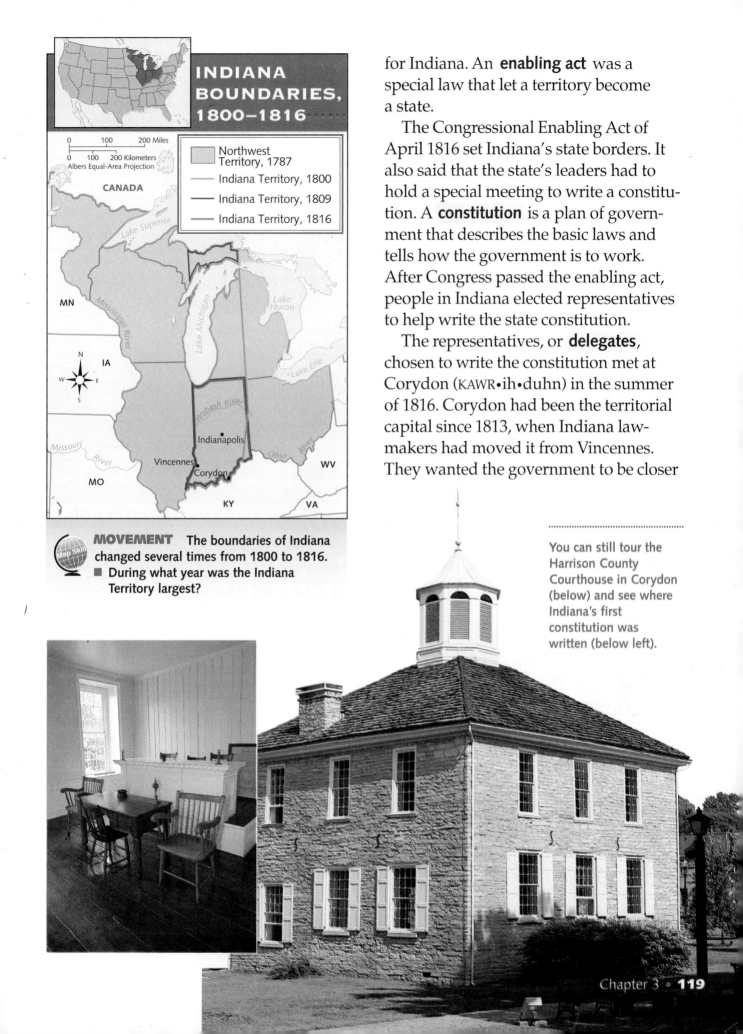

INDIANA BOUNDARIES, 1800–1816

0   100   200 Miles
0   100   200 Kilometers
Albers Equal-Area Projection

CANADA

Northwest Territory, 1787
Indiana Territory, 1800
Indiana Territory, 1809
Indiana Territory, 1816

Lake Superior
Lake Michigan
Lake Huron
Lake Erie
Mississippi River
MN
IA
N W E S
Wabash River
Indianapolis
Vincennes
Corydon
Missouri River
Ohio River
WV
MO
KY
VA

MOVEMENT The boundaries of Indiana changed several times from 1800 to 1816.
■ During what year was the Indiana Territory largest?

for Indiana. An **enabling act** was a special law that let a territory become a state.

The Congressional Enabling Act of April 1816 set Indiana's state borders. It also said that the state's leaders had to hold a special meeting to write a constitution. A **constitution** is a plan of government that describes the basic laws and tells how the government is to work. After Congress passed the enabling act, people in Indiana elected representatives to help write the state constitution.

The representatives, or **delegates**, chosen to write the constitution met at Corydon (KAWR•ih•duhn) in the summer of 1816. Corydon had been the territorial capital since 1813, when Indiana lawmakers had moved it from Vincennes. They wanted the government to be closer

You can still tour the Harrison County Courthouse in Corydon (below) and see where Indiana's first constitution was written (below left).

Members of Indiana's constitutional convention often met under the shade of a huge elm tree—now known as the Constitutional Elm.

to the more settled part of the Indiana Territory, along the Ohio River.

The constitutional **convention**, as the special meeting was called, was held at the Harrison County Courthouse. But many of the days that summer were hot and humid. So the 43 delegates often met outside the courthouse in the shade of a huge elm. This tree came to be known as the Constitutional Elm. One of the first things the delegates did was choose Jonathan Jennings to lead the convention. As the convention president, he helped write the state's constitution.

 How did Jonathan Jennings help Indiana become a state?

INDIANA'S FIRST CONSTITUTION

The constitution that the delegates at Corydon wrote in 1816 set up a state government with three parts. The General Assembly would make the laws. A governor would carry out the laws. The state supreme court would decide whether the laws were fair.

Indiana's constitution provided for the rights and freedoms of its citizens. It also promised a state public school system, the first in the United States. It even set aside the land in one township for a public university. Indiana University, in Bloomington, was later built in this township.

The delegates did not always agree on what the constitution should say. They argued over slavery. Some delegates wanted to allow it. Others, such as Jonathan Jennings, did not. They said it was wrong for one person to take away the freedom of another. In the end the delegates voted to make slavery illegal, or against the law, in Indiana.

LEARNING FROM DOCUMENTS The page shown below is from Indiana's first constitution.

■ Why is it important to preserve historical documents such as this one?

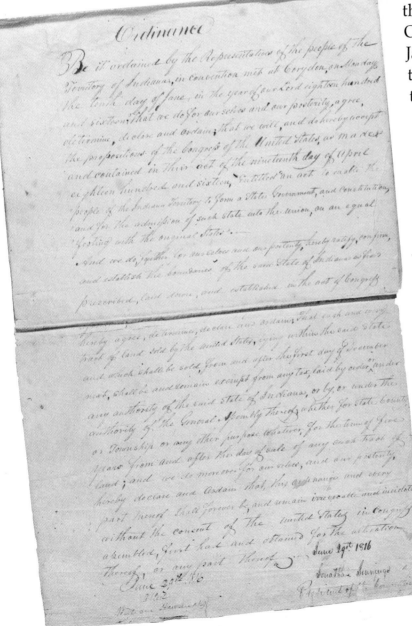

The delegates wrote in the constitution that "all power is inherent in [belongs to] the people." That is, the people of Indiana would control their government. They would make their laws by voting. Their rights would be protected. But not everyone in Indiana would be given all the rights of citizenship. Only white men would. Under this first state constitution, women, Africans in the United States, and Native Americans were not allowed to vote.

When the delegates finished writing the state constitution, they sent it to Washington, D.C. On December 11, 1816, President James Madison signed the law that made Indiana the nineteenth state in the United States.

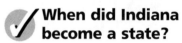
When did Indiana become a state?

CHOOSING A CAPITAL

After the constitution was written, the new government went to work. Jonathan Jennings was elected the first governor. The first Indiana General Assembly and Indiana Supreme Court met at Corydon, Indiana's first state capital.

The new Indiana Constitution made the town of Corydon the capital. But in 1820 a committee of the General Assembly chose the **site**, or place, for a new capital where Fall Creek joins the

White River. The whole General Assembly approved the site in 1821 and gave the future capital the name Indianapolis. *Indianapolis* includes the Latin word for Indian (*Indiana*) and the Greek word for city (*polis*). Some legislators had wanted to name the city Tecumseh.

The General Assembly hired Alexander Ralston to prepare a street plan for the city. Ralston laid out Indianapolis with four major diagonal streets leading to a city center, where most of the government buildings were located. Ralston had worked earlier with Benjamin Banneker in mapping Washington, D.C. Ralston's plan was used to buy land in the new capital city. Finally, by 1825, Indiana's state records had been moved from Corydon to Indianapolis, and the state lawmakers began meeting there.

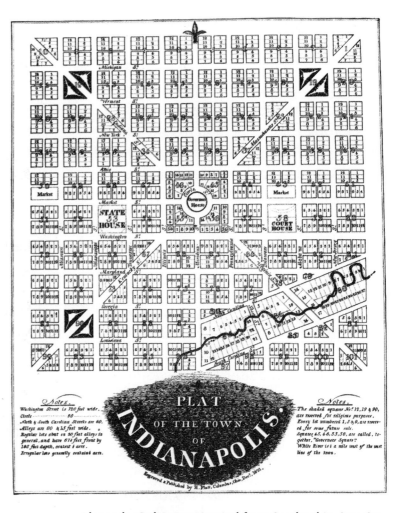

Alexander Ralston emigrated from Scotland to America and surveyed western lands before he planned the streets of Indianapolis.

 How was the site for the new state capital chosen?

LESSON 3 REVIEW

Check Understanding

1. **Recall the Facts** What document set up Indiana's state government?
2. **Focus on the Main Idea** How did the people of Indiana work to set up their new state?

Think Critically

3. **Cause and Effect** What was the effect of the Enabling Act of April 1816?
4. **Think More About It** What do you think it might have been like to serve as a delegate to the constitutional convention in Corydon?

Show What You Know

 Writing Activity Imagine that you are a landowner in Indiana in 1820. Write a letter to the committee of the General Assembly that must decide where to build the state's new capital. Try to persuade the committee members to choose your land. Share your letter with a partner.

Compromise to Resolve Conflicts

Why Is This Skill Important?

Throughout your life you will meet people you disagree with. Knowing how to **resolve,** or settle, conflicts with other people is an important life skill. You can walk away and let the strong feelings fade over time. You can talk about the conflict and explain your way of thinking. You also can compromise. To **compromise** means to give up some of what you want to reach agreement with someone.

Remember What You Have Read

You have read that the delegates to Indiana's constitutional convention did not always agree. One of the most serious disagreements at the convention was over allowing slavery. To resolve this conflict, delegates from both sides had to compromise. To get some of what they wanted, both sides had to give up other things they wanted.

Understand the Process

To resolve a conflict by compromise, you can use the following steps.

- Before you begin to talk with the person you disagree with, be aware that you may have to give up some of the things you want.
- Tell the other person clearly what you want.
- Decide which of the things you want are the most important to you.
- Present a plan for a possible compromise. Let the other person present his or her plan.
- Talk about any differences in the two plans.
- If you still do not agree, present another plan for a compromise, this time giving up one of the things that is important to you. Continue talking until the two of you agree on a compromise plan.
- If you begin to feel angry, take a break and calm down before you go on talking.

Think and Apply

With your classmates, choose an issue that you do not all agree on, such as a school rule. Form sides to discuss the issue, using the steps in Understand the Process.

As part of Indiana's General Assembly, members of the Senate (right) often must compromise when deciding the best way to use state resources.

CHAPTER 3
REVIEW

CONNECT MAIN IDEAS

Use this organizer to show that you understand how the chapter's main ideas are connected. Copy the organizer onto a separate sheet of paper. Then complete it by filling in the missing information.

From Territory to Statehood

Cause Thousands of settlers come to the Northwest Territory.
Effect _____
_____
_____

Cause _____
_____
_____
_____

Effect Tecumseh and the Prophet begin to unite Indians against the American settlers.

Cause The United States Congress passes the Enabling Act of 1816.
Effect _____
_____
_____
_____

WRITE MORE ABOUT IT

1. Write a Poem Imagine that you are forced to move out of your house so someone else can move in. Write a poem that describes how you feel.

2. Write a Descriptive Letter Suppose you are a delegate to the Indiana constitutional convention. Write a letter to a family member. Describe the work you are doing at the convention.

USE VOCABULARY

Write a paragraph explaining the difference between the Land Ordinance of 1785 and the Northwest Ordinance. Use the following vocabulary terms in your paragraph.

ordinance   Congress
township   slave
section   deed

CHECK UNDERSTANDING

1. What was the Northwest Territory?

2. How did Governor William Henry Harrison gain more land for American settlers?

3. Why did Tecumseh meet with William Henry Harrison at Vincennes in 1810?

4. Why did Tecumseh become an ally of the British?

5. What was important about Oliver Hazard Perry's victory on Lake Erie in the War of 1812?

6. What did the census of 1814 show about Indiana?

7. What did the Enabling Act of 1816 do for Indiana?

8. In what year did Indiana become a state?

9. Who was the first governor of Indiana?

10. Who prepared the street plan for the city of Indianapolis?

THINK CRITICALLY

1. **Think More About It** Why was it important to many people that Indiana become a state?

2. **Explore Viewpoints** Why do you think some Indian leaders signed the Treaty of Fort Wayne? Why do you think others did not?

3. **Personally Speaking** As an American settler, how would you have felt toward the British? How would you have felt toward the Indians?

4. **Cause and Effect** What caused the War of 1812? How did the war affect the Indian confederation of the Northwest Territory?

5. **Past to Present** How did Indiana come to have the state borders it has today?

APPLY SKILLS

How to Identify Cause and Effect
Make a poster that shows the causes and effects of the conflicts between Tecumseh and William Henry Harrison. Use both words and drawings on your poster.

How to Compromise to Resolve Conflicts Think of something that you and a friend disagree about. Then list the steps that you might follow to resolve your conflict. What things are you willing to give up to reach a compromise?

READ MORE ABOUT IT

Tecumseh, Shawnee War Chief by Jane Fleischer. Troll Associates. This book is an easy-to-read account of the Indian leader's life.

William Henry Harrison by Christine Maloney Fitz-Gerald. Childrens Press. This is a good biography of Harrison's life with excellent pictures.

CHAPTER 4

PIONEERS IN INDIANA

> 66 On summer evenings, beside a smudge fire which kept the mosquitoes at bay, my grandfather would tell me tales of the early days, the Indians, the wolves, the deer, the struggles of the pioneers. Immense stretches of land now devoted to corn and oats, melons and potatoes, had been covered with forest when he came west. 99
>
> A description of Indiana in pioneer days, from the book *Dune Boy* by Edwin Way Teale

Elizabeth Chapman Conner, early pioneer and wife of William Conner

PIONEER SETTLEMENTS

Link to Our World

How do people today solve the problems of living in a new place?

Focus on the Main Idea
Read to find out how Indiana's pioneers solved the problems of living on the frontier.

Preview Vocabulary
claim
loft
gristmill

In the early 1800s it seemed as if everyone was moving to the lands west of the Appalachian Mountains. From Philadelphia one person wrote, "I can scarcely walk a square without meeting [someone] . . . whose destination is principally Ohio and Indiana." This person predicted that in 20 years most of the people in the United States would be living in that region.

Thousands of people, with their household goods and animals, arrived in Indiana by covered wagon and flatboat. Some traveled down the Ohio River from the Northeast region of the United States. Many others came from the Southeast through the mountains of Kentucky, crossing the Ohio River there. The newcomers came as single persons and as families. Some came in groups of several hundred people or more. Most settled first in southern Indiana.

THE LINCOLN FAMILY IN INDIANA

One Indiana pioneer family was the Lincoln family. Tom and Nancy Lincoln and their children left their home in Kentucky in 1816 and moved to Indiana to make a better life.

One reason they left Kentucky was that many people there owned slaves. The enslaved people did much of the work. Because of this, there were few jobs for people like the Lincolns.

In Lincoln City you can visit the Lincoln Boyhood National Memorial (above) and see the fireplace where young Abraham Lincoln used to sit and read.

Tom and Nancy Lincoln knew that Indiana's constitution did not allow slavery, so they decided to move there. They traded their small Kentucky farm for ten barrels of whiskey and $20 cash. Tom Lincoln was not a drinking man, but at that time whiskey was used as money.

Leaving his family in Kentucky, Tom Lincoln crossed the Ohio River by flatboat and then set off on foot into the thick forests of what is now Spencer County. He decided to farm a small piece of land on Little Pigeon Creek.

When Tom Lincoln got to the site, he cleared away the brush and piled it, as the Indiana land laws required settlers to do. He marked with his ax the trees on the borders of his land. This showed his **claim**. Later he filed a deed at the land office in Vincennes and paid $2 an acre.

Tom Lincoln returned to Kentucky and told his family "he reckoned they'd all put in the winter up in 'Indianny.'" With their daughter Sally, age 9, and son Abraham, age 7, Tom and Nancy Lincoln moved to their new home on Little Pigeon Creek. Abraham Lincoln would later grow up to become a President of the United States.

 What is one reason the Lincoln family moved to Indiana?

BUILDING A HOME

As soon as the Lincolns arrived, they built a simple shelter the pioneers called a half-faced camp. It had a slanted roof over three walls—the fourth was left open. The shelter was made of poles, branches, or anything that would provide some protection from the wind and rain.

Pioneer families usually lived in an open shelter like this until they could build a proper home made of logs.

The log cabin the Lincolns built later was like the homes most Indiana pioneers lived in. It had one room with a dirt floor. There were no windows. Light came through the open door and from the fireplace, where a fire burned day and night. Pioneer families used the fireplace for cooking and for warmth. Usually they burned wood. They also burned bear fat when they had it. In time families made their homes more comfortable. Some added windows. Others covered their dirt floors with wooden planks.

LEARNING FROM DIAGRAMS Most log cabins had a simple design.
■ What was used to fill the cracks between the logs?

A LOG CABIN

Chimney

Cracks between logs, filled with moss, clay, or mud

Door and latch

At night the adults in a family spread their blankets over a pile of dry leaves on the floor. The children slept in the loft, the part of the cabin between the ceiling and the roof. They climbed up to the loft on a ladder, which might be just wooden pegs driven into the wall.

Another pioneer, Oliver Johnson, remembered sleeping in a loft when he was a child growing up in Marion County.

66If you slept in the loft, you pulled your head under the covers during a storm. When you got up in the mornin[g], you [would] shake the snow off the covers, grab your shirt and britches [pants] and hop down the ladder to the fireplace, where it was good and warm.99

The Lincoln family lived in their cabin on Little Pigeon Creek for 14 years. By then Indiana was getting crowded. The Lincolns decided to move on again, this time to the Illinois frontier.

 **What was a half-faced camp?**

BUILDING A COMMUNITY

Most pioneer families lived a long way from their neighbors, but even so they found it necessary to cooperate. Pioneers helped one another clear land and plant crops. Neighbors got together to build cabins and barns. When the men gathered to build, the women often held quilting bees. At quilting bees they turned bits and pieces of fabric into quilts, or bedcoverings. When the work was finished, everyone shared a meal. The day often ended with music and dancing.

The pioneers enjoyed these times with their neighbors. They also came to

What?

Pioneer Schools

"Come to books!" That was what teachers in pioneer schools said to begin the school day. School on the frontier was held in the winter, if there was a teacher. Children went to school only when they were not needed to do chores at home. In school they learned the basics of reading, writing, arithmetic, and spelling. Much learning, however, was done at home. When young Abraham Lincoln could not go to school, he read everything he could. He read the family's Bible. He would walk miles to neighboring farms to borrow books, which he often read at night by firelight.

depend on their neighbors for certain kinds of help. With no doctors around, pioneers depended on neighbors who were known for their skill in treating the sick. Even so, accidents and disease killed many pioneers. In 1818 Nancy Lincoln died in Indiana of the "milk disease." This disease is caused by drinking milk from cows that have eaten poisonous plants.

How did pioneer families cooperate with one another?

BUILDING A TOWN

Some pioneer families moved to the Indiana frontier not only to build a better life but also to have religious freedom. In 1814 a Christian minister named George Rapp and his followers came from Pennsylvania to build a community on the Wabash River south of Vincennes. More than 800 people arrived by flatboat and built the town of Harmonie. The word *harmony* means "getting along together." Rapp and his followers were often called Harmonists.

The Harmonists were hardworking people. They cleared forests and drained wetlands. In just five years they planted more than 1,400 acres in crops and fruit trees. They built homes, a church, sawmills to cut logs into boards, and **gristmills** to grind corn and wheat into flour. The Harmonists sold their goods in markets as far away as New Orleans. Because of Harmonie's prosperity, or success, people began calling it the "Wonder of the West."

In 1824 George Rapp and his followers decided to leave Harmonie and return to Pennsylvania. In 1825 Robert Owen, who owned some factories in Scotland, bought the land and the town. He renamed it New Harmony.

Why did the Harmonists move to Indiana?

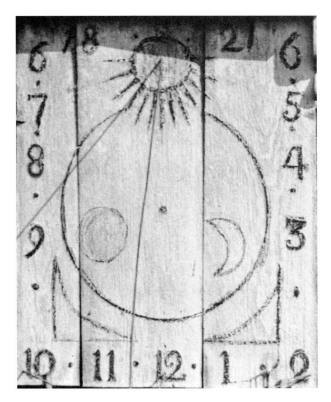

The sundial shown above was built by Harmonists. A wire is strung from the sun symbol to the number 12. You can tell what time it is by reading the number on which the wire's shadow falls.

NEW HARMONY

Robert Owen hoped to make New Harmony a center of learning on the frontier. He believed that education is the key to a better life. More than 1,000 people went to live in New Harmony. Among them were world-famous writers, scientists, and teachers from the United States and Europe. They are sometimes called Owenites.

Most Owenites wanted to study new ideas. They did not want to work farming the land. When they ran out of food, Robert Owen had to spend his own money to feed them. By 1827 Owen had run out of money. He left Indiana, but his sons and many of the other Owenites stayed in New Harmony.

Robert Owen (above)
and the community of
New Harmony (right)

The work of these Owenites helped the whole nation. They had formed a model community and many of their ideas were copied by other communities. They started the first kindergarten, the first trade school, and the first free public library. Their public school system was the first to have equal education for boys and girls.

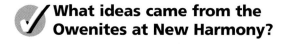 **What ideas came from the Owenites at New Harmony?**

LESSON 1 REVIEW

Check Understanding

1. **Recall the Facts** What are the people who lived in New Harmony sometimes called?

2. **Focus on the Main Idea** How did some of Indiana's pioneers solve the problems of living on the frontier?

Think Critically

3. **Past to Present** What kinds of people are today's pioneers? Explain your answer.

4. **Personally Speaking** Why do you think people form model communities?

Show What You Know

Planning Activity Imagine that you are a pioneer in the 1800s. Describe the steps you would follow to claim and settle your land. Review the steps Tom Lincoln followed to claim land for his family. Share your plan with a family member.

How To

Use a Map to Show Movement

During the early 1800s many settlers moved to the uncrowded West.

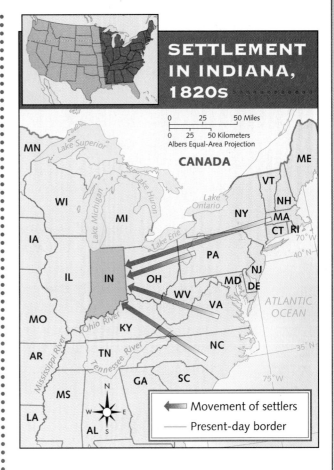

SETTLEMENT IN INDIANA, 1820s

0   25   50 Miles
0   25   50 Kilometers
Albers Equal-Area Projection

Movement of settlers
Present-day border

Why Is This Skill Important?

To help people know direction when they use a map, mapmakers add a small drawing called a compass rose. The compass rose identifies the cardinal directions—north, south, east, and west—and the intermediate directions. The intermediate directions are the in-between directions—northeast, southeast, southwest, and northwest. The compass rose can help you describe the directions of movement shown on the map.

Understand the Process

The map on this page shows the regions of the United States that people left in the 1820s to find a better way of life. The map key shows you that the arrows stand for the movement of people. Use your finger to trace each arrow from beginning to end.

1. In which places do the arrows begin?
2. Where do the arrows go?

Now trace each arrow again with your finger. Look at the compass rose to see the direction each arrow follows from where it

starts to where it ends. In which direction does the arrow go toward Indiana from each state listed below? Be sure to use both cardinal and intermediate directions in your answers.

- Virginia
- North Carolina
- Massachusetts
- Pennsylvania

Think and Apply

With a partner, draw a map of Indiana. Show your city or town and five others on the map. Then draw an arrow from each of the other cities or towns to yours. Draw a compass rose on your map. Write sentences that tell in which direction people would travel to get from each of those other towns to your town.

LEARN with LITERATURE

Focus on Pioneer Life

Log Cabin in the Woods

by Joanne Landers Henry

"Going to the mill" was an important part of pioneer life in Indiana. As soon as a boy was old enough to ride a horse, he would go with his father to the gristmill. There the corn or wheat that the family had grown would be ground into cornmeal or flour for baking. When a boy was old enough and could manage the heavy sacks of cornmeal or flour, he would be sent alone. It was often a trip of ten miles or more. If he waited for the grinding to be done, he was gone all day. Read now the story of 11-year-old Ollie Johnson's first trip to the gristmill.

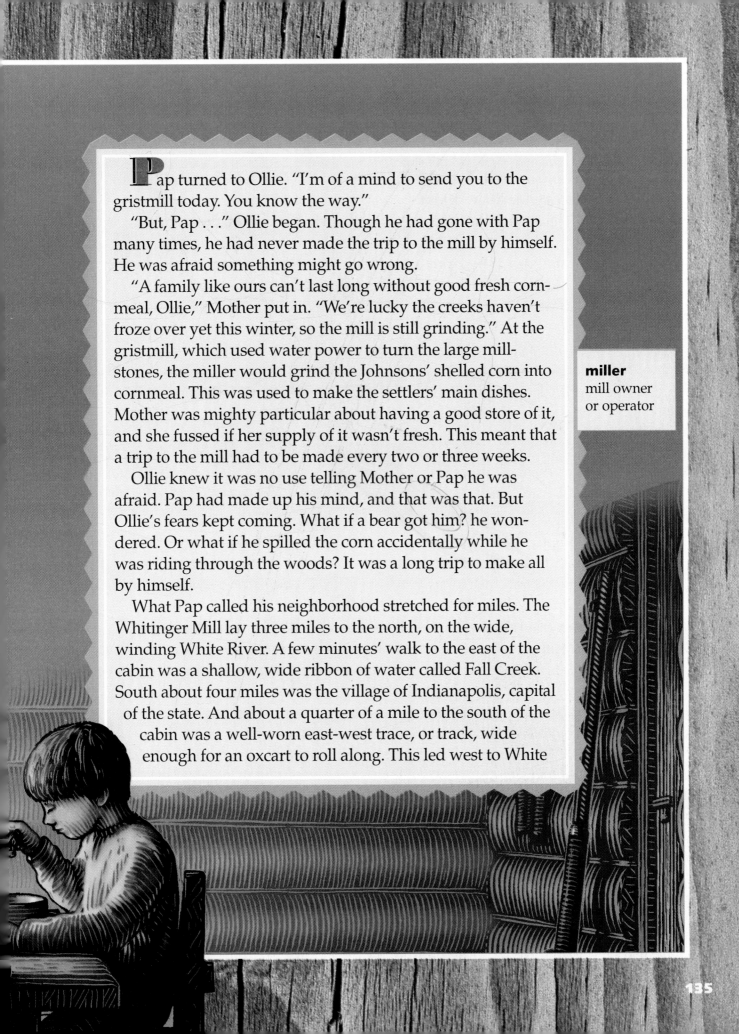

Pap turned to Ollie. "I'm of a mind to send you to the gristmill today. You know the way."

"But, Pap . . ." Ollie began. Though he had gone with Pap many times, he had never made the trip to the mill by himself. He was afraid something might go wrong.

"A family like ours can't last long without good fresh cornmeal, Ollie," Mother put in. "We're lucky the creeks haven't froze over yet this winter, so the mill is still grinding." At the gristmill, which used water power to turn the large millstones, the **miller** would grind the Johnsons' shelled corn into cornmeal. This was used to make the settlers' main dishes. Mother was mighty particular about having a good store of it, and she fussed if her supply of it wasn't fresh. This meant that a trip to the mill had to be made every two or three weeks.

Ollie knew it was no use telling Mother or Pap he was afraid. Pap had made up his mind, and that was that. But Ollie's fears kept coming. What if a bear got him? he wondered. Or what if he spilled the corn accidentally while he was riding through the woods? It was a long trip to make all by himself.

What Pap called his neighborhood stretched for miles. The Whitinger Mill lay three miles to the north, on the wide, winding White River. A few minutes' walk to the east of the cabin was a shallow, wide ribbon of water called Fall Creek. South about four miles was the village of Indianapolis, capital of the state. And about a quarter of a mile to the south of the cabin was a well-worn east-west trace, or track, wide enough for an oxcart to roll along. This led west to White

miller
mill owner
or operator

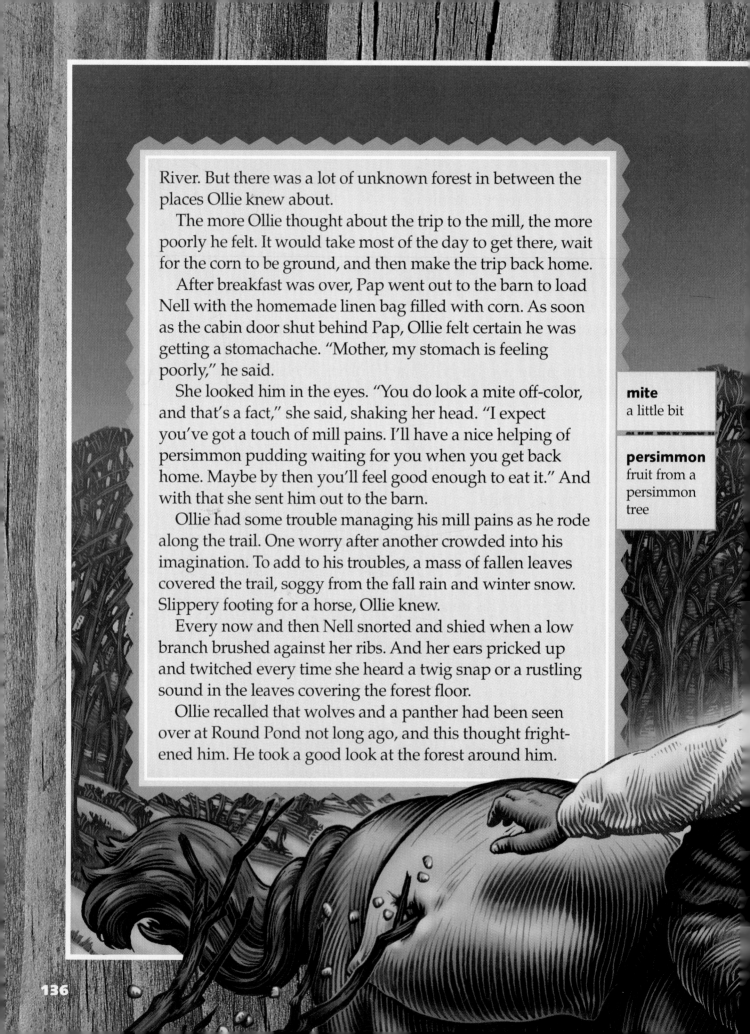

River. But there was a lot of unknown forest in between the places Ollie knew about.

The more Ollie thought about the trip to the mill, the more poorly he felt. It would take most of the day to get there, wait for the corn to be ground, and then make the trip back home.

After breakfast was over, Pap went out to the barn to load Nell with the homemade linen bag filled with corn. As soon as the cabin door shut behind Pap, Ollie felt certain he was getting a stomachache. "Mother, my stomach is feeling poorly," he said.

She looked him in the eyes. "You do look a mite off-color, and that's a fact," she said, shaking her head. "I expect you've got a touch of mill pains. I'll have a nice helping of persimmon pudding waiting for you when you get back home. Maybe by then you'll feel good enough to eat it." And with that she sent him out to the barn.

Ollie had some trouble managing his mill pains as he rode along the trail. One worry after another crowded into his imagination. To add to his troubles, a mass of fallen leaves covered the trail, soggy from the fall rain and winter snow. Slippery footing for a horse, Ollie knew.

Every now and then Nell snorted and shied when a low branch brushed against her ribs. And her ears pricked up and twitched every time she heard a twig snap or a rustling sound in the leaves covering the forest floor.

Ollie recalled that wolves and a panther had been seen over at Round Pond not long ago, and this thought frightened him. He took a good look at the forest around him.

mite
a little bit

persimmon
fruit from a persimmon tree

High overhead the sunlight glittering through the tree branches made the forest seem peaceful and friendly enough. After all, he thought, Round Pond was well to the south and west of his trail. He should be safe enough here.

Suddenly Nell's right front foot slipped. "Steady, Nell, steady!" Ollie cried. He grabbed hold of the bag of corn and hung on tight. Nell bumped into a dead branch but caught herself before she fell. The bag saved her from being poked in the ribs, but the branch made a hole in the bag.

"Easy, Nell." Ollie soothed her with quiet talk, though his heart was thumping with fright. Then he saw a small, steady stream of corn spilling from the bag. "Oh, no!" he cried.

He jerked his hat from his head and stuffed a corner of it in the hole. But he had already lost about as much corn as

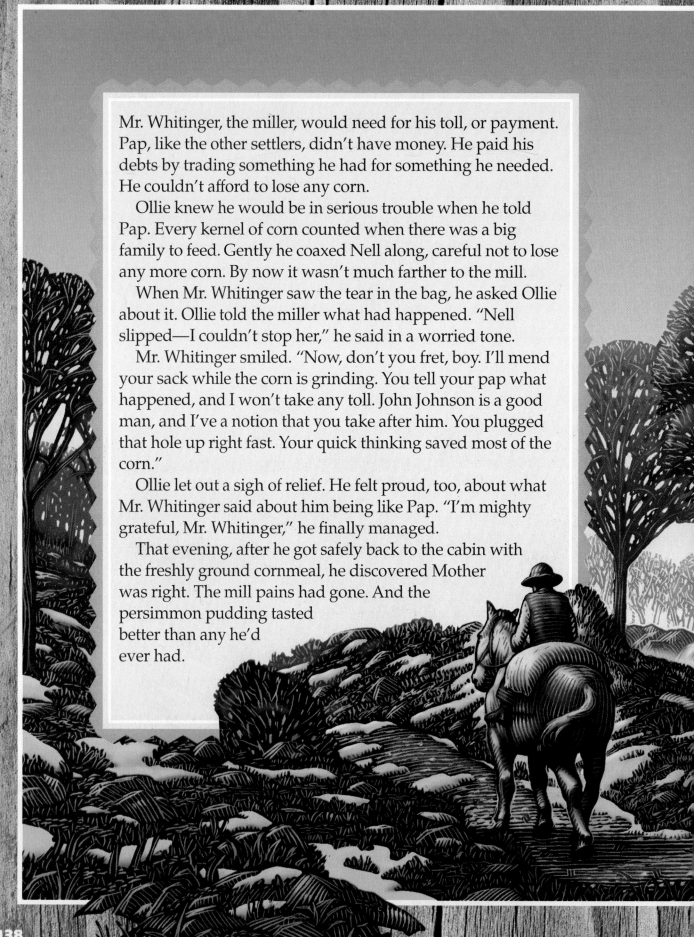

Mr. Whitinger, the miller, would need for his toll, or payment. Pap, like the other settlers, didn't have money. He paid his debts by trading something he had for something he needed. He couldn't afford to lose any corn.

Ollie knew he would be in serious trouble when he told Pap. Every kernel of corn counted when there was a big family to feed. Gently he coaxed Nell along, careful not to lose any more corn. By now it wasn't much farther to the mill.

When Mr. Whitinger saw the tear in the bag, he asked Ollie about it. Ollie told the miller what had happened. "Nell slipped—I couldn't stop her," he said in a worried tone.

Mr. Whitinger smiled. "Now, don't you fret, boy. I'll mend your sack while the corn is grinding. You tell your pap what happened, and I won't take any toll. John Johnson is a good man, and I've a notion that you take after him. You plugged that hole up right fast. Your quick thinking saved most of the corn."

Ollie let out a sigh of relief. He felt proud, too, about what Mr. Whitinger said about him being like Pap. "I'm mighty grateful, Mr. Whitinger," he finally managed.

That evening, after he got safely back to the cabin with the freshly ground cornmeal, he discovered Mother was right. The mill pains had gone. And the persimmon pudding tasted better than any he'd ever had.

Literature Review

1. Why was going to the gristmill so important to Indiana's early settlers?
2. Why was Ollie Johnson worried when he lost some of the corn?
3. Imagine that you are a young person living during pioneer days. Write a journal entry telling how you feel making your first trip to the gristmill.

Read a Diagram

Why Is This Skill Important?

Knowing how to read a diagram can help you understand how something works—in this case, a gristmill. Once you are able to read diagrams, you can use them to explain to another person the way something works.

Understand the Process

To grind their corn into cornmeal, pioneers in Indiana built gristmills next to rivers and creeks. The fast-moving water turned a water-wheel outside the mill. The following steps tell what happened inside the mill. Match the step numbers to those on the diagram.

Step 1 The waterwheel outside the mill turned a counterwheel inside the mill.

Step 2 The counterwheel turned a shaft, which turned a grinding stone.

Step 3 The corn was poured into a hopper to be ground by the stone.

Step 4 The cornmeal slid down a chute and was put into sacks.

Think and Apply

Draw a diagram that shows how something in your classroom or at home works. List the steps, and explain the diagram to a classmate.

LESSON 3

NEW WAYS OF TRAVEL BRING CHANGE

Link to Our World

How does transportation affect places today?

Focus on the Main Idea
Read to find out how roads, rivers, canals, and railroads affected the early growth and settlement of the state of Indiana.

Preview Vocabulary

trace
stagecoach
downstream
upstream
navigable
canal

locomotive
line
hub

Stone mile markers were used on some roads in the early to middle 1800s.

Between 1800 and 1850 it became easier to travel both by water and by land. As transportation improved, Indiana began to grow and change even more.

BUILDING ROADS

Most early pioneers walked or rode horses between settlements in Indiana. There were no real roads. People followed trails, or **traces**, through the woods and fields that connected rivers and creeks. Most traces were first made by animals.

Traces were wide enough for only one person or one animal. Soon pioneers began to widen the traces so that wagons could travel on them. One of the first roads built this way in Indiana was the Buffalo Trace. This former buffalo path connected the towns of New Albany and Vincennes.

In marsh areas pioneers laid logs across the trails. People called these "corduroy roads" because they were bumpy like corduroy cloth. These bumpy roads made riding in wagons uncomfortable. So pioneers began to split logs into flat planks to make "plank roads." When it rained, however, plank roads became slippery, so travel was still difficult.

In the 1820s the state began building roads to connect Indiana's main towns to one another and to the new state capital at Indianapolis. The first of these early state roads was the Michigan Road. It linked towns from

This artist's drawing shows a bridge on the National Road during the 1840s and 1850s. What river does the bridge cross?

north to south through the state, from Lake Michigan to the Ohio River.

In 1829 the National Road reached Indiana. The National Road was built westward from Maryland, and in time it crossed Indiana and reached as far as Vandalia, Illinois. The United States government paid for it to be built. The National Road was covered with a thick layer of gravel instead of logs or planks. This first gravel road in Indiana was not as bumpy as a corduroy road and did not get as slippery as a plank road did.

The National Road passed through Indiana from Richmond to Indianapolis and then to Terre Haute. It connected Indiana with states to the east and west. During the 1830s and 1840s, the National Road carried a steady flow of stage-coaches and freight wagons full of people and goods. A **stagecoach** was a covered passenger wagon pulled by horses. Today the National Road is also called U.S. Route 40.

 What was the National Road?

STEAMBOATS

The first people to settle in Indiana used rivers for transportation. Indians of the Eastern Woodlands, as well as French and British fur traders, traveled in canoes. Later most American settlers arrived in Indiana by way of the Ohio River.

Farmers on the frontier built flatboats to carry passengers and to take their goods to market by way of rivers. The problem with flatboats was that they could travel only **downstream**, or with the river's current. But sometimes travelers needed to go **upstream**, or against the river's current.

The invention of the steamboat by Robert Fulton in 1807 solved that problem. Steamboats had large paddle wheels that pushed them through the water. The power to turn the paddle wheel came from steam. Fuel, usually wood, was burned to turn water into steam in a boiler.

Because of its paddle wheel, a steam-boat could go downstream twice as fast as a flatboat. More important, it could also go upstream.

In 1811 steamboats began to chug up and down the Ohio River. By 1841 hundreds of them traveled the Mississippi, Ohio, and other rivers.

Steamboats could be used only on rivers that were navigable. A **navigable** river is one that is fairly deep and wide. In Indiana only the Ohio River and the lower part of the Wabash River were navigable for steamboats. However, steamboats could be used on the Great Lakes. As a result, Michigan City became an important port for lake steamboats.

 How were steamboats different from flatboats?

INDIANA CANALS

Many farmers in Indiana lived far from the two navigable rivers and the Great Lakes. This made it hard for them to ship their goods to market. To help them, the state of Indiana began to dig canals. A **canal** is a narrow waterway built to connect other waterways or bodies of water. Because they helped farm products and settlers reach the cities and towns, the canals were important to the early growth of Indiana.

The Wabash and Erie Canal was the longest canal built in Indiana. Building began in 1832, and the canal was completed in 1853. The Wabash and Erie Canal made it possible for canal boats to

Because flatboats could travel only downstream, they were often taken apart and sold as wood at the end of a journey.

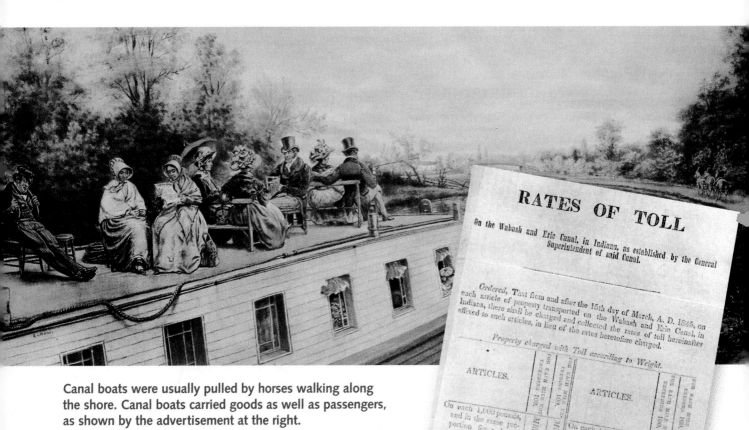

Canal boats were usually pulled by horses walking along the shore. Canal boats carried goods as well as passengers, as shown by the advertisement at the right.

travel all the way from the Great Lakes to the Ohio River. The route of the canal started at Lake Erie and followed the Maumee River to the city of Fort Wayne. From there it went to the Wabash River and on to Terre Haute. From Terre Haute the canal went south to Evansville, on the Ohio River.

Because Indiana's canals were so busy, many frontier settlements along them began to grow. More people started settling along the canal routes to open shops and build homes.

✓ Why were canals built in Indiana?

EARLY RAILROADS

By the 1850s, however, canals had become a less important form of transportation. Railroads were being built, bringing great changes to the whole country. Trains could haul many more goods than freight wagons, steamboats, and canal barges could—and often at a lower cost. They could carry more passengers, too, and could travel in all kinds of weather. Railroads linked towns in parts of the state where there were no rivers or canals. Railroads also linked Indiana with the rest of the United States.

Indiana's first railroad was a track about one mile (about 2 km) long. It was built in Shelbyville in 1834. The owner, Judge W. J. Peasley, did not have a **locomotive**, or train engine, so he used a

This drawing shows an early view of Union Station.

horse. The horse pulled a single passenger car. People rode it for fun.

Indiana's first railroad line was built in 1847. It connected Madison, on the Ohio River, with Indianapolis. A **line** is a transportation route. When the first train arrived in Indianapolis on October 1, 1847, the people there held a great celebration. The evening sky was lit with fireworks displays. A local newspaper called the event "a proud day for Indianapolis."

Of the first eight railroad lines in Indiana, five connected Indianapolis to other cities. People began calling Indianapolis "Railroad City." It became a **hub**, or center, of transportation. Being a transportation hub helped Indianapolis grow into the state's largest city.

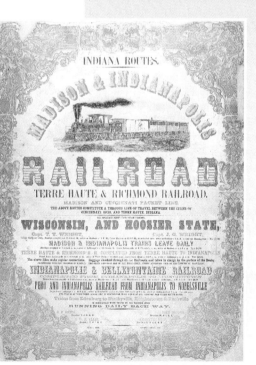

W̶hat?

Crossroads of America

Hoosiers chose Crossroads of America as their state motto because of Indiana's central location. It was on the path taken by many people moving west in the early 1800s. Travelers passed through the state by trail, by road, by river, and by canal. Later they traveled by railroad, and the word *crossroads* became popular. Crossroads of America is still a good motto for the state because more highways and railroads crisscross Indiana than any other state.

 Why did railroads become more important than rivers and canals for transportation?

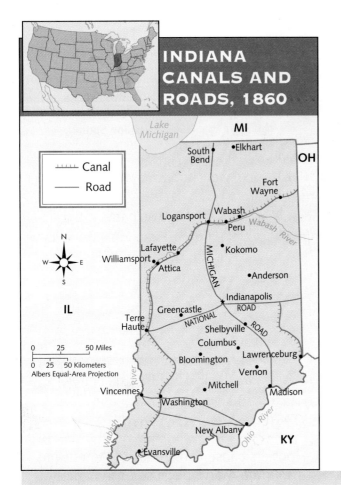

INDIANA CANALS AND ROADS, 1860

Canal
Road

N W E S

IL

0 25 50 Miles
0 25 50 Kilometers
Albers Equal-Area Projection

Lake Michigan
MI
OH

South Bend
Elkhart
Fort Wayne
Logansport
Wabash
Peru
Wabash River
Lafayette
Kokomo
Williamsport
Attica
MICHIGAN
Anderson
Indianapolis
ROAD
Greencastle
NATIONAL ROAD
Terre Haute
Shelbyville
Columbus
Bloomington
Lawrenceburg
Vernon
Mitchell
Vincennes
Madison
Washington
Wabash River
Ohio River
New Albany
KY
Evansville

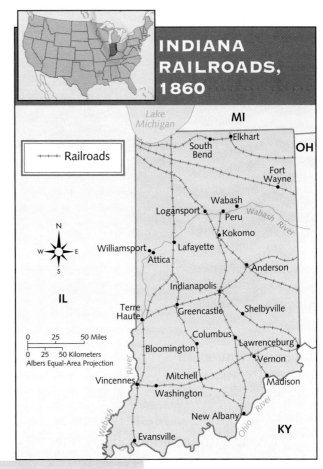

INDIANA RAILROADS, 1860

Railroads

N W E S

IL

0 25 50 Miles
0 25 50 Kilometers
Albers Equal-Area Projection

Lake Michigan
MI
OH

South Bend
Elkhart
Fort Wayne
Logansport
Wabash
Peru
Wabash River
Williamsport
Kokomo
Attica
Lafayette
Anderson
Indianapolis
Terre Haute
Greencastle
Shelbyville
Columbus
Lawrenceburg
Bloomington
Vernon
Mitchell
Vincennes
Madison
Washington
New Albany
Ohio River
Evansville
KY
Wabash River

MOVEMENT Indiana was an important transportation link between the eastern and western United States.

■ If a person was traveling from Logansport to Indianapolis in 1860, what methods of transportation could be used?

LESSON 3 REVIEW

Check Understanding

1. **Recall the Facts** Which roads first crossed Indiana from north to south and from east to west?

2. **Focus on the Main Idea** How did roads, rivers, canals, and railroads affect the early growth and settlement of the state of Indiana?

Think Critically

3. **Past to Present** Why do you think Indiana continues to depend on more than one kind of transportation?

4. **Cause and Effect** What effect did the Wabash and Erie Canal have on frontier settlements?

Show What You Know

Art Activity Draw a picture map showing different forms of early transportation and early transportation routes in Indiana. On your map, show where you could find steamboats, flatboats, freight wagons, stagecoaches, canal boats, and trains. Share your map with family members.

HowTo

Use a Line Graph to See Change

Why Is This Skill Important?

A line graph is a good way to show information and tell how that information changes over a period of time. This line graph shows how the **population**, or number of people, of Indiana grew between 1810 and 1850.

Understand the Process

The numbers at the bottom of the graph are the years from 1810 to 1850. The population is shown on the left side of the graph. The numbers go from 0 to 1,000,000.

There is a dot on the line above some of the years. Find the year 1810. With your finger, trace the line upward until you reach the dot. Then move your finger to the left to find the population number. This number is an estimate, or close guess, of the population in 1810. There were about 25,000 settlers in what is now Indiana.

Now find the year 1820. What was the population in that year? If you look at the line connecting the dots for 1810 and 1820, you can see clearly how the population changed in those ten years.

Think and Apply

Create a line graph to see the change in population of Africans living in Indiana between 1810 and 1850. Use this information— 1810 (630), 1820 (1,420), 1830 (3,632), 1840 (7,168), and 1850 (11,262).

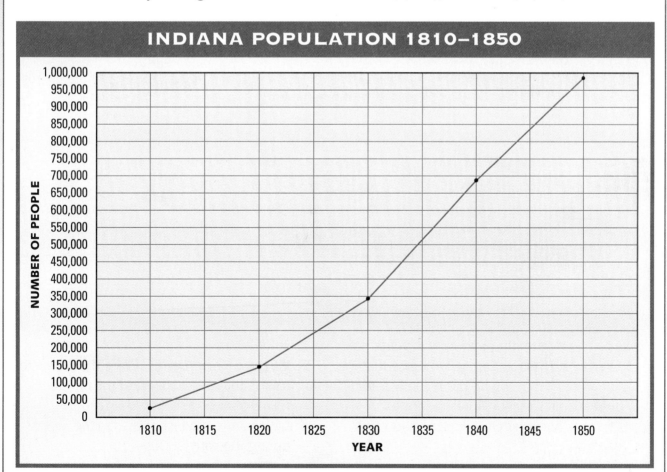

INDIANA POPULATION 1810–1850

CONNECT MAIN IDEAS

Use this organizer to show that you understand how the chapter's main ideas are connected. Copy the organizer onto a separate sheet of paper. Then complete it by writing two sentences to summarize each lesson.

Pioneers in Indiana

Pioneer Settlements
1. _____
_____
2. _____
_____

Pioneer Life
1. _____
_____
2. _____
_____

Early Transportation
1. _____
_____
2. _____
_____

WRITE MORE ABOUT IT

1. **Write a Journal Entry** Imagine that you are a pioneer who has recently settled in Indiana. Describe how you got to Indiana and what you did when you first arrived.

2. **Write a Song Lyric** Write the words to a song that describes ways the different forms of transportation changed in Indiana and the rest of the United States during the early 1800s.

USE VOCABULARY

Use the words below to make a crossword puzzle on a sheet of graph paper. Use the definitions of the words as *ACROSS* and *DOWN* clues. Give your puzzle to a partner to solve.

claim   trace
loft   canal
gristmill   line

CHECK UNDERSTANDING

1. Where did the Lincolns live in Indiana?

2. What was one of the first tasks settlers did when they arrived on their land?

3. Who built the town of Harmonie?

4. Who started New Harmony?

5. What was the advantage of having a farm near a navigable river?

6. Who built the National Road?

7. How did river transportation change with the invention of the steamboat?

8. Between which two towns did Indiana's first railroad line run?

THINK CRITICALLY

1. **Personally Speaking**   If you were a pioneer, what would you look for in choosing a site for a home and farm?

2. **Think More About It**   Why do you think pioneers cooperated in building and farming?

3. **Cause and Effect**   How did roads, canals, and railroads affect the growth of Indiana towns?

4. **Explore Viewpoints**   How do you think canal boat operators felt about having railroads built across Indiana?

5. **Past to Present**   How is transportation today like that in the early 1800s? How is it different?

APPLY SKILLS

How to Use a Map to Show Movement   Draw a map that shows your classroom and several other places in your school. Add a compass rose to your map. Then draw arrows from your classroom to the other places shown on your map. Write a sentence that tells in which direction you travel as you walk from one place to another.

How to Read a Diagram   Imagine that you are a gristmill operator. Write a description of the process for milling grain. Use the diagram on page 140 as a guide.

How to Use a Line Graph to See Change   Look in newspapers or old magazines for a line graph. Cut out a graph and tape it to a sheet of paper. Below the graph, describe the change being shown. What change happens over time?

READ MORE ABOUT IT

A Home in the Woods: Pioneer Life in Indiana by Oliver Johnson. Indiana University Press. A challenging book that gives one person's first-hand account of life as a pioneer in Indiana.

Abraham Lincoln by Lee Morgan. Silver Burdett. This book follows Lincoln's life from his childhood in Indiana until his death while he was President of the United States.

Conner Prairie

Like many students, you may think of history as something that happened to other people in other times. It may not seem real to you. It might even seem like a fantasy. At Conner Prairie, near Indianapolis, history comes alive. You can see it. You can hear it. You can smell it. You can even act it out.

Conner Prairie is a "living history" village. On a visit there you can experience the sights, sounds, and smells of Indiana pioneer life in 1836. You can see the homes. You can hear the hammering of the blacksmith. You can smell what's cooking at the inn. You can also try activities such as dipping candles, washing clothes on a washboard, and playing pioneer games.

Real history is more than just names and dates. It is the stories of people just like you who lived in another time.

THINK AND APPLY

BUILDING CITIZENSHIP

Imagine that you are making a living history museum to show life in your town today. What kinds of displays and exhibits would be in your museum? How would you help visitors make history come alive? Share your ideas with the class.

Some of the things you can do at Conner Prairie include visiting an 1836 schoolroom (left) or a carpenter's shop (right).

STORY CLOTH

Follow the pictures in this story cloth to help you review what you read about in Unit 2.

Summarize the Main Ideas

1. After the American Revolution thousands of people began to settle the land west of the Appalachian Mountains.

2. Tecumseh wanted the Native Americans to form a confederation. He felt that together they could stop the American settlers from moving onto western land.

3. Many Indians joined the British against the United States in the War of 1812. The defeat of the British and the death of the Indian leader Tecumseh made it easier for Americans to settle in the Indiana Territory.

4. The number of people living in the Indiana Territory grew quickly in the early 1800s. In 1816 the United States government made Indiana a state.

5. Pioneers arrived in Indiana by boat and wagon. Some pioneers walked and rode horses to the new land, where they hoped to start a better life.

6. Indiana's growth was helped by new transportation links with the rest of the country. Goods and people moved by way of rivers, roads, canals, and railroads.

Make Your Own Story Cloth   Choose a topic that is illustrated in this story cloth. Then create your own story cloth about that topic. Draw simple pictures. Ask a classmate to use your drawings to tell a story.

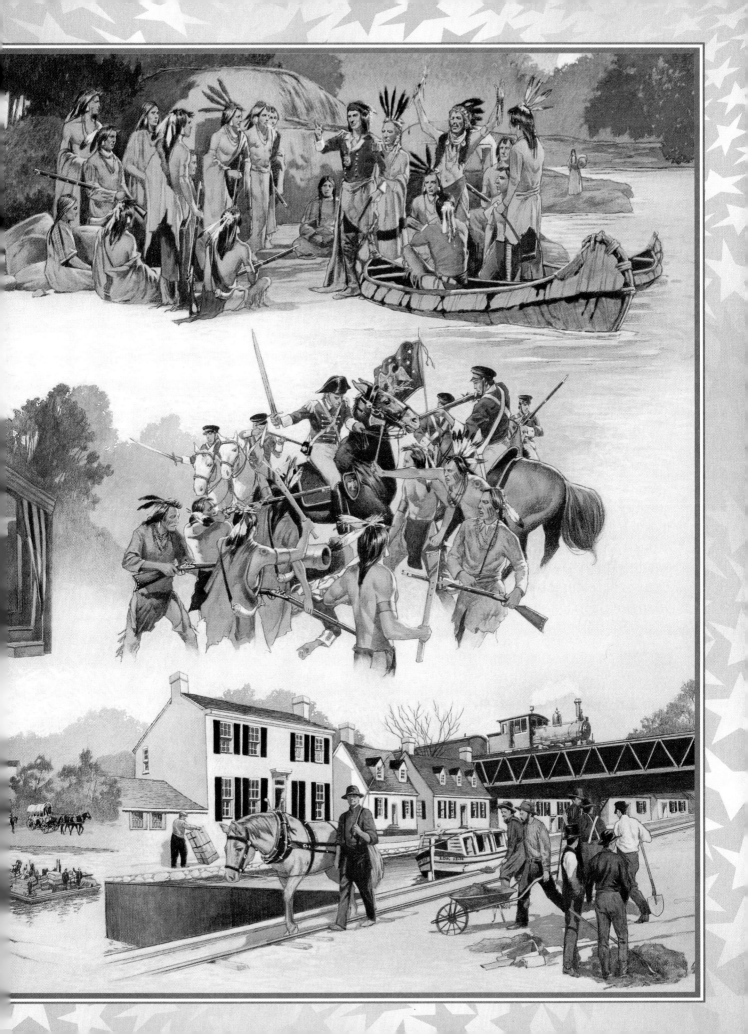

COOPERATIVE LEARNING WORKSHOP

Remember
- Share your ideas.
- Cooperate with others to plan your work.
- Take responsibility for your work.
- Show your group's work to the class.
- Discuss what you learned by working together.

Activity 1
Publish a Magazine

Work in small groups to write magazine articles and draw pictures to tell the story of Indian leaders in the Northwest Territory. Include articles on Little Turtle, Tecumseh, and the Prophet. Put all the articles and pictures together in a magazine. Display your group's magazine in the school library for other students to read.

Activity 2
Plan a Movie

As a class, plan a movie called *Coming to Indiana*. Look back at the unit for ideas. Work in small groups to write the script and design the scenery. Then choose actors to "rehearse" the movie for the directors—the rest of the class. Perform your play for other students who might want to learn about the early pioneers in Indiana's history.

Activity 3
Create a Display

Work in groups to design a multimedia display that shows the life of Jonathan Jennings. Some students may make pictures showing his contributions to Indiana history. Other students may write a short biography or act out a scene from his life.

Activity 4
Make Advertisements

With a group of your classmates, make an advertisement for one of the ways to travel in Indiana's pioneer days. For example, you might choose a flatboat. Use words and pictures to "sell" your kind of transportation to the pioneers. Display your advertisement in the classroom.

USE VOCABULARY

Write a short story about pioneer days in Indiana. Use the following vocabulary terms in your story.

loft	deed
claim	township
gristmill	section
trace	ordinance

CHECK UNDERSTANDING

1. What law helped the American settlers in the Northwest Territory pay for public schools?

2. What effect did the Battle of Tippecanoe have on Native Americans living in the Northwest Territory?

3. Where did many of the Indiana pioneers come from?

4. What does the name *Indianapolis* mean?

5. How was New Harmony different from most pioneer communities?

6. Why did settlers living long ago in Indiana build gristmills?

7. Why was the Wabash and Erie Canal important to Indiana?

THINK CRITICALLY

1. **Think More About It** Why do you think it was important for a new state to have a constitution?

2. **Personally Speaking** Would you rather have lived in Indiana during pioneer days, or do you prefer living here now? Explain your answer.

3. **Cause and Effect** What effect did statehood have on the American settlers living in Indiana?

APPLY GEOGRAPHY SKILLS

How to Use a Map to Show Movement Since Indianapolis became the state capital, members of the Indiana General Assembly have traveled there to make laws for the state. In which direction would a lawmaker today travel to Indianapolis from each of the following cities?

1. Evansville
2. Gary
3. South Bend
4. Fort Wayne
5. Terre Haute
6. Richmond

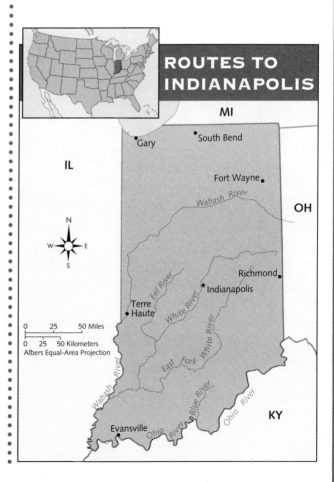

ROUTES TO INDIANAPOLIS

MI
Gary
South Bend
IL
Fort Wayne
Wabash River
OH
N
W — E
S
Eel River
Richmond
Indianapolis
Terre Haute
White River
0 25 50 Miles
0 25 50 Kilometers
Albers Equal-Area Projection
East Fork White River
Wabash River
Blue River
Ohio River
KY
Evansville
Ohio River

UNIT 3

PROGRESS AS A STATE

1855

1863
Civil War battle fought at Corydon

1875

1867
Oliver H. Kelley starts the Grange

1894
Elwood Haynes test-drives one of the first automobiles

1895

1909
City of Gary becomes a center for the steel industry

1911
First Indianapolis 500 automobile race is held

1915

1916
Indiana celebrates 100 years as a state

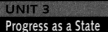

In the years after gaining statehood, Indiana progressed, or developed, to become a top agricultural state. Farmers produced larger and richer harvests, and their hard work helped Indiana's cities grow. By 1916, when Indiana celebrated 100 years as a state, more than one-third of its people lived in cities. Today, most of its people live in cities, working in jobs no one could have dreamed of in 1816. In this unit you will read about how Indiana has progressed in the years since it became a state. How do you think your state will progress in the future?

← Painting by Theodore Groll showing Indianapolis around 1900

1935

1941
United States enters World War II

1945
World War II ends

1955

1949
Indiana legislature makes school segregation against the law

1975

1970
Port of Indiana at Burns Harbor opens

1995

Unit 3 • **157**

ESCAPE FROM SLAVERY

by Doreen Rappaport

The first free Africans to come to Indiana arrived in the early 1800s. Many settled on land deeded to Ishmael Roberts, an African veteran of the American Revolution. Their settlements became important rest stops for Africans escaping slavery in southern states. In *Escape from Slavery* Selena and Cornelia Jackson were two young slaves running away to Canada. On their journey they got some very important help from a boy named Dosha and the other settlers at Cabin Creek in what is now Randolph County.

It was a week since folks in Cabin Creek had gotten the news that slave hunters were around, tracking down the Jackson girls. Selena Jackson was eleven, a year older than Dosha. Her sister, Cornelia, was a couple of years younger. Dosha didn't much like girls, but these two were different from most. He had to admit that. They'd made their way to Cabin Creek, Indiana, from somewhere in Tennessee, over two hundred miles away. Hiding in thickets and caves during the day. Scrounging for food in barns, eating pig slop to keep from starving. They had traveled in the pitch black of night, crossing mountains and swamps. Their only guide had been the North Star. He didn't know how they'd done it, and had to admit that he wasn't sure that he could have.

Folks in Cabin Creek were used to slave hunters coming after runaways. The black settlement was just north of a six-mile stretch of wilderness that had been leveled by a tornado. Many slaves lost their pursuers in this tangle of huge, downed trees and thick underbrush and ended up in Cabin Creek. Hounds couldn't follow the human scent when escaping slaves waded in the swamp or ran above ground, jumping from fallen limb to fallen limb. When the runaways got to Cabin Creek, folks hid them until they could get them farther north to Canada.

Cabin Creek was only one of about twenty rural [free African] settlements in Indiana. Slavery was forbidden in the Indiana Constitution, so free blacks

FREE AFRICAN RURAL SETTLEMENTS, INDIANA, 1860

- Free African rural settlement

0 25 50 Miles
0 25 50 Kilometers
Albers Equal-Area Projection

Huggart
Rush
Bassett
Weaver
Greenville
Snow Hill
Roberts
(name unknown)
Cabin Creek
Beech
Lost Creek
Underwood
(name unknown)
Burnett
(name unknown)
Seymour
Vallonia
(name unknown)
Lyles Station
Lick Creek
Beck's Mill
Sand Hill
Roundtree
Pinkston

LOCATION Cabin Creek was located in eastern central Indiana.
■ What settlements were located near Cabin Creek?

and freed slaves immigrated here. Around fifteen years earlier, in 1826, Dosha's parents and other free blacks from
North Carolina had come to Cabin Creek. They'd drained
the boggy land that white settlers didn't want. They'd
turned it and tended it until the soil was rich enough to
yield plentiful harvests. A group of white Quakers, who had
also immigrated from North Carolina, raised money to tide
the black community over until it was self-sufficient.

Now Cabin Creek had over a hundred residents. It also
had a whole system worked out to help runaways. Dosha's
watch duty was only one part of the system.

Dosha blinked his eyes at a flurry of motion about a mile
or so away. Definitely riders. He waited another minute
hoping to distinguish how many, but he
couldn't make it out. They were getting closer.
He scampered down the tree, mounted Free
and kicked him hard. Free broke into a
gallop almost immediately. A bullet
from a shotgun whizzed by.
Dosha's heart jumped like a
scared rabbit. Another shot.
He kicked Free harder.

In the center of town Dosha pulled in Free's reins, put a horn to his lips, gave a loud blast, then galloped off to a secluded spot about a quarter mile away. His friend Samuel was already there, with his horse. Dosha left Free with him and ran back to the center of town.

When Bessie Watkins heard the horn, she ran to the window. Four men on horseback were riding straight toward her cabin. There was no back door or back window to the cabin, and the men were too close to risk letting the girls out the front door. *How did they find out?* she thought. There hadn't been any strangers around Cabin Creek for weeks, and it was unthinkable that anyone in town might have given them away. She rummaged through a drawer to get the clothes she'd saved for just this occasion.

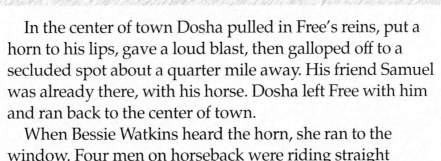

Dressed as boys, Selena and Cornelia were taken by Dosha to another settlement 20 miles (32 km) away. There they were hidden for a few weeks until the slave hunters gave up their search.

INDIANA GROWS AND CHANGES

> ❝ I am a woman who came from the cotton fields of the South. . . . I promoted myself into the business of manufacturing. . . . I have built my own factory on my own ground. ❞
>
> Madam C. J. Walker,
> 1867–1919

Madam C. J. Walker was born Sarah Breedlove and married Charles Joseph Walker in 1906. As was the custom of women in business then, she added the title "Madam" to her husband's name.

INDIANA IN THE CIVIL WAR

LESSON 1

Link to Our World

What can happen today when groups of people do not agree?

Focus on the Main Idea
Read to find out what happened in the middle 1800s when the northern and southern states did not agree.

Preview Vocabulary
slave state   civil war
free state   cavalry
Underground
  Railroad
Union
Confederacy

Leg shackles were used by slave owners to prevent slaves from escaping.

Indiana grew and changed in many ways from the time it became a state in 1816 until the 1850s. Many people came to live in the state. Brick buildings and wooden houses replaced log cabins. New inventions made travel and work easier. Yet a dark cloud hung over the nation. Arguments about slavery were dividing the people of the United States.

SLAVERY IN THE UNITED STATES

By the 1850s more than 4 million Africans in the United States were forced to work as slaves. Most of the enslaved people lived in the South, in the states that were known as **slave states**. Slavery was allowed in these southern states. The slaves worked on farms, planting, caring for, and harvesting crops, mostly cotton. They also worked as house servants, doing cooking, cleaning, and sewing.

Slaves had no freedom and little free time. They worked from dawn to sunset, or as the slaves said, "from can see to can't see." Enslaved children worked, too. Young children gathered firewood, helped in the gardens and kitchens, and looked after animals. Older enslaved children worked with the adults.

Many slaves in the South lived in small cabins (above) on their owners' property. Rewards were offered for the return of runaway slaves (left).

$150 REWARD

RANAWAY from the subscriber, on the night of the 2d instant, a negro man, who calls himself *Henry May*, about 22 years old, 5 feet 6 or 8 inches high, ordinary color, rather chunky built, bushy head, and has it divided mostly on one side, and keeps it very nicely combed; has been raised in the house, and is a first rate dining-room servant, and was in a tavern in Louisville for 18 months. I expect he is now in Louisville trying to make his escape to a free state, (in all probability to Cincinnati, Ohio.) Perhaps he may try to get employment on a steamboat. He is a good cook, and is handy in any capacity as a house servant. Had on when he left, a dark cassinett coatee, and dark striped cassinett pantaloons, new—he had other clothing. I will give **$50** reward if taken in Louisville; **100 dollars** if taken one hundred miles from Louisville in this State, and **150 dollars** if taken out of this State, and delivered to me, or secured in any jail so that I can get him again.

WILLIAM BURKE.
Bardstown, Ky., September 3d, 1838.

Even slaves who were treated well by their owners were not free. They were not allowed to choose where they would live or what work they would do. Some slaves could not even choose whom they would marry.

Some slaves tried to escape. Alone or in small groups, most who got away headed for Canada. They knew they faced a terrible beating if they were caught. Many owners sent slave hunters to bring their runaway slaves back. Under the law, anyone caught helping slaves to escape would be punished.

 What work did enslaved children do?

UNDERGROUND RAILROAD

The first goal of many runaway slaves was to reach the Ohio River, the boundary line between the slave states and the free states. In **free states**, such as Indiana, slavery was not allowed. One of the places where the slaves crossed the river into Indiana was the city of Evansville. There they could find a place to hide with free Africans, many of whom had been slaves themselves. Some had run away, and some had been given their freedom. They had jobs in Evansville and provided services by working as barbers, painters, tailors, carpenters, laundry workers, and blacksmiths.

One of the free Africans who helped ferry slaves across the Ohio River was Chapman Harris. When he was ready to cross the river in his rowboat, Harris would strike a large iron block that he had hung in a tree near the river. That was the signal that he was on his way. The sound was the sound of freedom for many runaway slaves.

After crossing the Ohio River, many runaway slaves heading for Canada stopped in central Indiana. Those traveling through east-central Indiana often stopped at Levi and Katherine "Aunt Katie" Coffin's farm in Fountain City. The Coffins were members of the Society of Friends, often called Quakers. This religious group believed that all people should have the same rights. Many Quakers helped runaway slaves. Over time more than 2,000 slaves hid at the Coffins' farm. One angry Kentucky slave owner said, "They must have an underground railroad running hereabouts, and Levi Coffin must be the president of it."

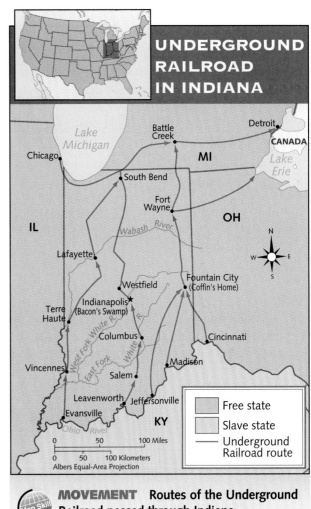

UNDERGROUND RAILROAD IN INDIANA

MOVEMENT Routes of the Underground Railroad passed through Indiana.
■ Where would a runaway slave hiding in Fountain City most likely go next?

Runaway slaves arrive in eastern central Indiana (below), near the home of Levi Coffin (left). Coffin's house had hiding places in it for runaway slaves.

165

THE UNION AND THE CONFEDERACY

CANADA

WASHINGTON TERRITORY

OREGON

DAKOTA TERRITORY

MINNESOTA

WISCONSIN

MICHIGAN

Lake Superior

MAINE

VT

NH

NEW YORK

MA

CT

RI

NEVADA TERRITORY

NEBRASKA TERRITORY

IOWA

PENNSYLVANIA

NJ

UTAH TERRITORY

COLORADO TERRITORY

KANSAS

ILLINOIS

INDIANA

OHIO

MD

DE

WEST VIRGINIA (1863)

VIRGINIA

CALIFORNIA

MISSOURI

KENTUCKY

NORTH CAROLINA

NEW MEXICO TERRITORY

INDIAN TERRITORY

ARKANSAS

TENNESSEE

SOUTH CAROLINA

ATLANTIC OCEAN

PACIFIC OCEAN

TEXAS

MISSISSIPPI

ALABAMA

GEORGIA

LOUISIANA

FLORIDA

MEXICO

Gulf of Mexico

0   200   400 Miles
0   200   400 Kilometers
Albers Equal-Area Projection

Legend:
- Union state
- Border state
- Confederate state
- Territory

REGIONS This map shows how the United States was divided at the beginning of the Civil War.
■ How many territories are shown on this map?

The **Underground Railroad**, as it came to be known, was not a real railroad and was not underground. It was a route along which runaway slaves knew they could find help in getting to Canada. Homes where slaves could hide were called stations. Three routes of the Underground Railroad met at the Coffin farm. One route was from Cincinnati, Ohio. Another was from Madison. The third route was from Jeffersonville. For this reason the Coffin farm was later called "the Grand Central Station of the Underground Railroad."

People who hid runaway slaves at a station were called stationmasters. Hiram Bacon was one of the stationmasters in Indianapolis. He hid many runaway slaves in a barn on the east bank of his swamp. At night other helpers, called conductors, moved the slaves from Bacon's Swamp to Westfield, the next stop on the way to Canada. Any slave who made it as far as Westfield on the Underground Railroad felt safe—the slave hunters did not search that far north.

William Wells Brown, a runaway slave, described how the help he was given made him feel. "I was encouraged to press forward, my heart strengthened, and I forgot that I was tired or hungry."

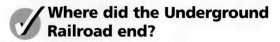 **Where did the Underground Railroad end?**

THE CIVIL WAR

People in the United States had disagreed about slavery for many years. The idea that slavery was wrong was not new. However, owners of plantations, or large farms in the southern states, said they had to have slaves as workers. Many people, even those who did not own slaves, felt that the question of slavery should be decided by each state, not by the national government.

Then, in 1860, Abraham Lincoln was elected President of the United States. Many people in the southern states did not want Lincoln to be President. They worried that he would end slavery. After Lincoln was elected, people in the South began to talk about not being a part of the **Union**, or the United States of America. In February 1861, seven of the southern states formed their own country. They called it the Confederate States of America, or the **Confederacy**. In April and May four more states joined it.

From 1861 to 1865 the people of the Union and the Confederacy fought a war. This war was called the Civil War. A **civil war** is a fight between groups of citizens in what was once the same country.

✓ **What two groups fought in the Civil War?**

HOOSIERS FIGHT FOR THE UNION

President Lincoln said that he would fight the war to "save the Union." He wanted to keep the United States together. Indiana's governor, Oliver P. Morton, agreed. Recalling the American Revolution, Morton said, "If it was worth a bloody struggle to establish this nation, it is worth one to preserve it."

The Civil War started in April 1861. Soldiers of the Confederacy fired on Fort Sumter, a United States fort in South Carolina held by Union soldiers. A few days later the first Hoosier soldiers went to Camp Morton in Indianapolis for training. Camp Morton was also used as a prison for captured Confederate soldiers.

Who?

Drummers

Many Hoosiers who fought in the Civil War were young people between 18 and 21 years old. One Hoosier was 8 years old when he joined the Union army. Edward Black of Hagerstown served as a drummer. The main job of a drummer was to wake the soldiers in his group for another day of fighting. Drummers also kept rhythm for the soldiers to march to. Many boys who became drummers did so to stay with fathers who were soldiers. Others signed up because they had no relatives to take care of them.

One group of soldiers from Indiana was made up of free Africans. Garland White, a soldier in the group, told people that his reason for fighting was to see "the flag of the Union waved over a nation of freemen."

More than 190,000 Hoosiers fought in the Union army and navy during the Civil War. Of every eight who fought, one died. More than 3,000 Indiana soldiers died in one battle alone in Tennessee.

 On which side did Hoosiers fight in the Civil War?

MORGAN'S RAID

Most of the battles in the Civil War were fought in states other than Indiana. Only one battle took place in Indiana. This happened when a Confederate officer, John Hunt Morgan, led a raid into southern Indiana.

Morgan was in charge of 2,500 **cavalry**, or soldiers on horses. On July 8, 1863, Morgan's cavalry crossed the Ohio River from Kentucky and landed south of Corydon. The next day they moved north, stealing horses and supplies at Corydon and setting fire to Salem. Near Corydon a group of citizens tried to stop Morgan's raiders in a battle. But since there were not nearly as many of them, the Hoosiers lost the battle.

One of the Hoosiers in the group that was defeated at Corydon later wrote,

66It was not expected at the start that so small a force could whip Morgan, but it was expected we could punish him some.99

On July 10, Governor Oliver P. Morton called for Indiana citizens to form a Home Guard to protect Indianapolis. When Morgan heard this, he moved his cavalry

Confederate general John Hunt Morgan, shown here as a colonel (right), led raids (below) into Corydon, Salem, Vernon, and Versailles before he was captured in Ohio.

Robert Dale Owen (right) wrote a letter (above) to President Lincoln, urging him to end slavery. Owen also worked for better education, prison reform, and women's rights.

into Ohio. A few weeks later a Union army captured Morgan's raiders.

 Where did the only Civil War battle in Indiana take place?

THE END OF SLAVERY AND THE WAR

The Civil War was still being fought when President Lincoln signed the Emancipation Proclamation. This important statement gave freedom to all enslaved people in the Confederacy.

Robert Dale Owen, son of New Harmony's Robert Owen, had written a letter to President Lincoln in 1862. In it he said that ending slavery would be a way to get more soldiers—the freed slaves could join the Union army. This was one reason Lincoln signed the Emancipation Proclamation in 1863.

The Civil War ended two years later in 1865. The Union victory meant that the southern states would remain in the Union. It also meant that slavery was ended. One week after the war's end, however, President Abraham Lincoln was shot while he watched a play in Washington, D.C. He died the next day and never had the chance to lead the nation in peace.

 **When did the Civil War end?**

LESSON 1 REVIEW

Check Understanding

1. **Recall the Facts**   What was the Underground Railroad?
2. **Focus on the Main Idea**   What happened in the middle 1800s when the northern and southern states did not agree?

Think Critically

3. **Cause and Effect**   How did Robert Dale Owen think freeing the southern slaves would help the Union?
4. **Think More About It**   Why do you think people worked as stationmasters and conductors on the Underground Railroad?

Show What You Know

Journal-Writing Activity
Imagine that you are an enslaved African escaping north on the Underground Railroad in Indiana. Use the information in this lesson to describe your journey and the people you meet along the way.

Tell Primary from Secondary Sources

Why Is This Skill Important?

People who study history learn about the past from many sources. The best sources of information are **primary sources**. A primary source gives the real words and pictures of people who were there when an event took place and who saw what happened. Their words may be found in letters or diaries, records of interviews, and other old papers. Their drawings or photographs may show people, places, or events as they really were.

Sometimes the only way to learn about the past is from a secondary source. A **secondary source** gives information written at a later time by someone who did not actually see what happened. Your social studies book is one kind of secondary source. Encyclopedias and other reference books are also secondary sources.

Remember What You Have Read

Primary sources let a reader "hear the voices" of people telling about their own experiences. In this lesson you "heard" enslaved workers describe their workday as lasting "from can see to can't see." You heard a slave owner complain about Levi and Katherine Coffin helping runaway slaves. He said, "They must have an underground railroad running hereabouts, and Levi Coffin must be the president of it."

You also read much information about slavery and the Civil War. Most of this information came from secondary sources.

Understand the Process

The words used in a source can sometimes help you tell if the source is primary or secondary. Words like *I, we, my,* and *our* are often found in primary sources.

Each kind of source can be helpful. A primary source can give a reader the feeling of being there. A secondary source may give more facts, such as names and dates.

There can also be problems with each kind of source. Primary sources might give just one person's view of what happened. The people writing secondary sources might not understand what really happened, since they were not there. And they, too, might give their own opinions as facts.

On the following page you can read a report about Morgan's Raid in Corydon. Compare it with what you read about the raid in Lesson 1. Which is a primary source and which is a secondary source? How do you know?

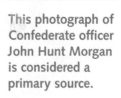

This photograph of Confederate officer John Hunt Morgan is considered a primary source.

MORGAN'S RAID

as remembered by Charles N. Dome of Corydon when he was a boy

We were on the lookout for the approach of the rebels and just at dusk twenty or more men came riding swiftly up the road toward our place. The men ran through our orchard north of the house and into the woods beyond. The women and children fled into the woods west of the house. Morgan's men saw us as we were fleeing and came riding into the woods in pursuit, ordering us to halt, which we did. I remember the leader dismounted and got up on the body of a large fallen tree and said he thought we were a bunch of men. Since we were only women and children, we were told to come back to the house as they would not harm us. They wanted the women to get supper for them. . . .

While the women were getting the meal, several men gathered in the house. I wanted to see what was going on so I edged into the room where the guns were stacked in a pyramid in one corner and the men were sitting around the room talking.

I was a little towhead [blond] and very small for my age. One of the men took me on his lap and as I looked up into his face, I said to him, "You are good rebels, ain't ye? You wouldn't hurt nobody, would ye?"

The men all laughed and he said, "Of course not. We wouldn't hurt nobody."

The man had such a pleasant expression that I felt he was a friend, so I said, "You don't know where my Pa is."

"No, where is he?"

"He's in the woods hidin' from you." This brought a hearty-laugh from all the men.

After supper was over, the leader told our folks to go to bed, that they would not be disturbed during the night. I do not know where the men slept. . . .

Morgan's men were gone when I got up next morning. I remember going into the barn lot. We had a stake and "ridered" fence around the lot and they had tied the horses to the fence corners and fed them sheaf oats. They had plenty, for the ground was still covered with it. So far as I know the raiders were well behaved and offered no indignities [rude treatment] to anyone.

Think and Apply

Write a short journal entry telling what you thought and did during one afternoon. With a classmate, read your journal entries to each other. Write another paragraph based on what your classmate says. Together, compare the primary sources with the secondary sources. How closely does your classmate's report match your real experience?

CHANGES ON THE FARMS

LESSON 2

Link to Our World

How have new inventions and ideas changed the lives of children since your parents or grandparents were your age?

Focus on the Main Idea
Read to find out how new inventions and ideas changed the lives of Indiana farmers in the years after the Civil War.

Preview Vocabulary
isolated   sod
self-sufficient   agriculture
surplus   Grange

Before the 1830s, wheat was harvested with hand tools such as the scythes shown here.

Most of the soldiers from Indiana who fought in the Civil War were the children and grandchildren of pioneers. They grew up in the early 1800s in small communities and on farms that were **isolated**, or far from any neighbors. Going off to war, they saw other parts of the country for the first time. They saw other ways of life and ways of doing things. Their lives would never be the same.

PIONEER FARMS

This was also a time of great change on Indiana's farms. Pioneer farm families had to be almost self-sufficient. Being **self-sufficient** means being able to produce everything needed to live without help from others. The pioneers raised much of their own food and made most of their own goods. From the milk of their cows, they made butter and cheese. From the wool of their sheep, they made clothing.

Pioneer farmers took some of the wheat they grew to a mill to be ground into flour. They used the flour to make their bread. They sold their **surplus**, the part of their crop they did not need for their own use. By selling the surplus to storekeepers in towns, farmers got money to buy things they could not make themselves, such as steel knives, needles, and metal pots and pans. Until the 1830s, surpluses on pioneer farms were not large. Farmers could harvest and send to market only small amounts.

 How were pioneer farmers self-sufficient?

NEW FARMING MACHINES

In 1831 Cyrus McCormick of Virginia invented the first of many new machines for farmers. These machines made farmers' work easier and gave them larger surpluses. McCormick's new invention was a machine called a reaper for cutting wheat.

Wheat grew well in most of Indiana. To harvest it, however, farmers had to cut it by hand with a curved knife called a sickle or other tool. Harvesting a small field took days, even when family members helped. McCormick's reaper, pulled by a horse, cut the wheat faster and with less work. A field of wheat that had taken several workers days to cut now took one person only hours!

Oliver's plow made it possible to grow crops on land that had been too hard to farm before.

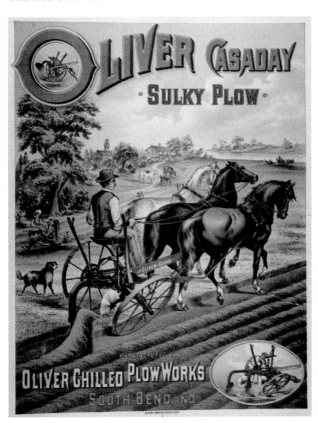

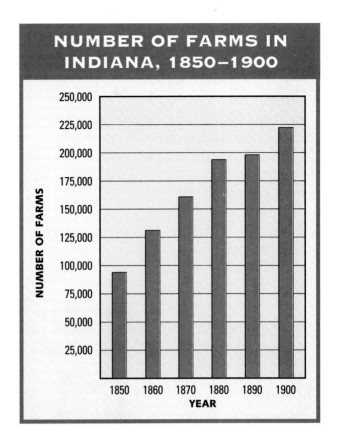

NUMBER OF FARMS IN INDIANA, 1850–1900

LEARNING FROM GRAPHS The number of farms in Indiana grew as new farming machines were invented and new farming methods were developed.
■ Which year shows the greatest number of farms?

With McCormick's reaper, farmers could harvest more wheat—if they could plant more. James Oliver of South Bend invented a better plow to help them do just that.

Pioneer farmers had been making their own plows out of wood and iron, but these plows were not very sharp. This made it difficult to cut through sod. **Sod** is soil in which grass is growing. The sharp edges of Oliver's chilled iron plow easily cut through sod. Using Oliver's plow, farmers could prepare more land for planting in the same amount of time. This meant that the farmers could plant more crops.

 How did Cyrus McCormick and James Oliver help farmers?

What?

The Indiana State Fair

Each year since 1852, people from all over Indiana have come to Indianapolis for the state fair. In its early days, the Indiana State Fair was a yearly show of farm products and new farm machines. It was a place where farmers could meet and share new ideas. Over the years it has become a place for all kinds of businesses to show their latest goods and services. The Indiana State Fair is one of the oldest state fairs in the United States.

Ad for the Indiana State Fair of 1885 (right) and a present-day Indiana State Fair (below)

NEW IDEAS ABOUT FARMING

In pioneer days farmers grew only what they needed for their own food. After the Civil War, farmers all over the United States began to specialize. They grew or raised more of the crops or animals that did well in their area. In Indiana many farmers specialized in growing wheat or corn or in raising hogs or dairy cattle. This way they were able to sell larger amounts of a few farm products and to use the money to buy what they no longer produced themselves.

Scientists at that time were also learning new things about agriculture (AG•rih•kuhl•cher). **Agriculture** is another word for "farming." Scientists learned, for example, that adding certain minerals, or fertilizers, to the soil helped crops grow well. Scientists worked with farmers to learn which fertilizers worked best for each kind of crop.

During the Civil War the United States Congress passed a law giving each state land on which to build a college for the study of agriculture. Indiana's leaders could not agree on a site for Indiana's agriculture college until John Purdue of Lafayette gave the state $150,000 to build the college near his town. Purdue University became Indiana's first agricultural school in 1865. Research done there helped Indiana become one of the top agricultural states in the United States.

 **For what purpose was Purdue University founded?**

THE GRANGE

Although new inventions and ideas brought changes, farming was still a hard, lonely life. Farmers did not make much money because prices for farm products were low. To make matters worse, many farmers owed money, which they had borrowed to buy seeds, fertilizers, and machines.

In 1867 Oliver H. Kelley started a club called the Grange. **Grange** is an old word meaning "farm." The purpose of the club was to bring isolated farm families together. Members of the Grange often cooperated to do things they could not do alone.

Grange meetings were often held in schools or in people's homes. At the meetings farm families shared good times and talked about their problems. This helped them feel less isolated. But the Grange

This Grange poster shows many of the things that were important to farm families in Indiana.

was important in other ways. Working together, Grange members persuaded lawmakers to help them get mail delivery and better schools. They also asked for laws to limit the amounts railroads could charge to carry farm products to market.

The Grange was the first national farm organization in the United States. By 1875 there were more than 21,000 Grange groups in the United States with more than 850,000 members. The Grange is still important to farm families in Indiana.

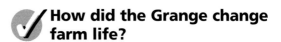 **How did the Grange change farm life?**

LESSON 2 REVIEW

Check Understanding

1. **Recall the Facts**   Name two people who helped make life better for farmers.
2. **Focus on the Main Idea**   How did new inventions and ideas change the lives of Indiana farmers in the years after the Civil War?

Think Critically

3. **Past to Present**   What kinds of inventions or discoveries might help agriculture today?
4. **Cause and Effect**   What effect do you think McCormick's reaper had on the number of workers needed on a farm?

Show What You Know

Table-Making Activity
Make a table to compare and contrast farm life in 1820 and 1880. Under the heading 1820, use words and drawings to show what farm life was like in pioneer days in Indiana. Under the heading 1880, use words and drawings to show how farm life changed.

MANUFACTURING AND THE GROWTH OF CITIES

Link to Our World

How do people build businesses today?

Focus on the Main Idea
Read to find out how people built new businesses in Indiana in the years after the Civil War.

Preview Vocabulary
manufacturing immigrant
industry   free enterprise
refinery   entrepreneur
sharecropper pharmaceutical

By the time of the Civil War, some of Indiana's small towns were becoming cities. Almost 20,000 people lived in Indianapolis. New Albany, Madison, and Evansville, three cities along the Ohio River, each had more than 10,000 people. Many of the people living in the cities had come from Indiana farms. With the new farm machines, fewer workers were needed to raise crops. Many people moved to cities hoping to find jobs in manufacturing. **Manufacturing** is the making of products in factories.

NEW INDUSTRIES

The Civil War helped make manufacturing grow in Indiana. This happened as farmers and factory owners worked to meet the needs of the Union army for food and supplies.

Before the war, factories in Indiana mostly packed pork, milled grain, and made household goods. After the war, new industries moved to the state. An **industry** is all of the businesses that make one kind of product or provide one kind of service.

In 1886 natural gas was discovered near Portland, in northern Indiana. Government leaders of many towns in that area knew that this fuel source could help their people. They offered free natural gas to businesses outside Indiana that would build factories in their communities. In 1889 Standard Oil Company of Ohio built one of the world's largest refineries in the little village of

A Ball brothers' glass jar

Whiting, on the Illinois border near Lake Michigan. A **refinery** is a factory where resources such as oil are made into products people can use. Soon many other large factories were built in the area.

The offer of free natural gas also brought the five Ball brothers—Edmund, William, Lucius, George, and Frank—to Indiana. Government leaders in Muncie offered them free natural gas and land and the money to move their glass factory from Buffalo, New York. In Indiana the Ball brothers'

Natural gas displays, like this one in 1888, were held to show that Indiana had enough natural gas to power large industries.

company became the largest maker of glass jars in the United States. The brothers used some of the money they made to start a college, Ball State University.

The supply of natural gas in Indiana lasted only about 15 years. However, many industries stayed in Indiana. Their factories switched to coal for energy.

✓ **Why did businesses from other states move to Indiana?**

The Standard Oil Refinery was one of the first large industrial plants to be built along the shore of Lake Michigan in northwestern Indiana.

Steel production drew many workers. The steel mills (above) made Gary a prosperous town. By 1920 Gary was the sixth-largest city in Indiana.

A NEW CITY

New businesses helped other Indiana towns grow into cities. Many people moved to South Bend to work in the factory that made the chilled iron plows invented by James Oliver. Workers came to Elkhart to make musical instruments in the factory started by C. G. Conn. Other workers came to Jeffersonville to make steamboats and to Fort Wayne to make socks. Later, workers would flock to Gary to make steel. But in the 1800s there was no Gary!

In the early 1900s the United States Steel Corporation was looking for a place in the Middle West to build a new steel mill. Steel making had become an important industry. Steel was used for making railroad tracks, bridges, buildings, and many kinds of machines. The place for the new mill had to be near supplies of coal, iron, and limestone, which are needed for making steel. It also had to be on good transportation routes for movement of resources in and finished goods out.

United States Steel chose to build its new mill in the Calumet region of northwest Indiana on Lake Michigan. There, ships on the Great Lakes could bring iron ore from northern Minnesota. Railroads could bring limestone from southern Indiana and coal from Pennsylvania. The mill, completed in 1909, was one of the largest steel mills in the world.

Farther south on the Grand Calumet River, United States Steel built a town for all of the new mill workers. The town was named for Elbert H. Gary. He was the head of the United States Steel Corporation at that time. Gary is the only Indiana city that was founded in the twentieth century.

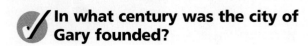

In what century was the city of Gary founded?

NEWCOMERS FROM NEAR AND FAR

As industries grew in Indiana, so did the number of people living in the state. In the early 1900s people began moving to cities in the Calumet Region and other parts of Indiana. They came from other parts of the United States and the world.

In the early 1900s many African Americans moved to Indiana from the southern states. After the Civil War many former slaves had farmed in the South as sharecroppers. A **sharecropper** rented land to farm, paying the landowner with a share of the crops. The sharecropper was given a cabin, tools, and seed. The worker then farmed the land. At harvest time the landowner took part of the crops. What was left was the worker's share. Often, however, this was little or nothing at all. So when sharecroppers heard about jobs in northern factories, many left the South. They moved to cities such as New York, Chicago, Detroit, Pittsburgh, Cleveland, Indianapolis, and Gary to find work and to make better lives for their families.

....

This illustration from *The Great Migration* by Jacob Lawrence shows African Americans moving to the North during the early 1900s.

work and to make better lives for their families.

Other people who came to live in northern cities after the Civil War were immigrants. An **immigrant** is a person who moves to a country from another country. Many immigrants in the early 1900s came to the United States from European countries such as Germany, Greece, Italy, Poland, and western Russia. Like the African Americans, the European immigrants came to Indiana to find jobs and make better lives for themselves and their families.

 What groups of people moved to Indiana to work in its factories?

FREE ENTERPRISE AND NEW BUSINESSES

Many industries grew in Indiana because of free enterprise. **Free enterprise** means that people are free to start and run their own businesses.

New businesses are started by people who are sometimes called entrepreneurs (ahn•truh•pruh•NERZ). An **entrepreneur** is a person who starts and runs a business. To do this, most entrepreneurs must have three kinds of resources. (1) They must have natural resources, such as land, water, and fuel. Businesses that make products also need raw materials. (2) Entrepreneurs must have human resources, or workers. (3) They must have capital resources, or the money, buildings, machines, and tools needed to run their business.

If the business does well, the entrepreneur makes a profit. If people do not want the goods or services the business sells, the business fails. Some entrepreneurs in Indiana lost their money, while others became rich. Two of the most successful entrepreneurs in Indiana at this time were Madam C. J. Walker and Eli Lilly.

Madam C. J. Walker's Manufacturing Company in Indianapolis made hair care products for African American women. Walker's business had more than 3,000 workers, mostly women. These "Walker Agents" traveled all over the country selling Walker products.

In 1876 Eli Lilly started a pharmaceutical (far•muh•SOO•tih•kuhl) company in Indianapolis. Pharmaceuticals are medicines. Both Madam Walker's and Eli Lilly's businesses did well, making these entrepreneurs rich. Walker and Lilly used some of their money to help other people who lived in their communities.

 What is an entrepreneur?

Eli Lilly (above right) was a Union officer in the Civil War. Later he started a business (below right) that would make medicines.

L SSON 3 REVIEW

Check Understanding

1. **Recall the Facts**   What three kinds of resources does an entrepreneur need to start and run a business?
2. **Focus on the Main Idea**   How did people build new businesses in Indiana in the years after the Civil War?

Think Critically

3. **Cause and Effect**   What effect did free enterprise have on the growth of industries in Indiana?

4. **Think More About It**   Why was the Calumet Region a good place to build a steel mill?

Show What You Know

Simulation Activity
Imagine that you and a partner are entrepreneurs. You want to start your own business. What kind of business would you start? Why? Make a list of the resources you would need. Share your list with the class.

Read Symbols on a Product Map

Why Is This Skill Important?

Maps use symbols to show where places are located or where goods are made. This map of Indiana in the early 1900s uses symbols to show where certain products were made at that time.

Understand the Process

Look at the map key to see the symbols used on this map. Each symbol tells you something different about the place it is near.

The ⚒ symbol tells you that factories in Elkhart made musical instruments. In what Indiana cities did workers make glass?

What cities have the 🏭 symbol next to their names? What does the symbol tell you about those cities?

Find the symbols next to Terre Haute. What do they tell you about the kind of work many people did in that town?

Think and Apply

Draw a map of your neighborhood or part of town. Use one symbol for your home. Use other symbols for other buildings, roads, and places of interest. Add a map key to tell what each symbol stands for. How is your map like the map below?

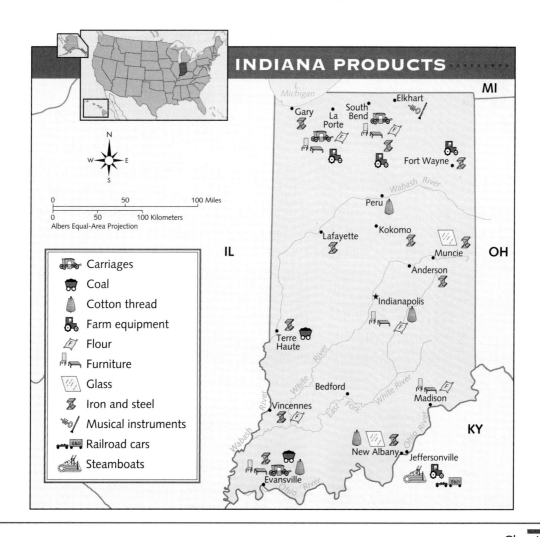

INDIANA PRODUCTS

Key:
- 🛒 Carriages
- ⬛ Coal
- 🧵 Cotton thread
- 🚜 Farm equipment
- Ⓕ Flour
- 🪑 Furniture
- ◹ Glass
- 🏭 Iron and steel
- ⚒ Musical instruments
- 🚃 Railroad cars
- 🚢 Steamboats

INTO A NEW CENTURY

Link to Our World

How does the automobile affect your life?

Focus on the Main Idea
Read to find out how the automobile affected the lives of Hoosiers and the state's economy.

Preview Vocabulary
**automobile
centennial
preserve
memorial**

As the twentieth century began, Indiana was becoming a state of cities and small towns rather than of isolated farms. By 1900 one-third of Indiana's 2.5 million people lived in cities. As Indiana changed, so did the way its people lived. Much of this change came from one invention. For Indiana and the rest of the country, the new century brought a new age—the Automobile Age.

INDIANA AND THE AUTOMOBILE

On July 4, 1894, Kokomo inventor Elwood Haynes took a ride that made him famous. He test-drove his first gasoline-powered **automobile**. The word *automobile* means "self-moving." Haynes tried out his automobile along the twisting Pumpkinvine Pike, a road outside Kokomo. The Kokomo police, fearing the automobile might explode, would not let him drive in town. Haynes drove a mile and a half (more than 2 km) at a speed of 7 miles (about 11 km) an hour. The test went well.

Haynes and his partners, Elmer and Edgar Apperson, were sure people would buy "horse-less carriages," so they decided to make more. Their automobiles were some of the first that were sold in the United States. Soon 88 Indiana cities and towns had automobile factories. South Bend's was the largest. It was owned by the Studebaker (STOO•duh•bay•ker) Company.

An old speed limit sign from Brookston, Indiana, warns speeding drivers of a $10 fine. What speed limit is shown on the sign?

Henry and Clem Studebaker had first made wagons. Their advertisement said,

> 66 The Studebaker won't wear out
> No matter how you drive about.
> Pile on your rocks, this is no joke,
> This wagon is as stout as oak. 99

In 1904 the Studebaker brothers turned from making wagons to making automobiles in their factory.

Indianapolis was another center of the automobile industry in Indiana. It had at least 64 automobile factories, the greatest number of any city. The Duesenbergs (DOO•suhn•burgs), which were among the

Although the cars and the speedway have changed through the years, the Indianapolis 500 has always been one of the most popular racing events in the world.

finest automobiles ever built, were made by Fred and August Duesenberg.

Interest in comparing automobiles was high. Indiana began to hold a race each year to show what the new automobiles could do. On May 30, 1911, the first Indianapolis 500 automobile race was held at the Indianapolis Motor Speedway. Ray Harroun won the first race in his Marmon "Wasp," with an average speed of about 76 miles (122 km) an hour. Today cars in Indianapolis 500 races run at speeds of more than 160 miles (257 km) an hour each Memorial Day weekend in Speedway.

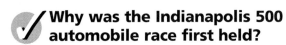 **Why was the Indianapolis 500 automobile race first held?**

THE AUTOMOBILE BRINGS CHANGE

At first only rich people could afford automobiles. Automobiles were costly

Studebaker automobiles were made in Indiana from 1899 to 1963.

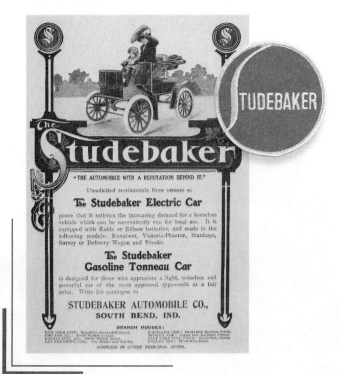

because they were made by hand. It took a long time to produce just a few. Also, the price of gasoline to run them was high. Because they cost so much, automobiles became a status symbol for many Americans. In time the cost went down as ways were developed to make many automobiles quickly. The price of gasoline went down, too, after rich deposits of oil were discovered in Texas.

As more people began to use automobiles, ways of life changed greatly. Farm families were no longer isolated. With their automobiles they could easily get to cities and towns. City people used automobiles to explore the countryside.

The wide use of automobiles in Indiana and the rest of the United States brought many things we know well today. Paved roads and state highway systems were built. Later came motels, shopping centers, and fast-food restaurants. At the same time, automobile accidents began to be a serious problem.

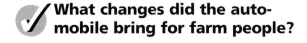 **What changes did the automobile bring for farm people?**

INDIANA'S STATE CENTENNIAL

In the early 1900s Hoosiers were looking ahead to a bright future. They could see that the automobile and other inventions would make their lives easier. Hoosiers also remembered the past. In 1916 the people of Indiana celebrated the state's centennial (sen•TEN•ee•uhl). A **centennial** is the one-hundredth anniversary of a special event.

Cities and towns all over Indiana had parades and fireworks displays. Some held special days for learning about

President Woodrow Wilson (left) visited Indianapolis during the 1916 state centennial.

Indiana's history. Others started new museums and historical societies. People put on plays about George Rogers Clark, Tecumseh, and other heroes of Indiana's past.

The centennial made people realize the need to **preserve**, or save, the natural environment that first brought the pioneers to their state. In 1916 the state government set aside land for Indiana's first state parks—Turkey Run State Park near Marshall and McCormick's Creek State Park near Spencer.

Since the time of the centennial, more state parks and also state forests have been created. The state has also built museums and memorials. A **memorial** is anything created to honor a person or an event in the past. It may be a statue, or it may be a special garden, nature trail, or other place named for the person or event being honored.

 **Which two state parks were the first in Indiana?**

 **LESSON 4 REVIEW**

Check Understanding

1. **Recall the Facts**   Who test-drove the first automobile in Indiana?
2. **Focus on the Main Idea**   How did the automobile affect the lives of Hoosiers and the state's economy?

Think Critically

3. **Think More About It**   What do you think life might have been like before there were automobiles?
4. **Past to Present**   Why do you think the Indianapolis 500 automobile race is still held each year?

Show What You Know

Planning Activity   Indiana's bicentennial, or two-hundredth anniversary, will be in the year 2016. Imagine that you and a partner have been asked to plan a day of celebration. Prepare a list of community activities, such as plays and poster contests.

REVIEW

CONNECT MAIN IDEAS

Use this organizer to show that you understand how the chapter's main ideas are connected. Copy the organizer onto a separate sheet of paper. Then complete it by writing two sentences to summarize each lesson.

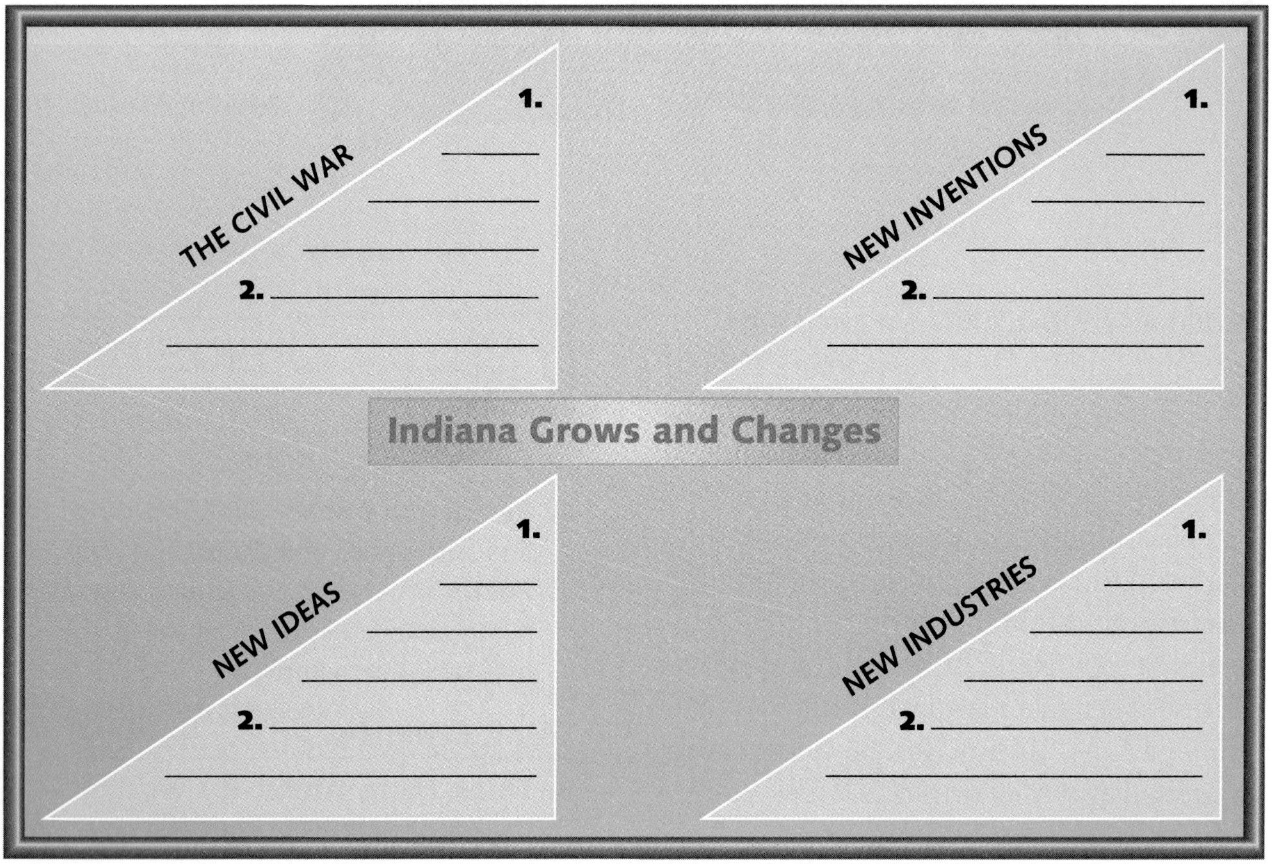

THE CIVIL WAR
1. _____
_____
_____
2. _____
_____

NEW INVENTIONS
1. _____
_____
2. _____
_____

Indiana Grows and Changes

NEW IDEAS
1. _____
_____
_____
2. _____
_____

NEW INDUSTRIES
1. _____
_____
_____
2. _____
_____

WRITE MORE ABOUT IT

1. **Write a Poem**   Imagine that you are living in Indiana in the late 1800s. Write a poem about what you see or hear either on a farm or in a city. Your poem does not have to rhyme.

2. **Write an Interview**   List five questions you would like to ask Elwood Haynes about his famous automobile ride in Kokomo.

3. **Write a Postcard**   Use library resources to find information about the Indiana State Fair in the year 1900. Then imagine you are at the fair. Write a postcard to a friend, describing what you see.

USE VOCABULARY

Write one paragraph in which you use each of these vocabulary words at least once.

manufacturing   free enterprise
industry   entrepreneur
immigrant   self-sufficient

CHECK UNDERSTANDING

1. What was Levi Coffin's part in the Underground Railroad?

2. Why did most of the southern states join the Confederacy?

3. Name the town in Indiana where Hoosiers fought against soldiers led by Confederate officer John Hunt Morgan.

4. What did James Oliver invent?

5. At what university in Indiana could students learn about agriculture?

6. How did the Grange help farm families?

7. How did the discovery of natural gas in Indiana bring new businesses to the state?

8. What kind of industry did people move to Gary to work in?

9. What products did Madam C. J. Walker and Eli Lilly make?

10. What brothers turned from making wagons to making automobiles in South Bend?

THINK CRITICALLY

1. **Cause and Effect** What effects did the Emancipation Proclamation and the Civil War have on slavery?

2. **Explore Viewpoints** How did runaway slaves feel about the Underground Railroad? How did slave owners feel about these escape routes?

3. **Think More About It** How did changes in farming help Indiana's cities grow? How, in turn, did the growth of cities help farmers?

4. **Think More About It** How did the oil industry help the automobile industry grow? Explain your answer.

APPLY SKILLS

How to Tell Primary from Secondary Sources Choose one of the quotations in this chapter. What tells you that the quotation is a primary source? How does it let you "hear the voice" of the person who said or wrote the words?

How to Read Symbols on a Product Map Using the map on page 181, list the main products that were made in Indiana in the early 1900s. Then write a sentence about the product that had the most to do with the growth of industries in Indiana.

READ MORE ABOUT IT

Corydon, The Forgotten Battle of the Civil War by W. Fred Conway. FBH Publishers. Maps, pictures, and primary sources help tell the story of the only Civil War battle fought in Indiana.

Follow the Drinking Gourd by Jeanette Winter. Knopf. A song helps lead escaping slaves in the right direction on their journey north to freedom.

INDIANA IN THE MODERN WORLD

> 66 I think when you have gone from horse and buggy to outer space travel, you have covered a good many miles. 99
>
> Elizabeth McCullough in *Buggies and Bad Roads*, one in a series of books featuring Hoosier women, 1985

Virgil ("Gus") Grissom of Mitchell was the first Hoosier astronaut.

CHANGING TIMES

LESSON 1

Link to Our World

How do events outside the state affect people in Indiana today?

Focus on the Main Idea
Read to find out how events outside Indiana affected Hoosiers in the early 1900s.

Preview Vocabulary
war bond   depression
shortage   unemployment
suffrage
amendment
consumer good
aviation

In 1916 Hoosiers celebrated Indiana's first centennial as a state and looked ahead with hope to its second hundred years. In Europe, however, a war was being fought at this time. It had started in 1914 with Britain, France, and Russia fighting Germany and Austria-Hungary. Soon many countries around the world took sides. At first the United States stayed out of the fighting. In time, however, the nation's leaders decided that the United States needed to take part in what later became known as World War I.

WORLD WAR I

When the war started, the United States sent supplies to Britain and France but did not send soldiers. Then, in 1917, German submarines attacked United States supply ships and passenger ships in the Atlantic Ocean. Because of those attacks, President Woodrow Wilson asked the United States Congress to declare war on Germany and send soldiers to Europe to fight.

More than 130,000 of the Americans who went to fight in Europe were from Indiana. Hoosiers at home helped the war effort as well. Many women worked in factories, doing the jobs of men who had left to fight. Many students spent a dime a week to buy war bonds. When people buy bonds, they are letting the government use their money for a certain amount of time. After that time, they turn in the paper

Soldiers in World War I wore steel helmets.

bonds and get their money back. Buying war bonds was a way of loaning money to the government to help pay for the war.

The war caused shortages of food and other goods. A shortage of something means that there is not enough of it for everyone. Because of shortages, the government allowed people to buy only small amounts of certain foods and other items so there would be enough for the soldiers.

World War I ended when Germany surrendered, or gave up, in 1918. American soldiers and supplies had helped win the war.

More than 3,000 Hoosiers had died in the fighting. Many others returned home wounded. People hoped for a lasting peace. They thought of World War I as "the war to end all wars."

This war bond poster (above left) and American soldier pin (above right) are from World War I.

✓ **How did Hoosiers at home help fight World War I?**

James Gresham of Evansville (left) was the first Hoosier killed in World War I. The invention of new weapons (below) led to massive destruction on both sides.

Many Indiana citizens were harmed by the Ku Klux Klan during the early 1920s.

THE KU KLUX KLAN

During World War I many African Americans and immigrants moved to Indiana and other Middle West manufacturing states. They came to find jobs in factories. Factory owners needed workers to fill in for those who had left to fight in Europe. When the soldiers returned, however, there were problems. In Indiana some Hoosiers did not want the newcomers to stay. They believed the newcomers were taking away their jobs.

Many people did not want the newcomers as neighbors. In the early 1920s thousands of white Hoosiers joined a hate group called the Ku Klux Klan, or KKK. The group's goal was to make African Americans and immigrants leave. Soon the KKK had members in every county in Indiana. Some state and local government officials were members.

KKK members dressed in white robes and wore hoods to hide who they were. They marched along city streets and held outdoor meetings where they burned crosses. The KKK hoped this show of hate would scare the newcomers away. When it did not, some KKK members harmed people they did not like. In the mid-1920s a KKK leader in Indiana was arrested for murder. That arrest caused many members to leave the secret group.

✓ **What was the goal of the Ku Klux Klan in Indiana?**

WOMEN GAIN THE RIGHT TO VOTE

The years after World War I were a time of great change for women. Before 1920 most women in the United States were not allowed to vote. Women in Indiana

In 1851 Amanda Way held the first meeting in Indiana to help women gain the right to vote.

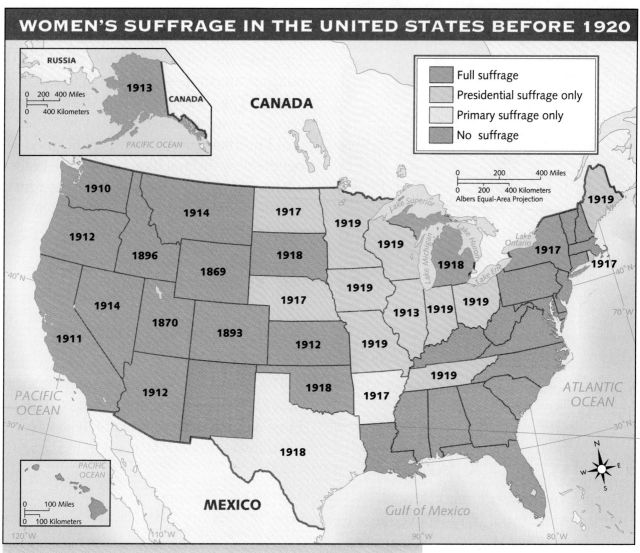

WOMEN'S SUFFRAGE IN THE UNITED STATES BEFORE 1920

RUSSIA
1913
CANADA

0   200   400 Miles
0   400 Kilometers

PACIFIC OCEAN

CANADA

Full suffrage
Presidential suffrage only
Primary suffrage only
No suffrage

0   200   400 Miles
0   200   400 Kilometers
Albers Equal-Area Projection

Lake Superior
Lake Michigan
Lake Huron
Lake Ontario
Lake Erie

1910
1914
1917
1919
1919
1919
1918
1912
1896
1918
1919
1917
1869
1918
1914
1917
1913   1919   1919
1870
1893
1911
1912
1919
1912
1919
1917
1918
1917

PACIFIC OCEAN

ATLANTIC OCEAN

1912

1918

PACIFIC OCEAN

0   100 Miles
0   100 Kilometers

MEXICO

Gulf of Mexico

120°W   110°W   90°W   80°W
40°N   30°N   70°W

LOCATION Many states gave partial or full suffrage to women before 1920.
■ What is the earliest full suffrage date shown?

had worked for many years for **suffrage** (SUH•frij), or the right to vote. In 1869 they held a Women's Rights Convention in Indianapolis. By 1900, women in Indiana, like women in most other states, could own property and businesses but still could not vote.

Leaders such as Ida Harper of Fairfield and May Wright Sewall and Sara Lauter of Indianapolis held meetings and made speeches about women's suffrage. They helped people understand that all citizens should have the right to vote.

Finally, in 1920, Indiana joined with other states to add the Nineteenth Amendment to the United States Constitution. An **amendment** to the Constitution makes a change in it. The Nineteenth Amendment said that women across the country were to be allowed to vote in national elections. In 1921 Indiana passed a law allowing women to vote in state elections.

How did women work to gain the right to vote?

This airplane, which was partially built by the Ford automobile company, was used to carry mail and passengers.

GROWTH IN INDUSTRY

The period after World War I brought many economic changes to Indiana. By 1920 the state's two leading industries were the making of steel and the manufacturing of automobiles. For the first time more Hoosiers worked in manufacturing than in agriculture.

In the 1920s a new industry began— the making of electrical consumer goods. A **consumer good** is a product made for personal use. Vacuum cleaners, radios, washing machines, and other electrical products for the home were sold for the first time in the 1920s. Indiana soon became a leader in the making of consumer goods.

Aviation, the making and flying of airplanes, was another new industry in the 1920s. The first flight had been made in 1903 at Kitty Hawk, North Carolina, by Orville and Wilbur Wright. Wilbur Wright was born in New Castle, Indiana. By the 1920s airplanes were large enough and safe enough to carry passengers. Soon Indianapolis became an important stop for passenger airplanes.

The demand for consumer goods and for new services, such as air travel, grew in the 1920s. Because of this, more businesses were started and factories made more products.

 What new industries became important in Indiana after World War I?

THE GREAT DEPRESSION

The 1920s were good times for those Hoosiers who had the money to spend on consumer goods and services. But the good times did not last long. In 1929 Indiana and the rest of the United States faced a depression. A **depression** is a time when there are few jobs and people have little money. The depression of the 1930s came to be called the Great Depression.

The Great Depression started because many people had made poor business decisions. Banks that had loaned too much money to businesses had to close. When the banks closed, many people lost the money they had put in them. Because those people had less money, they bought fewer goods. This caused businesses that made or sold goods to fail. Workers in those businesses lost their jobs. For much of the 1930s, **unemployment**, or the number of people without jobs, was high in Indiana and the rest of the country.

Hoosiers looked to the national government for help. In 1932 Franklin D. Roosevelt was President of the United States. Under his leadership Congress passed laws to give many people new jobs. The government paid people to build roads, dams, and state parks. Workers also built post offices, schools, and other buildings. Congress passed laws to help people save their farms and houses.

In Indiana the state government did its best to help Hoosiers. Under Governor Paul V. McNutt, the state provided money for older people who had little money to live on.

By 1940 the United States had begun to come out of the Great Depression. Businesses opened once again, and many people were able to find jobs in the kinds of work they wanted. By this time,

During the Great Depression, the Works Progress Administration, or WPA, created many jobs that helped rebuild local communities.

however, countries in Europe and Asia were fighting again. Soon Hoosiers and other Americans were taking part in another world war.

 **What caused the Great Depression?**

L SSON 1 REVIEW

Check Understanding

1. **Recall the Facts**   In what ways did Indiana change after World War I?
2. **Focus on the Main Idea**   How did events outside Indiana affect Hoosiers in the early 1900s?

Think Critically

3. **Cause and Effect**   How did the making of electrical consumer goods bring change to Indiana and its people during the 1920s?

4. **Explore Viewpoints**   If you had been an African American or an immigrant in Indiana in the 1920s, why might you have worried about the Ku Klux Klan?

Show What You Know

 Poster Activity   Imagine that you are living in the year 1919. Make a poster that asks Hoosiers to support the idea for a Nineteenth Amendment to give women the right to vote.

Tell Fact from Opinion

Why Is This Skill Important?

A good listener or reader can tell facts from opinions. Knowing how to do this can help you better understand what you hear or read.

Understand the Process

A **fact** is a statement that can be checked and proved true. Facts often give dates, numbers, or other pieces of information. If you cannot find a particular piece of information in a source such as an almanac or encyclopedia, it may not be a fact.

The following statements are examples of facts.

- Before 1920 women in Indiana were not allowed to vote in state elections.
- The first airplane flight was made in 1903 at Kitty Hawk, North Carolina.

An **opinion** tells what a person thinks or believes. Words such as *think* and *believe* can be clues that you are reading or hearing an opinion. Other words, such as *greatest* or *more important*, also may tell you what someone thinks or believes about something.

The following statements are examples of opinions.

- I think World War I will be "the war to end all wars."
- A citizen's most important right is the right to vote.

Even though opinions cannot be proved, some of them can be helpful. Some opinions are based on facts. Historians use historical facts to help them form opinions about the past. Historians also use primary sources to help them figure out what people in the past may have thought or believed.

Think and Apply

Write six sentences, some of them facts and some opinions. Ask a classmate to identify which are facts and which are opinions and how he or she can tell.

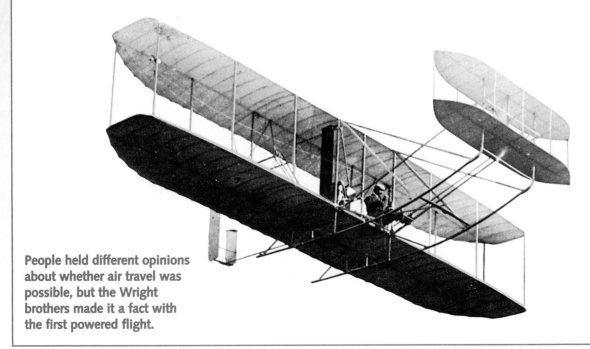

People held different opinions about whether air travel was possible, but the Wright brothers made it a fact with the first powered flight.

LEARN
with
LITERATURE

Focus on Everyday
Farm Life

When I Was Young In Indiana

by Dorothy Strattan Hinshaw

Dorothy Strattan Hinshaw was born on her family's farm near Knightstown, Indiana. When she went to Knightstown High School, she played basketball in the gymnasium where the movie *Hoosiers* would later be filmed. Her life was like the lives of most other young people on farms and in small towns during the time of the Great Depression. Read now to discover what everyday life was like in rural Indiana in the 1930s.

1935

Everyone called my grandmother Louie, short for Louisa. She often sat in a very small rocking chair reading the newspaper. I imagine she sat in this chair when she made rag balls. One of my games was to toss the rag balls up the stairs and watch them bounce back down. I did this again and again. They were soft and safe to throw in the house.

Outside the house was a big grassy lawn with maple trees. Near the barn was a big water tank for the animals. The horses and cows would come for many cool drinks on hot summer days. When I was small I used to get into the water tank to cool off! Clean spring water ran into the tank, and it was the best drinking water for miles around. A tin cup always was handy for our family, neighbors, and thirsty travelers.

The horses that drank from the water tank were named Daisy and Beauty. When Beauty grew old, she was the ugliest horse on the farm. They worked very hard pulling wagons and plows and the manure spreader. Phew! Sometimes I was allowed to ride on one of these horses as they pulled a wagon. Later, I had a regular riding horse. Much later when I was in college, I sold the horse to buy a car!

The same spring water that watered the animals also fed into grandmother's house. She had a special room which was like a natural refrigerator. Spring water flowed into the room in a little stream. Water ran around the room in a trough. Containers of food and milk were placed on rocks in the very cold water. The spring water was also piped into the kitchen for drinking and cooking. Grandmother had a bathroom with plumbing in her house, but at our house, we had an outhouse. The outhouse was some distance from the house. It was a cold, dark walk on a winter's night! We had a big round metal tub for Saturday night baths in the warmest room of the house: the dining room!

In the Spring, I enjoyed eating maple sugar cookies. Grandma made them from the big old sugar maple trees in our woods. Wooden buckets collected the sap and Grandmother and Dad boiled it in a big kettle in the shed until it was thick and sugary. Grandmother pressed it and made nice designs with a cookie cutter. Yum! Yum!

It was a real treat to visit my Grandmother Johnson in town. Her name was Matilda but most people called her Tillie. My grandfather, Josiah Johnson, died before I was born. I enjoyed taking a bath in Grandmother's tub which had hot running

trough a channel, or pathway, for water

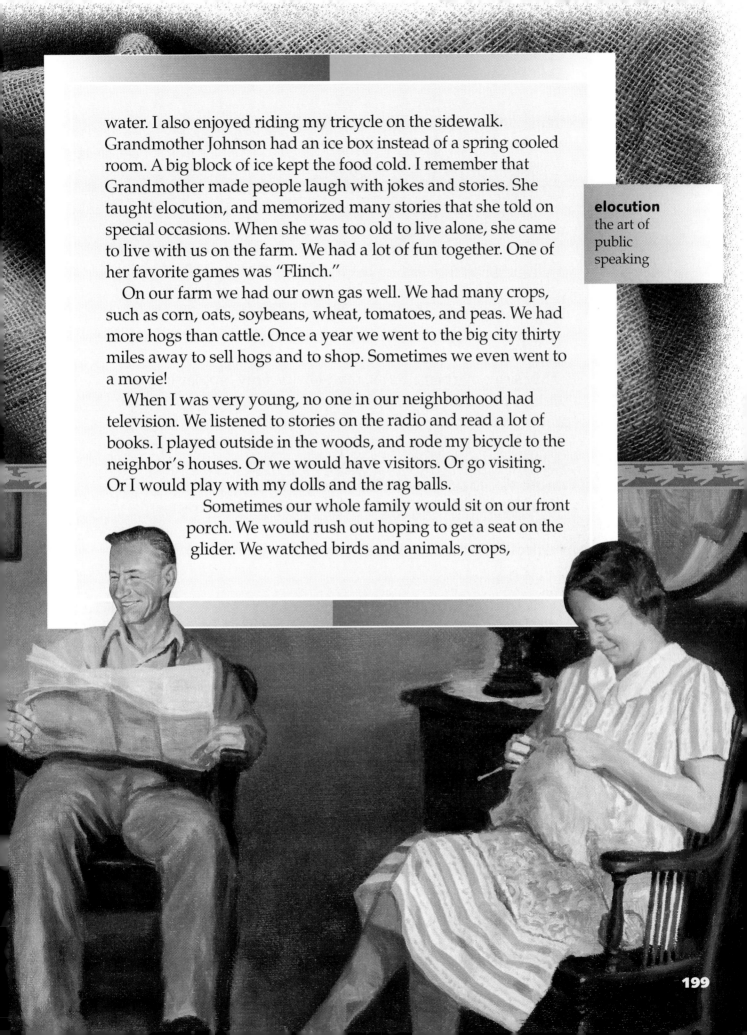

water. I also enjoyed riding my tricycle on the sidewalk. Grandmother Johnson had an ice box instead of a spring cooled room. A big block of ice kept the food cold. I remember that Grandmother made people laugh with jokes and stories. She taught elocution, and memorized many stories that she told on special occasions. When she was too old to live alone, she came to live with us on the farm. We had a lot of fun together. One of her favorite games was "Flinch."

On our farm we had our own gas well. We had many crops, such as corn, oats, soybeans, wheat, tomatoes, and peas. We had more hogs than cattle. Once a year we went to the big city thirty miles away to sell hogs and to shop. Sometimes we even went to a movie!

When I was very young, no one in our neighborhood had television. We listened to stories on the radio and read a lot of books. I played outside in the woods, and rode my bicycle to the neighbor's houses. Or we would have visitors. Or go visiting. Or I would play with my dolls and the rag balls.

Sometimes our whole family would sit on our front porch. We would rush out hoping to get a seat on the glider. We watched birds and animals, crops,

elocution
the art of public speaking

traffic, and weather. The most exciting weather was lightning and thunder. Sheet lightning was fascinating. Streak lightning was frightening. We had some fierce storms in Indiana. Once a terrible tornado blew down my sister's garage!

My sister, Marilyn June, was ten years older. I could not understand why I was not allowed to accompany her on her dates with her boyfriend. But she was a good pal most of the time and I had fun visiting her in college. One time my mother played a trick on her. Mother thought her boyfriend had stayed long enough, so she lowered an alarm clock down from the upstairs heating duct into the living room and it went off in their faces!

My sister married a farmer and I helped my brother-in-law and my father on the farm. When I was old enough, I drove the tractor and helped put hay in the hayloft. Here is how they did this: A wagon of hay would be driven into the barn. A rope on a pulley had giant hooks which would grab the hay, and a horse or tractor would drive away from the barn pulling the giant hooks of hay up into the hayloft. Back and forth went the tractor pulling up the hay.

I could drive a tractor and a jeep before I learned to drive a car.

Can you guess what noises I heard when I was young? Squealing pigs, mooing cows, crickets, locusts, farm machinery, the piano, and the sewing machine. When Mother was not practicing the piano, crocheting, knitting, or tatting, she sewed. Sometimes she made dresses from flowered feed sacks (ask your grandma what these were). My dad was a good mechanic and often worked on the farm machinery, took care of the animals, and planted and harvested crops. He often worried about the weather.

tatting
making lace by hand

Literature Review

1. What did some people on farms in the 1930s do in their free time?
2. How do you think town life at this time might have been different from farm life?
3. Use the information in this selection to write a journal entry as if you were on an Indiana farm in the 1930s. Include a description of your home, favorite foods, entertainment, and special trips or activities.

WORLD WAR II AND AFTER

Link to Our World

How is Indiana changing today?

Focus on the Main Idea
Read to learn about the changes that took place in Indiana and the United States after World War II.

Preview Vocabulary
defense plant
recycle
commute
leisure time
segregation
civil rights
orbit

On the morning of December 7, 1941, Japanese planes attacked United States Navy ships at Pearl Harbor, Hawaii. Most of the ships were destroyed, and many people were killed. Helen Musselman of Hamilton County, Indiana, remembers that day. "We knew we were going to be in war," she said, and she was right. On the following day President Franklin D. Roosevelt asked Congress to declare war on Japan. The United States joined the Allies—Britain, France, and the Soviet Union—in their fight against Japan, Germany, and Italy.

HOOSIERS AND WORLD WAR II

As they had more than 20 years earlier, Hoosiers went off to fight in a world war. They fought on land, at sea, and in the air in Europe, Africa, Asia, and the islands of the Pacific Ocean. More than 300,000 men and women from Indiana served in the United States armed forces in World War II.

At home in Indiana workers made supplies for the soldiers. Factories that had been making automobiles began making army trucks and jeeps. Steel mills in Gary produced much of the metal that was used to make ships and tanks. These factories were called **defense plants**, because they made things needed to defend the country.

The Indianapolis News headline, December 8, 1941

What?

USS *Indianapolis*

Three U.S. ships have been named for the city of Indianapolis. The first *Indianapolis* was used in World War I. The second, and most famous, was active in the Pacific Ocean in World War II. Near the end of the war, it was attacked by a Japanese submarine. The ship sank so fast that its crew could not even call for help. Of the 1,196 sailors aboard, 850 were able to jump into the ocean. For more than 80 hours, they fought cold, hunger, and sharks. When rescuers finally came, only 318 had survived. Today a submarine carries the name USS *Indianapolis*.

Indiana journalist Ernie Pyle (above) met many people as he traveled through Europe and Asia during World War II.

During World War II many women worked in Indiana's defense plants. Once again they took the places of the men who had become soldiers. Young people collected scrap metal, old tires, and paper. Defense plants **recycled**, or reused, these materials to make supplies that were needed for the war.

Americans at home learned what the war was like by reading newspaper articles written by Hoosier Ernie Pyle. Pyle was born in Dana and went to Indiana University. As a war reporter he traveled with soldiers, sharing the hardships and facing danger. In one article he wrote,

66 Some days they shelled us hard, and some days hours would go by without a single shell coming over. Yet nobody was wholly safe, and anybody who said he had been around Anzio [Italy] two days without having a shell hit within a hundred yards of him was just bragging. 99

By the end of the war in 1945, more than 10,000 Hoosiers had been killed. Among them was Ernie Pyle.

 How did Hoosiers at home help soldiers fight World War II?

People all over the United States celebrated the end of World War II. Indianapolis residents hold up newspapers in this photo from 1945.

LIFE AFTER THE WAR

"Bells and whistles blew like crazy," one woman said about the day World War II ended. All over Indiana, stores and city offices were closed while people celebrated. Some people in Indianapolis showed their joy by jumping into the Monument Circle pool. September 2, 1945, marked the end of 16 years of depression and war.

Life was good for many Americans in the years after World War II. New businesses provided more jobs that paid higher wages than ever before. A new way of living took shape.

Many Hoosier families moved to suburbs, or smaller towns and cities on the edges of large cities. With higher wages people were able to afford automobiles. People in the suburbs **commuted**, or traveled, to jobs in the cities. The first freeways and shopping centers were built in the 1950s and 1960s.

Many people had more money, so they were able to work fewer hours. This gave them more **leisure time**, or time away from work. Many enjoyed watching television and movies. They visited the new amusement parks. They played and watched sports.

The sport many Hoosiers seemed to like best was basketball. High school, college, and major league games all brought huge crowds. Major league teams are made up of the best professional, or paid, players. Among Indiana's first professional basketball teams were the Fort Wayne Zollner Pistons and the Indianapolis Kautskys, named for their owner, Indianapolis grocer Frank Kautsky. Later, in 1967, the Indiana Pacers started playing. The Pacers joined the National Basketball Association in 1976.

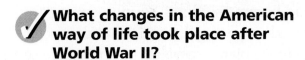
What changes in the American way of life took place after World War II?

THE FIGHT FOR CIVIL RIGHTS

Some people did not share in the good times that followed World War II. Many of those people were African Americans. Many African Americans in Indiana and other states earned low wages. Their children went to poor schools, partly because of segregation. **Segregation** means keeping people in separate groups based on race or culture.

State and local laws were taking away some of the civil rights of African Americans. **Civil rights** are the rights and freedoms given to all citizens by the Constitution.

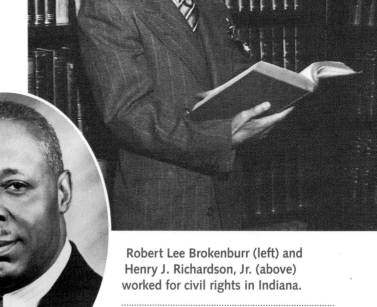

Robert Lee Brokenburr (left) and Henry J. Richardson, Jr. (above) worked for civil rights in Indiana.

African Americans were not allowed to take some kinds of jobs or go to some public places. They were not allowed to go to the parks, theaters, and schools that other Americans went to. An African American woman from East Chicago described her feelings about this, saying,

66We have any number of places [that] display signs in their windows, 'Whites Only.' . . . We need some action out here. . . . I want justice for all.99

In this photo from 1960, the National Association for the Advancement of Colored People (NAACP) holds a protest against a business that refused to serve African Americans.

DEMAND FULL SERVICE Everywhere DON'T PATRONIZE WOOLWORTH STORES Anywhere SUPPORT SOUTHERN "LUNCH COUNTER PROTEST" IND. STATE CONFERENCE NATIONAL ASSOCIATION FOR THE ADVANCEMENT OF COLORED PEOPLE • YOUTH AND COLLEGE CHAPTERS

Some people in the government did take action. Henry J. Richardson, Jr., of Indianapolis worked to end one form of segregation in Indiana. In 1949 Richardson, an African American lawyer, led the fight against segregation in the state's public schools. In 1961 state senator Robert Lee Brokenburr, also an African American, fought to have a civil rights law passed for the state—and won. Brokenburr's law gave all citizens an equal chance of being hired for jobs.

The need for change became known all over the United States through the work of an African American minister from Georgia. Dr. Martin Luther King, Jr., worked to persuade leaders to protect the civil rights of African Americans. Millions of Americans marched in demonstrations to support King and his work.

By the 1960s Congress had passed new laws that made segregation illegal. African Americans began voting in large numbers, electing leaders at all levels of government. In 1967 the citizens of Gary elected Richard Hatcher as their mayor—one of the country's first African American mayors of a large city. Hatcher was elected four more times and was the mayor of Gary for 20 years.

✓ **Who was one of the first African American mayors of a large city in the United States?**

Virgil ("Gus") Grissom

HOOSIERS IN THE SPACE AGE

During the 1950s and 1960s, great advances were made in science and technology in the United States. Some of the greatest of these were made through the United States space program.

In May 1961 astronaut Alan B. Shepard, Jr., became the first American launched into space. In July of that year, Virgil ("Gus") Grissom, who grew up in Mitchell, Indiana, became the second American in space.

The purpose of the Apollo program, a series of space flights in the 1960s, was to put an astronaut on the moon. In 1967 Grissom was chosen to be the command pilot of the first Apollo flight. But during a ground test, the *Apollo 1* spacecraft caught fire. He and two other astronauts in the spacecraft were killed.

In December 1968 Frank Borman of Gary, Indiana, and two other astronauts made history when the *Apollo 8* spacecraft became the first to **orbit**, or circle around, the moon. They took photographs and sent back videotaped pictures of the surface of the moon. Their work helped other astronauts land on the moon—the first on July 20, 1969.

Today astronauts orbit the Earth in space shuttles. Among the Hoosiers who have flown in shuttles are Joseph P. Allen of Crawfordsville, Jerry Ross of Crown Point, and Donald E. Williams of Lafayette. In 1990 Janice E. Voss of South Bend was chosen to be the first woman astronaut from Indiana. She also will fly on a shuttle mission.

 Who was the first astronaut from Indiana?

Janice Voss (right) is the first woman astronaut from Indiana.

LSSON 3 REVIEW

Check Understanding

1. **Recall the Facts**   In what years did the United States fight in World War II?
2. **Focus on the Main Idea**   How did life in Indiana and the United States change after World War II?

Think Critically

3. **Think More About It**   Why do you think it was important for African Americans to be able to vote for government leaders?

4. **Past to Present**   What kinds of activities do you do in your leisure time that people also enjoyed in the years after World War II?

Show What You Know

Letter-Writing Activity
Imagine that you are a civil rights leader in the 1950s. Write a persuasive letter to a member of the Indiana General Assembly, asking for laws to end segregation.

Understand Point of View

Why Is This Skill Important?

Artists and photographers share their feelings and beliefs in their works, just as writers do. If you learn to look for an artist's point of view, you will have a better idea of why the artist took the photograph or made the drawing. Then you may learn more about the picture's meaning.

Understand the Process

Look again at the picture on page 204. It shows Hoosiers celebrating the end of World War II. Now look at the photograph on this page. It shows a sailor about to go off to war. Like the photograph on page 204, it tells

something about feelings at the time of World War II.

Follow these steps as you think about the two photographers' points of view.

1. Think about how the picture makes you feel. Your own feelings can help you understand the photographer's point of view. Look at the peoples' faces in both pictures. How do they make you feel?

2. Study the details of the pictures for any information they can give you. What details tell you when each photograph might have been taken?

3. Ask yourself what the photographer wants to show you about other people. What does each photographer seem to want to show about how people felt about the war?

4. Think about how the photographer shows you his or her own point of view. What feelings of their own about the war are the photographers sharing with you? How is that point of view different with each photographer?

Think and Apply

Look for a photograph or painting that gives you a strong feeling. You can use books, magazines, or newspapers to find a picture. Describe how the picture makes you feel. What did the photographer or artist show you to make you feel as you do? What is his or her point of view?

RECENT YEARS

LESSON 4

Link to Our World

How do changes in the state economy affect you and your family?

Focus on the Main Idea
Read to learn how changes in the Indiana economy have affected Hoosiers in the 1970s, 1980s, and 1990s.

Preview Vocabulary

St. Lawrence Seaway	service industry
demand	high-tech
debt	supply
diverse economy	

Burns Harbor is located in northwest Indiana on the stretch of land that borders Lake Michigan. This area is one of the busiest industrial centers in the world.

In the early 1900s Indiana went through economic ups and downs. For many Hoosiers the ups and downs of good times and hard times were repeated in the 1970s, 1980s, and 1990s.

THE 1970S

During the 1970s the state's economy grew greatly. This growth was helped by the building of the Port of Indiana, which opened in 1970 at Burns Harbor on Lake Michigan. Now oceangoing ships that travel through the **St. Lawrence Seaway** can stop at the Port of Indiana. They can bring products from other countries into the state and take Indiana's products to the rest of the world.

Canada and the United States had worked together to build the St. Lawrence Seaway in the 1950s. Its canals link the St. Lawrence River, Lake Ontario, and Lake Erie. By using the seaway, ships can travel from the Atlantic Ocean through all the Great Lakes. They can reach ports as far inland as Duluth, Minnesota, on Lake Superior.

Besides building a new port on Lake Michigan, the state also opened a new port at Mount Vernon on the Ohio River. It is Indiana's busiest port and the second-largest port on the Ohio River. Barges from the port at Mount Vernon carry mostly grain to markets in the United States and all over the world.

Indiana also faced problems in the 1970s. It cost the state more and more money to keep up highways and

Chapter 6 • **209**

pay for other services. To pay the higher costs, the Indiana General Assembly in 1973 raised the state sales tax, a tax on products sold in the state. The sales tax was raised again in the middle 1980s.

✓ What large project helped Indiana's economy in the 1970s?

THE 1980s

During the 1980s unemployment increased in Indiana. Many jobs in the steel industry were lost. This happened when the **demand**, or the desire, for American goods made of steel, such as automobiles, decreased. More workers in Indiana lost their jobs when other countries began selling large amounts of their steel and automobiles in the United States.

Unemployment became a serious problem during the 1980s. Because of it, many Hoosiers moved to other states to find jobs. As a result, Indiana's population went down for the first time.

The 1980s brought hard times to Indiana farmers, too. Like farmers in other states, they faced higher costs for fuel, fertilizer, and other supplies. To buy what they needed, many farmers went into **debt**. They borrowed money from banks. Some farmers could repay their debts only by selling their farms.

✓ What caused some of the unemployment in Indiana in the 1980s?

THE 1990s

By the 1990s Indiana's economy began to get better. New kinds of businesses opened, making the economy more diverse. A **diverse economy** is made up of many kinds of industries. Indiana no longer depended mostly on metal products and farming.

The state government passed laws to help new businesses. Many of these businesses did not make goods. Instead, they provided services. Among the businesses in **service industries** are hotels, law and insurance offices, and hospitals.

High-technology, or high-tech, industries made the state's economy even more diverse in the 1990s. **High-tech** businesses are those that invent, build, and use computers and other electronic equipment.

By the 1990s the demand for computers had grown. Many people were using them at work, at school, and at home. To

High-tech industries such as medical research grew in Indiana during the late 1980s and early 1990s.

Union Station in Indianapolis reminds Hoosiers of their history.

meet the greater demand, a greater **supply**, or number, of computers was needed. Producing these computers has provided new jobs for Hoosiers.

The growth of new businesses in Indiana has helped many of the state's cities. Indianapolis has become an important center for service industries. Many kinds of businesses moved into Union Station, the city's old railroad station. New office buildings and apartments, the Circle Centre Mall, and the Hoosier Dome, which is now called the RCA Dome, have been built in other old parts of Indianapolis. A great deal of building and rebuilding is taking place in other Indiana cities such as Fort Wayne, Evansville, and South Bend, as well.

✓ **How has Indiana's economy changed in the 1990s?**

LESSON 4 REVIEW

Check Understanding

1. **Recall the Facts** What new port was opened on Lake Michigan in 1970?

2. **Focus on the Main Idea** How have changes in the economy of Indiana affected Hoosiers in the 1970s, 1980s, and 1990s?

Think Critically

3. **Link to You** What are some high-tech inventions you use in your home or at school?

4. **Think More About It** How do you think changes in the demand for and supply of a product might affect its price?

Show What You Know

Time Line Activity Make a time line that shows events in Indiana in the 1970s, 1980s, and 1990s. Begin with the events given in this lesson. Use reference books to find other events to add. Display your time line in the classroom.

CHAPTER 6
REVIEW

CONNECT MAIN IDEAS

Use this organizer to show that you understand how the chapter's main ideas are connected. Copy the organizer onto a separate sheet of paper. Then complete it by listing people and events that were part of the history of Indiana from the 1920s to today.

Indiana in the Modern World

1920s and 1930s _____
_____
_____

1940s and 1950s _____
_____
_____

1960s and 1970s
_____
_____

1980s and 1990s
_____
_____

WRITE MORE ABOUT IT

1. **Write a Conversation** Write a conversation between two people in the 1950s who are comparing life in the United States before and after World War II.

2. **Write Headlines** Write two headlines, one announcing the beginning of the

Great Depression and the other announcing the end of World War II.

3. **Write a Persuasive Letter** Imagine that you are living in Indiana in the 1950s. Write a letter to the newspaper telling why civil rights are so important.

USE VOCABULARY

For each pair of vocabulary terms, write a sentence or two explaining how the words are related.

1. war bond, debt

2. suffrage, amendment

3. depression, unemployment

4. commute, leisure time

5. segregation, civil rights

6. supply, demand

CHECK UNDERSTANDING

1. Name two ways Hoosiers at home helped America fight World War I.

2. What change did the Nineteenth Amendment make to the Constitution of the United States?

3. What new industries began in Indiana in the 1920s?

4. What happened in the Great Depression?

5. What kinds of supplies did Indiana defense plants make during World War II?

6. How did life in Indiana change after World War II?

7. What two African American lawmakers worked to end segregation in Indiana?

8. How did life change for African Americans in Indiana once segregation was against the law?

9. How did the high rate of unemployment during the 1980s affect Indiana?

10. What new kinds of industries grew in Indiana in the 1990s?

11. What is a diverse economy?

THINK CRITICALLY

1. **Cause and Effect** What event or events made the United States decide to enter World War I? World War II?

2. **Personally Speaking** How are your leisure activities different from those of Hoosiers after World War II?

3. **Think More About It** Why do you think Indiana leaders believed that building a port for oceangoing ships would help the state's economy?

4. **Link to You** The federal government helped people during the Great Depression. How does the government today help citizens in hard times?

APPLY SKILLS

How to Tell Fact from Opinion Read a letter to the editor in your newspaper. Underline all the phrases or sentences that are facts. Circle the opinions. Write a paragraph explaining your choices.

How to Understand Point of View Find a painting or photograph that you like. Tell what it shows, and describe the artist's or photographer's point of view.

READ MORE ABOUT IT

The Aces: Pilots and Planes of World War I by Christopher Maynard and David Jefferis. Franklin Watts. Learn about the planes and the people who flew them during World War I.

The Civil Rights Movement by Stuart Kallen. Abdo and Daughters. This book tells the story of the civil rights movement, describing its leaders and important events.

HOOSIER HYSTERIA

Milan High School had only 161 students in 1954, when it played Muncie Central High School for the Indiana state basketball championship. Muncie Central had more than 2,000 students! To many it would be a miracle for tiny Milan to keep up—but it did.

With only seconds left in the game, the score was tied. Then Milan's Bobby Plump grabbed the ball for a final shot at the basket. Those who were there said the ball left Plump's fingers and sailed in a huge arc above the Muncie Central players. It dropped into the basket as the horn sounded, ending the game. Milan had won the state championship, 32-30.

Exciting games like that one have caused "Hoosier Hysteria." It was the name given to the high school basketball state tournament in the 1920s when fan interest first became high excitement. In the early days of the tournament, about 15,000 fans filled the fieldhouse at Butler University in Indianapolis. Today the tournament is held at the RCA Dome with more than 40,000 people watching. It is also televised.

Bob Knight

Hoosier Hysteria gave people in Indiana happy moments during the hard times of the Great Depression and World War II. Hoosiers take great pride in their basketball heritage, which includes not only high school but also college and professional basketball teams.

Oscar Robertson

Milan High School during the 1954
Hoosier Hysteria tournament

THINK AND APPLY

Design a postage stamp to celebrate
Hoosier Hysteria, or write a paragraph
describing how it might look. Your design
should show the place of basketball in Indiana
history and culture. Display your design or paragraph
in the classroom.

BUILDING CITIZENSHIP

STORY CLOTH

Follow the pictures shown in this story cloth to help you review the events in Unit 3.

Summarize the Main Ideas

1. Disagreements over slavery divided the country and led to the Civil War. Some Hoosiers helped runaway slaves escape.

2. After the Civil War, new inventions and ways of farming changed Indiana from a pioneer frontier to a farm state.

3. New businesses and new factories helped many cities in Indiana grow.

4. By its centennial, Indiana had become a state of many cities and small towns. The automobile brought great changes to the lives of Hoosiers.

5. The United States entered World War I and many Hoosiers went to Europe to fight. In 1920 women gained the right to vote.

6. The economy grew in the early 1900s, but the good times ended in 1929 with the Great Depression. President Franklin D. Roosevelt created government jobs to get people back to work.

7. Hoosiers joined the fighting in World War II. After the war, life changed for many Americans. African Americans worked hard to gain their civil rights.

8. In recent years, Indiana's economy has become more diverse.

Choose an Event From this story cloth, choose the event that you think has had the greatest effect on your life. Explain your choice.

EQUALITY

COOPERATIVE LEARNING WORKSHOP

Remember
- Share your ideas.
- Cooperate with others to plan your work.
- Take responsibility for your work.
- Show your group's work to the class.
- Discuss what you learned by working together.

Activity 1
Make a Picture Book
With a partner, write a story for younger students about one of the events described in this unit. Tell your story with pictures and easy sentences. Share your book with a group of younger students in your school.

Activity 2
Make a Set of Postcards
Work in a group of five classmates to draw pictures on index cards, showing people or events from this unit. Be sure to draw on only one side of each card. Stack all the drawings from the class upside down, and have your teacher shuffle them. Have someone in your group take five cards from the top of the stack. Work together to write descriptions of the people or events shown on those cards.

Activity 3
Plan a State Fair Display
Work in a group to plan a display for next year's state fair. Your display title can be *Changes on the Farm, Indiana's Steel City of Gary,* or *New Businesses and Industries.* Use the information in Chapter 5 to help you. Also use other books and electronic resources. Describe your display plan to the rest of the class.

Activity 4
Conduct an Interview
With a partner, prepare a list of questions to ask an older adult about World War II. You might want to ask what he or she remembers about the day the war started and the day it ended. Conduct your interview, and share what you learn with the rest of the class.

USE VOCABULARY

Use each term in a complete sentence that shows its meaning.

1. civil war
2. Union
3. isolated
4. self-sufficient
5. agriculture
6. sharecropper
7. pharmaceutical
8. war bond
9. aviation
10. service industry

CHECK UNDERSTANDING

1. Why did some people in the southern states want to keep slavery?

2. Where did the only Civil War battle in Indiana take place?

3. What new inventions and ideas helped farmers? What changes did they bring?

4. Why did people from all over the world move to Gary in the early 1900s?

5. For what are Madam C. J. Walker and Eli Lilly remembered?

6. What industries were the most important in Indiana in the 1920s?

7. What problems did African Americans face in the years after World War II?

THINK CRITICALLY

1. **Think More About It** Was the Underground Railroad a good name for the system of routes and hiding places slaves used to escape? Explain your answer.

2. **Cause and Effect** In a free enterprise system, what would happen if a business offered a good or service nobody wanted?

3. **Past to Present** Why was recycling important during World War II? Why is recycling important today?

APPLY GEOGRAPHY SKILLS

How to Read Symbols on a Product Map During World War II many factories in Indiana made supplies for the war. The map below shows where some supplies were made. Use the map to answer the questions that follow.

WORLD WAR II GOODS MADE IN INDIANA

Airplanes/parts
Gunpowder/bullets
Uniforms
Fuel
Engines
Ships/parts
Trucks/parts

1. In what city were uniforms made?

2. How many cities made gunpowder?

3. Which Indiana cities made airplanes or parts for airplanes?

UNIT 4

INTO THE TWENTY-FIRST CENTURY

INDIANA TODAY

people

jobs

challenges

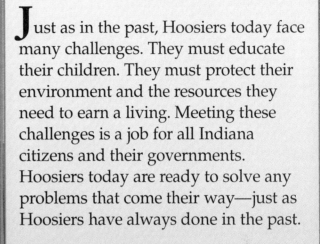

J ust as in the past, Hoosiers today face many challenges. They must educate their children. They must protect their environment and the resources they need to earn a living. Meeting these challenges is a job for all Indiana citizens and their governments. Hoosiers today are ready to solve any problems that come their way—just as Hoosiers have always done in the past.

← **Present-day Indianapolis**

GOVERNMENT

national

state

local

citizens

On the Banks of the

words and music by Paul Dresser

In 1897 Paul Dresser of Terre Haute described how he and others felt about living in Indiana. His words live on today as Indiana's official state song.

'Round my Indiana homestead wave the cornfields,
In the distance loom the woodlands clear and cool.
Often times my thoughts revert to scenes of childhood,
Where I first received my lessons, nature's school;
But one thing there is missing in the picture,
Without her face it seems so incomplete.
I long to see my mother in the doorway,
As she stood there years ago, her boy to greet!

homestead
a house and the land around it

The Indiana flag, the Soldiers and Sailors Monument, the red cardinal, and the yellow poplar tree are all symbols of Indiana.

Wabash, Far Away

Refrain:
Oh, the moonlight's fair
    tonight along the Wabash,
From the fields there comes the
    breath of new-mown hay,
Through the sycamores the candlelights
    are gleaming,
On the banks of the Wabash, far away.

The Star-Spangled Banner

by Francis Scott Key

The United States Congress agreed in 1931 to accept "The Star-Spangled Banner" as the national anthem. It had been written more than 100 years earlier during the War of 1812, which was fought between Britain and the United States. After a British attack on Fort McHenry in Baltimore, Maryland, Francis Scott Key was thrilled to see the American flag still waving. He wrote these words to show his pride in his country and in the flag under which the Americans had fought so hard.

Oh! say, can you see, by the dawn's early light,

hailed greeted

What so proudly we hailed at the twilight's last gleaming?

perilous dangerous

Whose broad stripes and bright stars, thro' the perilous fight,

ramparts
protective barriers

O'er the ramparts we watched were so gallantly streaming?

And the rockets' red glare, the bombs bursting in air,

Gave proof thro' the night that our flag was still there.

Oh! say, does that star-spangled banner yet wave

O'er the land of the free and the home of the brave?

The United States flag, the bald eagle, the Statue of Liberty, and the Liberty Bell are all symbols of the United States.

225

CHAPTER 7

INDIANA TODAY

66 Ours is a state of rolling hills and sandy dunes, thick woodlands and fertile farmland, large cities and rural communities, heavy industry and high technology, and people proud of their past who eagerly await the challenges of the future. 99

Former Governor Robert D. Orr in *Crossroads for World Trade*, 1986

People from many places in the world have come to live and work in Indiana.

MANY KINDS OF HOOSIERS

Link to Our World

What groups of people live near you?

Focus on the Main Idea
Read to find out more about the people of Indiana.

Preview Vocabulary
Hispanic   **fable**
rural

The fiddle is one of the main instruments used in bluegrass music.

In 1990 the United States Census counted more than 5.5 million Hoosiers. The 1990 census shows the diversity of Indiana. Nine out of ten Hoosiers are of European background. More than 430,000 Hoosiers are African Americans, and more than 12,000 are Native Americans and Native Alaskans. More than 37,000 have Asian or Pacific Island backgrounds. Almost 99,000 are **Hispanics**, or people whose families come from Spanish-speaking countries in North, Central, and South America.

CULTURES AND CELEBRATIONS

Most of Indiana's people were born in the state. However, their ancestors came from all over the world. The first people to live in what is now Indiana were Native Americans. The first Europeans to arrive were French. Next came British colonists and pioneers from the southeastern and northeastern United States. Later, African Americans from the southern states and immigrants from Europe came to work in Indiana's steel mills and factories. Today people come to Indiana from many Asian countries, such as India, China, Japan, and Vietnam. There are also Hispanic people from Cuba, Mexico, Puerto Rico, and the countries in Central and South America.

The many people who have come to live in Indiana give the state an interesting mix of cultures. This cultural mix has led to many shared

The Feast of the Hunters' Moon (above) and the Indiana Black Expo (right) are just two of the cultural celebrations that take place in Indiana every year.

celebrations. Hoosiers celebrate the German Oktoberfest and some Hispanic fiestas, as well as the French and Native American Feast of the Hunters' Moon and the African American Indiana Black Expo. The Feast of the Hunters' Moon, held at Fort Ouiatenon on the Wabash River, honors the American Indians and the early European settlers in Indiana. The Indiana Black Expo celebrates African American history and culture.

Every year Hoosiers also celebrate their ties with people from the southern United States. Many of Indiana's early pioneers came from Virginia, Kentucky, and other parts of the South. At the Beanblossom Bluegrass Festival, Hoosiers can enjoy the lively sounds of fiddles and banjos playing bluegrass, a kind of music first played in the Appalachian Mountains.

 Name two culture groups living in Indiana.

RELIGIONS IN INDIANA

The many people who have come to live in Indiana have brought with them their religious beliefs, which shape the way they think about themselves and others. Religion in Indiana is as diverse as the state's people. There are Methodists, Roman Catholics, Baptists, Presbyterians, Lutherans, Friends, Mormons, Muslims, Jews, Buddhists, Hindus, and others.

The Amish are one of the many religious groups in Indiana. The Amish religion began in Europe, in the country of Switzerland. The Amish people believe in living simply, just as their ancestors in Switzerland did more than 200 years ago. Because they wear plain clothes and do things in simple ways, the Amish are often called Plain People.

The Amish do not live in cities. They have their own communities, where they live on farms. Most of the Amish

Horse-drawn buggies are a common sight in Amish communities.

communities in Indiana are in the **rural** areas, or countryside, in the northern and southern parts of the state.

The Amish do their farmwork using hand tools and tools pulled by horses. They do not use automobiles but instead drive buggies pulled by horses. The Amish do not have electricity in their homes. They feel that radio and television would take time away from family life.

✓ **Name two religious groups in Indiana.**

These places of worship show some of the different building styles to be found in Indiana.

SOME FAMOUS HOOSIERS

Indiana has been the home of many well-known people. These people are remembered for being very good at what they did.

Some of America's most famous writers and poets have been Hoosiers. In the early 1900s James Whitcomb Riley of Indianapolis wrote poems about Hoosiers. Booth Tarkington, one of Riley's neighbors, wrote books describing life in Indianapolis. George Ade, who also lived at that time, became famous for his fables. A **fable** is a story that teaches a lesson. During the middle 1900s Jessamyn West of North Vernon became famous for her stories about Indiana's past.

Other famous Hoosiers have been musicians. Paul Dresser of Terre Haute wrote the words and music to many

songs, one of which became the state song, "On the Banks of the Wabash, Far Away." Hoagy Carmichael (HOH•gee KAR•my•kuhl) and Cole Porter wrote songs for shows. Indiana's musicians today include Michael and Janet Jackson of Gary and John Mellencamp of Seymour. Mellencamp lived in other places for a time but moved back to Indiana when he became famous. "I wouldn't want to live anyplace else," he says.

Hoosiers have been famous artists, too. The work of painters such as William Forsyth and Theodore C. Steele came to be called the Indiana school of painting. Members of this Hoosier Group, as it was known, painted mostly scenes in nature. One of Indiana's best-known artists today is sculptor Robert Indiana. He was born Robert Clark but changed his name to show his Hoosier pride.

Many famous sports coaches have also been from Indiana. Knute Rockne (NOOT RAHK•nee) of Notre Dame University was known as one of the best football coaches in the nation. Hoosier John Wooden was just as famous as a basketball coach. He played at Purdue University and later coached at Indiana State University and at the University of California at Los Angeles, or UCLA. Today Indiana University's Bob Knight is known as one of the best basketball coaches in the nation.

Some of America's finest basketball players have also been from Indiana. Oscar Robertson of Indianapolis was the first Hoosier named most valuable player in the National Basketball Association, or NBA. Larry Bird of French Lick was named the NBA's most valuable player three years in a row, from 1984 to 1986.

Marshall W. ("Major") Taylor of Indianapolis was one of the fastest cyclists of his time. The photo at right was taken during his first European race, in Berlin in 1901.

Indiana artist William Forsyth shows one of Indiana's most famous trees in his painting *The Constitutional Elm* (left).

Indiana has also been home to many Olympic champions. One was Wilma Rudolph. She was born in Tennessee but lived in Indianapolis. When she was young, she had many serious illnesses. One was polio, a disease that left her unable to walk. Wilma Rudolph not only got well but also went on to become a track-and-field champion. At the 1960 Olympics she won three gold medals.

 Name one famous Hoosier writer, one musician, one artist, and one sports figure.

LESSON 1 REVIEW

Check Understanding

1. **Recall the Facts** Name some Indiana festivals and celebrations.
2. **Focus on the Main Idea** What groups of people live in Indiana today?

Think Critically

3. **Think More About It** Why do you think the Amish people choose not to use automobiles?
4. **Personally Speaking** Think of other Hoosiers of today that you would add to those in this lesson. Explain your choices.

Show What You Know

 **Interviewing Activity**
Think about the Hoosiers described in this lesson. They have different heritages and have done different things. If you could interview one of these famous Hoosiers or someone from one of the groups you read about, which person or group would you choose? Make a list of five questions you would ask the famous person or the group member you have chosen. Share your list with a family member.

Use a Population Map

Why Is This Skill Important?

Different kinds of maps show different kinds of information about places. A population map shows how many people live in a certain area. Knowing how to read a population map can help you find out which places have few people and which have many.

Understand the Process

The map key tells you that the colors on the map stand for different population densities. Population density is the number of people living in an area of a certain size. On this map the color yellow shows places with few people. Most of Indiana's farming and forest areas are shown in yellow. The color red shows places with many people. Large cities and the towns and suburbs around them are shown in red.

Use the map on this page to answer these questions.

1. Do more people live in the Fort Wayne area or in the Columbus area? Tell how you know.

2. Do more people live in the Bloomington area or in the Gary area? Tell how you know.

3. Do more people live in the Evansville area or in the Indianapolis area? Tell how you know.

4. Is the population density higher near Lake Michigan or along the Ohio River? Tell how you know.

5. Is the population density higher in the northwestern part of Indiana or in the northeastern part? Tell how you know.

6. Do you think the area north of Lafayette is more likely a farming area or a manufacturing area? Explain your answer.

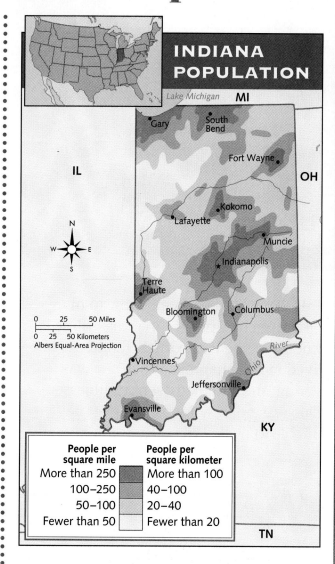

INDIANA POPULATION

People per square mile	People per square kilometer
More than 250	More than 100
100–250	40–100
50–100	20–40
Fewer than 50	Fewer than 20

7. Which parts of Indiana have the highest population density? Tell how you know.

Think and Apply

Find a population map of the United States in an encyclopedia or an atlas. In which parts of the United States is the population density the highest? In which parts is it the lowest? Is Indiana's population density higher or lower than that of New Jersey? Share your findings with a family member.

HOW HOOSIERS EARN THEIR LIVINGS

LESSON 2

Link to Our World

What are some kinds of work people in your community do?

Focus on the Main Idea
Read to find out about the kinds of work people do in your state.

Preview Vocabulary

commercial	export
farm	barge
Corn Belt	cargo
quarry	interstate
reclaim	highway

Steel production is important to Indiana's economy.

Indiana's workers earn their livings in many ways. They are factory workers, shopkeepers, and airplane pilots. They make and sell products; they farm and mine. They also provide services such as transportation.

MAKING PRODUCTS AND PROVIDING SERVICES

Indiana is ninth among the states in manufacturing. It has more than 9,600 factories.

In the early 1900s the United States Steel Corporation built its first steel mill in Gary, Indiana. Soon the making of steel and other metals became the state's top manufacturing industry. Most of Indiana's steel is made in the Calumet Region. From there it is shipped all over Indiana. Steel is used to make trucks in Indianapolis, recreational vehicles and school buses in Richmond, mobile homes in Elkhart, refrigerators in Evansville, and diesel engines in Columbus.

Other factories in Indiana prepare food products. Still others make furniture, pharmaceuticals, musical instruments, electric motors, and electronic products, such as televisions, computers, and telephones.

More than 665,000 Hoosiers earn their livings making products, and more than 710,000 have jobs selling these and other goods. Another 910,000 are service workers. Service workers do not make or sell goods. Instead they provide useful services for people. Service workers may be plumbers, automobile mechanics, lawyers, teachers,

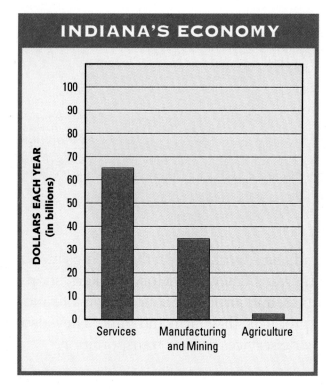

INDIANA'S ECONOMY

DOLLARS EACH YEAR (in billions)

Services	
Manufacturing and Mining	
Agriculture	

LEARNING FROM GRAPHS This graph shows the major parts of Indiana's economy.
■ How many billion dollars do Indiana services produce each year?

nurses, or doctors. Hotel workers and others in the tourism industry provide services for people who are traveling on vacation. Other service workers have jobs in government.

Service industries are very important to Indiana's economy. They provide more jobs for people and make more money for the state than the manufacturing and farming industries put together.

✓ What is the top manufacturing industry in Indiana?

FARMING

Indiana has more than 60,000 farms. Most are owned by families, but some of the largest ones are commercial farms. A **commercial farm** is a farm owned by a company. All of its crops are sold to make money for the company.

Corn and soybeans are the state's leading crops. Hoosiers grow more than 712 million bushels of corn each year, making Indiana fourth of all states in growing corn. The state is third in the country in growing soybeans.

Indiana lies in the eastern part of the Corn Belt. The **Corn Belt**, a region in the middle part of the United States, grows more corn than any other region in the

MAJOR CORN AND SOYBEAN GROWING REGIONS

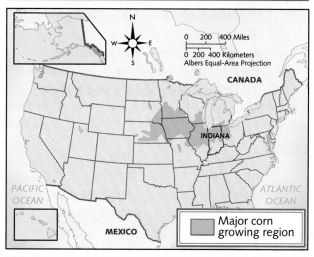

Major corn growing region

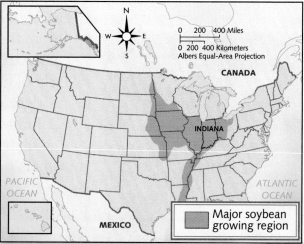

Major soybean growing region

REGIONS Indiana is part of a major corn growing region as well as a major soybean growing region.
■ Which growing region covers more of Indiana?

Reclaiming of land (far left, above) repairs the environment after damage by an activity such as strip mining (center).

world. The states of Ohio, Indiana, Illinois, and Iowa, as well as parts of Kansas and Nebraska, make up the Corn Belt.

Other farm products besides corn and soybeans are also important to Indiana. The state is fifth in raising hogs and poultry. Poultry is the name given to birds raised for food—for example, chickens, turkeys, and ducks.

One hundred years ago most Hoosiers lived and worked on farms. Today only 1 Hoosier out of about 40 makes a living from farming.

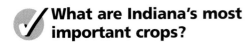 **What are Indiana's most important crops?**

MINING

More than 9,000 Hoosiers work in Indiana's mining industry. Most of them mine limestone in the quarries near Bedford and Bloomington. A **quarry** is a large, open pit from which stone is cut.

These quarries, located in southern Indiana, produce much of the limestone used in the United States for building. Quarries in other parts of Indiana produce crushed limestone, which is used in making steel, cement, and other products.

Coal, another important natural resource, is mined in southwestern Indiana. Because the coal there lies close to the surface, it is removed by strip mining. First, large machines remove the earth above the coal. Then other machines shovel the coal into trucks to be hauled away.

Strip mining can leave land bare of soil and plants. Laws today say that mining companies must reclaim the land after they have removed the coal. To **reclaim** the land means "to make it usable by people again." The coal companies must put back the soil they removed and plant it with grasses and trees.

 **What resources are mined in Indiana?**

TRANSPORTING PEOPLE AND GOODS

Indiana received its motto, "The Crossroads of America," from its location at the center of many transportation routes. Farm products, manufactured

INDIANA EXPORTS

MANUFACTURING
steel, wood products,
food products, electronics,
pharmaceuticals

AGRICULTURE
corn, soybeans,
poultry, hogs, cattle,
dairy products

MINING
oil, coal, limestone,
clay, gypsum, sand,
gravel

LEARNING FROM CHARTS This diagram shows some of Indiana's major exports.
■ What are some of Indiana's mining exports?

goods, and raw materials such as limestone and coal must all be moved to market. Shipping them is an important part of Indiana's economy.

Much of the state's limestone is exported to other states. To **export** means "to send to be sold in other places." Some of the state's agricultural products are also exported. These products are shipped to other places by water, land, and air.

Water transportation has always been important to Indiana. On the Ohio River and the Great Lakes, barges carry coal, iron, oil, and grain. **Barges** are large, flat-bottomed boats. Some barges carry cargo containers, the large steel boxes in which goods are shipped. The containers protect the **cargo**, or the goods being shipped.

Shipping goods by barge is usually the cheapest way to send them. However, it is slow, and barges can travel only along waterways. Railroads in Indiana are important for moving raw materials and

finished products over land. Railroads often carry cargo containers to and from Indiana's river and lake ports.

Trucks are also important to Indiana because they can take goods anywhere. Trucks use the state's system of highways. Some of these highways are interstates. An **interstate highway** goes from one state to another. Interstate highways link cities all over the United States.

Airplanes have become the most common way for people to travel near and far. Airplanes also carry cargo such as mail and other items that are not heavy. Airplanes fly into and out of 116 airports in Indiana. The largest of these is Indianapolis International Airport.

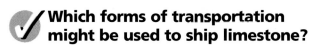 **Which forms of transportation might be used to ship limestone?**

LESSON 2 REVIEW

Check Understanding

1. **Recall the Facts** In what kinds of industries do the greatest number of people in Indiana earn their livings?
2. **Focus on the Main Idea** Name three industries in which Hoosiers work.

Think Critically

3. **Personally Speaking** How would you like to earn your living as an adult?
4. **Cause and Effect** Why is transportation important to Indiana's economy?

Show What You Know

 **Poster Activity** Think of a job you might like to have. Make a poster that tells about the knowledge·or skills needed to do this job.

How To

Use a Pictograph

Why Is This Skill Important?

Graphs can help you compare amounts. Some graphs use bars or lines. **Pictographs** use symbols to stand for amounts. The graph on this page compares the numbers of Hoosiers in different kinds of jobs. From the pictograph you can easily see which industries have the most workers.

Understand the Process

A pictograph makes it easy to compare numbers, but it does not give exact amounts. In this pictograph each symbol stands for about 25,000 people. Six symbols are shown for the construction industry. To find the number of workers these symbols stand for, you need to multiply 25,000 by 6. The total is 150,000, so the number of workers in construction in Indiana is about 150,000.

Now use the pictograph to answer these questions.

1. About how many Hoosiers work in the manufacturing industry?
2. About how many Hoosiers work in the agriculture industry?
3. Which industry has the fewest workers?
4. Which industry has the most workers?

Think and Apply

Make a pictograph to compare the populations of Indiana's five largest cities. Create a symbol to stand for 50,000 people. Use your symbol to show the following populations.

- Indianapolis—740,000
- Fort Wayne—175,000
- Evansville—130,000
- Gary—120,000
- South Bend—110,000

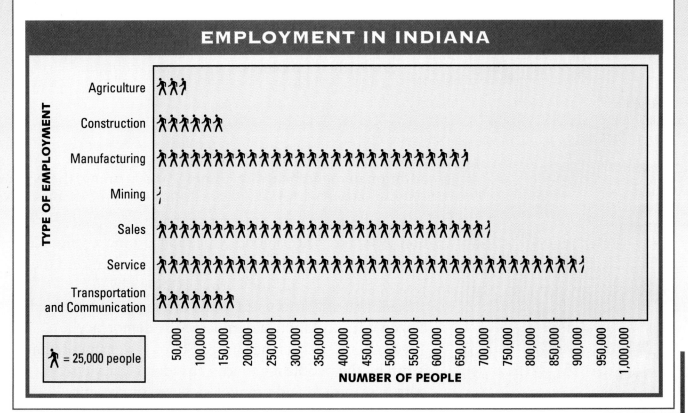

EMPLOYMENT IN INDIANA

TODAY'S CHALLENGES

Link to Our World

What do you do when you face a challenge?

Focus on the Main Idea
Read to find out how the people of Indiana are working to meet today's challenges.

Preview Vocabulary
human resource
democracy
informed citizen
metropolitan area
conserve

Providing a good education for Indiana citizens is one of the main goals of the Indiana state government.

There have always been people in Indiana who have worked to solve problems. George Rogers Clark worked to solve the problem of British rule. Pontiac, Little Turtle, and Tecumseh sought to protect Indians' rights from being taken away by British and American settlers. Both William Henry Harrison and Jonathan Jennings worked to solve the problems of the Indiana Territory and to prepare it for statehood. Other Hoosiers worked to solve the problems of war and economic depression. Today's Hoosiers face new kinds of challenges. They are ready to work to solve these problems, just as Hoosiers in the past worked to solve their problems.

IMPROVING EDUCATION

Indiana's economy has become more diverse. In addition to manufacturing, mining, and farming, there are now many high-technology industries. People who work in high-tech industries must have a good education. A worker with a good education is a more valuable human resource. **Human resources**  are workers and the knowledge and skills they bring to their jobs.

Besides being important to the economy, an educated citizen is important to a democracy. A **democracy** is a government, such as the United States government, that is run by the people it governs. In a democracy every person's opinion and point of view are important.

Voting allows informed citizens to make political decisions and to choose their national, state, and local government leaders.

An educated citizen is an informed citizen. An **informed citizen** is one who understands why things happen in the community, the state, the nation, and the world. An informed citizen is one who is likely to take part in community government. An informed citizen is also more likely to understand other people's opinions and points of view.

Indiana's leaders are working to make public schools better so that children will grow up to be educated workers and informed citizens. Governor Evan Bayh wanted to make sure "that every child starts school ready to learn." So he set up a plan he called Step Ahead. Under this plan the state government pays for four-year-olds to go to preschool before they start kindergarten.

The state government is also taking other actions to make public schools stronger. It is encouraging teachers to get more advanced training and is helping schools buy computers and other equipment. High school students must now learn more before they can graduate. To see whether the schools are getting better,

the state government gives students in certain grades special tests in reading, writing, and other subjects.

 **Why must Indiana students take special tests?**

KEEPING CITIES SAFE AND CLEAN

One of every five Hoosiers lives in or near Indianapolis, the state's largest metropolitan area. A **metropolitan area** is a large city plus all of the suburbs, towns, and smaller cities around it. The 1990 census showed that the population of the city of Indianapolis was 741,952. The population of the Indianapolis metropolitan area, however, was more than 1 million.

As Indianapolis and Indiana's other large cities grow, they must be able to provide city services. Among these are water supply, garbage pickup, and police and fire protection.

Traffic is a problem in many metropolitan areas. More people using automobiles means that more highways and roads must be built. Some cities provide good public transportation, hoping that people will use it instead of their automobiles.

Indiana cities are working to solve another problem—crime. Some of the things that lead people into crime are having no job, dropping out of school, and using drugs. Helping people with these problems can stop a great deal of crime.

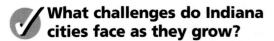

> **What challenges do Indiana cities face as they grow?**

PROTECTING THE ENVIRONMENT

Hoosiers today depend on the land, the air, and the water as much as Hoosiers of the past did. Today, however, most people understand that these natural resources must be protected. Leaders have worked to see that wastes do not pollute, or spoil, the environment. The national and state governments have passed laws about where harmful wastes must be dumped. Good citizens help by not littering and by obeying laws passed to cut down pollution.

Recycling is one way many people in Indiana protect the environment. People take metal cans, glass bottles, plastic containers, and newspapers to recycling centers. The centers then sell these items to businesses that use them to make new products. Old tires are used to make fuel and playground surfaces. Used lightbulbs are crushed to make tile for floors. Old newspapers are made into cereal boxes.

Recycling helps the environment in two ways. Land is saved because recycled items do not go into dumps. Resources are saved when new products are made from recycled materials. Also, the new businesses that do the recycling help Indiana's economy.

Another way Hoosiers protect the environment is by conserving the state's natural resources. To **conserve** a resource is to save it. Many farmers take care to conserve their soil. Some plant trees to block the wind. This keeps the soil from blowing away. Others plant crops without plowing, in order to help keep the soil in place.

As Indiana cities, such as Indianapolis, continue to grow, city services must grow with them.

Recycled materials (above) are used for many things. They have been used to make the surface of the playground at left.

As you read in Unit 1, Indiana was once covered with forests. Over time people cut down most trees to clear the land for planting and to get wood for building. Because of this, there are now few large forests left in Indiana. Many people are working to make sure the forests that are left are used wisely.

Today our government protects trees in state and national forests, such as Hoosier National Forest. Citizens, too, are working to conserve Indiana's forests. In 1985 Andrew Mahler started an organization called Protect Our Woods. People are also working to conserve Indiana's other natural areas, such as the dunes and marshes in northern Indiana.

How are Hoosiers protecting the environment?

LESSON 3 REVIEW

Check Understanding

1. **Recall the Facts**   What are three important challenges that the people of Indiana face today?
2. **Focus on the Main Idea**   How are the people of Indiana working to meet today's challenges?

Think Critically

3. **Link to You**   What things can you do in your community to help protect the environment?

4. **Personally Speaking**   What are you learning now that will help you as an adult? Explain your answer.

Show What You Know

Report-Writing Activity
Use your library to find out more about challenges Hoosiers face today. Write a report on your findings. Tell how citizens and their governments are working to solve problems.

WHAT IS THE BEST WAY TO USE INDIANA'S RESOURCES?

Just as people make choices, so must states. To help their economies grow, states need to decide on the best way to use their natural resources. By using their resources in one way, they give up the possibility of using them in other ways. For some states, these choices are difficult. If a state clears a forest for building, it no longer has the forest. If the state keeps the forest, it cannot use the land for building.

In 1989 the state of Indiana had to decide on the best way to use a piece of land on Patoka Lake in southern Indiana. Some people wanted to clear the forest there and build a theme park. The park, to be called Tillery Hill, would have thrill rides, a hotel, shops, and a zoo. Others wanted to keep the land as it was.

Read how some Hoosiers felt about how the state should use the land on Patoka Lake. Figure out what each person believes and why.

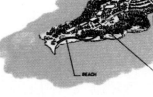

GOLF COURSE
RENTAL VILLAS
CONFERENCE CENTER
HOTEL
FISHING PIER
BEACH

William Reynolds is an entrepreneur. He is talking about the state's economy.

❝Tillery Hill will help all of southern Indiana—Evansville, Boonville, the entire area.❞

Bob Klawitter is a member of Protect Our Woods. He is speaking to people who own homes in the forest.

❝They're buying something from you, and what they're buying from you is this natural, fairly uncrowded, peaceful, crime-free environment where you like to live and bring up your kids. You want to sell that to bring Tillery Hill here?❞

John Duncan lives on the Patoka Lake land. He rents cabins to visitors.

❝They say public lands belong to the public. But how much of the public would be able to use that land if we don't allow this development?❞

Bill Edwards also lives on the Patoka Lake land.

❝Who's going to pay to fix the roads and dispose of the trash from all these visitors?❞

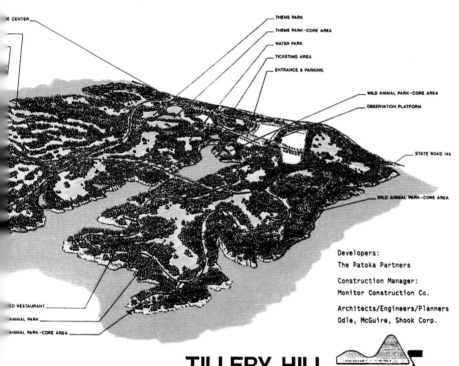

THEME PARK
THEME PARK-CORE AREA
WATER PARK
TICKETING AREA
ENTRANCE & PARKING
WILD ANIMAL PARK-CORE AREA
OBSERVATION PLATFORM
STATE ROAD 145
WILD ANIMAL PARK-CORE AREA

RESTAURANT
ANIMAL PARK
ANIMAL PARK-CORE AREA

Developers:
The Patoka Partners

Construction Manager:
Monitor Construction Co.

Architects/Engineers/Planners
Odle, McGuire, Shook Corp.

TILLERY HILL
THE RESORT AND RECREATIONAL DEVELOPMENT AT PATOKA LAKE
PRELIMINARY SITE PLAN

COMPARE VIEWPOINTS

1. What do you think each person wants done with the land at Patoka Lake?
2. Does William Reynolds agree with Bob Klawitter? How do you know?
3. Why do John Duncan and Bill Edwards, who both live on the Patoka Lake land, disagree?
4. Which side would you take? Give reasons for your answer.

THINK
–AND–
APPLY

People often have different points of view on a problem. At what other times have people from Indiana held different views about something? In the case of the Patoka Lake land, those who wanted it kept as it was won. Tillery Hill was never built.

BUILDING CITIZENSHIP

CONNECT MAIN IDEAS

Use this organizer to show that you understand how the chapter's main ideas are connected. Copy the organizer onto a separate sheet of paper. Then complete it by writing two sentences to summarize each lesson.

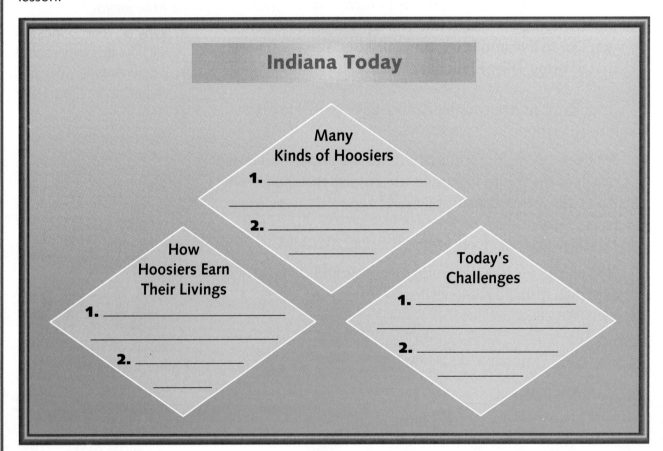

Indiana Today

Many Kinds of Hoosiers
1. _____
_____
2. _____
_____

How Hoosiers Earn Their Livings
1. _____
_____
2. _____
_____

Today's Challenges
1. _____
_____
2. _____
_____

WRITE MORE ABOUT IT

1. **Write a Letter** Imagine that members of your class are writing letters to members of a class in another country. Describe the people of Indiana today, and tell some ways they earn their livings.

2. **Write a Summary** In one paragraph tell how you think getting a good education will help you in the future.

3. **Write a Television Commercial** Imagine that you are starting a recycling center and you want people to bring in their recyclable goods. Write a 30-second television commercial about your center, telling how recycling will help your community. Share your commercial with the class.

USE VOCABULARY

Use each vocabulary term in a newspaper headline that shows the meaning of the term.

1. rural

2. reclaim

3. export

4. human resource

5. informed citizen

CHECK UNDERSTANDING

1. What cultures can be seen in Indiana today?

2. What are some religions that are followed in Indiana?

3. In what industries do the most workers in Indiana earn their livings?

4. How are service jobs different from manufacturing jobs?

5. What are Indiana's two most important crops?

6. What kind of road links cities all over the United States?

7. Why is it important for the state of Indiana to have educated and informed citizens?

8. How does recycling help protect the environment?

THINK CRITICALLY

1. **Think More About It**   How do Indiana's diverse cultures affect the state's people?

2. **Cause and Effect**   How might rapid growth in population affect a community's environment?

3. **Explore Viewpoints**   Why do you think some people might want a new factory built in their community, while others might not?

4. **Personally Speaking**   What do you think is the greatest challenge Indiana faces today?

5. **Link to You**   What do you think Indiana will be like when you are an adult? What will change? What will stay the same?

APPLY SKILLS

How to Use a Population Map
Look at the population map of Indiana on page 232. Imagine that you own a business and have enough money to advertise in only two cities. Which two cities would you choose? Why would you choose them?

How to Use a Pictograph   Look in old newspapers or magazines for a pictograph. Cut out the graph, and tape it onto a sheet of paper. Below the graph, write a short paragraph that describes the information it shows.

READ MORE ABOUT IT

Indiana by Jeannette Covert Nolan. Coward-McCann. This book describes Indiana as a leader in both manufacturing and farming.

The Play-Party in Indiana by Leah Jackson Wolford. Arno Press. This book is a collection of folk songs and games brought to Indiana by immigrants. The book also has songs about the environment.

GOVERNMENT IN INDIANA

> 66 If we really want good government, peace and unity, now's the time to practice what we preach. Good government comes in assorted colors and nationalities. 99
>
> Richard Hatcher,
> mayor of Gary, 1968 to 1988

INDIANA STATE GOVERNMENT

LESSON 1

Link to Our World

Why should the work of government be shared?

Focus on the Main Idea
Read to find out how the work of the Indiana state government is shared.

Preview Vocabulary

Bill of Rights	**veto power**
legislative	**majority**
branch	**agency**
budget	**judicial**
executive	**branch**
branch	**jury trial**

When the governor of Indiana takes the oath of office, he or she promises "to support the Constitution of the United States, and the Constitution of Indiana." The United States Constitution, which became law in 1789, set up the government of the nation. The Indiana Constitution of 1851 set up the state government that Hoosiers have today. It took the place of the Indiana Constitution of 1816, written when Indiana first became a state. Both the United States and Indiana constitutions list the rights of citizens and describe a plan for how the government should work.

The first state elections in Indiana were held on August 5, 1816.

THE INDIANA CONSTITUTION

The Indiana Constitution begins with a **Bill of Rights**, or list of rights and freedoms for citizens. The state Bill of Rights lists many of the same rights found in the United States Bill of Rights. Some of these are freedom of speech, freedom of the press, freedom of religion, and freedom to gather in groups.

The Indiana Bill of Rights also lists the rights of people who are victims of crimes and the rights of those accused of crimes that take place in the state. It makes clear that all the rights and freedoms it lists are for all citizens.

Like the United States Constitution, the Indiana Constitution set up a government with three branches, or parts. Each of these branches has its own work to do. One branch makes the laws. A second branch sees that these laws are obeyed. A third branch decides law cases.

What freedoms does the Indiana Bill of Rights list?

THE LEGISLATIVE BRANCH

The General Assembly is the name of the legislative (LEH•juhs•lay•tiv) branch of the Indiana state government. The **legislative branch** makes, or passes, laws.

The Indiana General Assembly has two houses, or parts. These are the House of Representatives and the Senate. The Indiana House of Representatives, sometimes called the House, has 100 members, who each serve terms of two years. The Indiana Senate has 50 members, who each serve terms of four years.

Indiana voters elect the members of both houses. But not all are elected at the same time. Half of the state senators, or 25 of the 50, are elected every two years.

The members of the House and the Senate meet at the Indiana State Capitol in Indianapolis. There they pass new laws to help protect the lives, freedoms, and property of the people of Indiana.

The General Assembly also passes state tax laws. State taxes are used to pay the costs of running the state government and providing state services. The General Assembly must plan how to spend the state's tax money. A written plan for spending money is called a **budget**.

State tax money is used for paying state workers and for building and repairing state roads, highways, and ports. It is used to keep state parks clean and safe. State tax money is spent on public schools and on state colleges and universities. State tax money also helps people who do not earn enough money to pay for their own food, shelter, and health care.

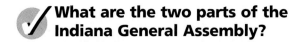
What are the two parts of the Indiana General Assembly?

The Indiana capitol (below) was built of Indiana limestone in 1888. Offices for the governor (speaking at right), the General Assembly (seated at right), and the Indiana Supreme Court are located in the capitol.

BRANCHES OF THE INDIANA STATE GOVERNMENT

LEGISLATIVE BRANCH	EXECUTIVE BRANCH	JUDICIAL BRANCH

Indiana House of Representatives and Indiana Senate	Governor and State Agencies	Courts

LEARNING FROM DIAGRAMS No branch of the Indiana state government is more powerful than the others.

■ Why do you think the Indiana state government is separated into three branches?

THE EXECUTIVE BRANCH

The **executive branch** of the Indiana state government makes sure that state laws passed by the General Assembly are obeyed. The governor of Indiana is the leader of the state's executive branch. The governor is elected by the voters and serves a term of four years.

The governor can suggest new laws to the legislative branch. New laws that the legislative branch wants to pass must be given to the governor. If he or she agrees with a new law by signing it, the law passes. The governor also has **veto power**, or the power to stop a new law by refusing to sign it. The General Assembly can still pass a law that has been vetoed by the governor if a **majority**, or more than half, of the House and the Senate vote to do so.

This medal shows the state seal of Indiana. Why is the date 1816 printed on it?

The governor shares the work of the executive branch with other leaders. One of these leaders is the lieutenant governor. The governor and the lieutenant governor always run for election as a team. Like the governor and lieutenant governor, some other leaders in the executive branch are elected by Indiana voters. Some, however, are chosen by the governor. The executive branch runs many **agencies**, or groups of state officials who make sure that laws passed by the General Assembly are obeyed.

✓ **Who is the leader of the executive branch of the Indiana state government?**

THE JUDICIAL BRANCH

As in the United States government, the state **judicial branch** is made up of courts and judges that hear and decide law cases. The judges make sure that Indiana laws are used fairly and that they agree with the state constitution.

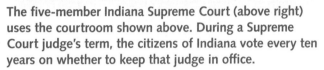

The five-member Indiana Supreme Court (above right) uses the courtroom shown above. During a Supreme Court judge's term, the citizens of Indiana vote every ten years on whether to keep that judge in office.

The highest court in Indiana is the state supreme court. It decides cases about the Indiana Constitution and the rights and freedoms of Indiana citizens. Five judges make up the supreme court. One of the judges is chosen to be the chief justice, or head judge. New judges for the supreme court are chosen by the governor.

Below the supreme court is the court of appeals. It hears cases asking for changes in decisions made in Indiana's county circuit and superior courts. Judges study the decisions to make sure they are fair.

Below the court of appeals are the county circuit and superior courts. Jury trials are often held in these courts. In a **jury trial** a group of citizens decides whether to believe that a person accused of a crime is guilty or not guilty. If the person is found guilty, the jury recommends the punishment.

 What is the highest court in Indiana?

LESSON 1 REVIEW

Check Understanding

1. **Recall the Facts**   What are the three branches of the Indiana state government?
2. **Focus on the Main Idea**   What does each branch of the state government do?

Think Critically

3. **Personally Speaking**   Describe three ways state tax money is spent in your community.
4. **Think More About It**   What might happen if the executive branch made the laws *and* made sure they were obeyed?

Show What You Know

Simulation Activity   With two partners, role-play a conversation between the governor of Indiana, a member of the General Assembly, and the chief justice of the Indiana Supreme Court. Each of you should describe your work.

Follow a Flow Chart

Why Is This Skill Important?

Some information is easier to understand when it is explained in a drawing. The drawing on this page is a flow chart. A **flow chart** is a drawing that shows the order in which things happen. The arrows on a flow chart are there to help you read the steps in the correct order. The flow chart on this page shows you how the Indiana state government makes new laws.

Understand the Process

The top box of the flow chart shows the first step in passing a law. In this step a member of the General Assembly writes a **bill,** or plan for a new law. In the second step the bill is given a number and sent to a special committee. The committee is a small group of members of the General Assembly. The members study the bill and tell the whole General Assembly whether they think it would make a good law. If the committee likes the bill, what happens next? Read the next step on the flow chart.

Read the remaining steps. What happens after both the Senate and the House of Representatives pass the bill? How can the bill become a law if the governor vetoes it?

Think and Apply

Work with a partner to make a flow chart that will explain to younger students how something works. Write each step on a strip of paper. Then paste the strips in order onto a sheet of posterboard, and connect the steps with arrows. Give your flow chart a title, and use it with a group of younger students.

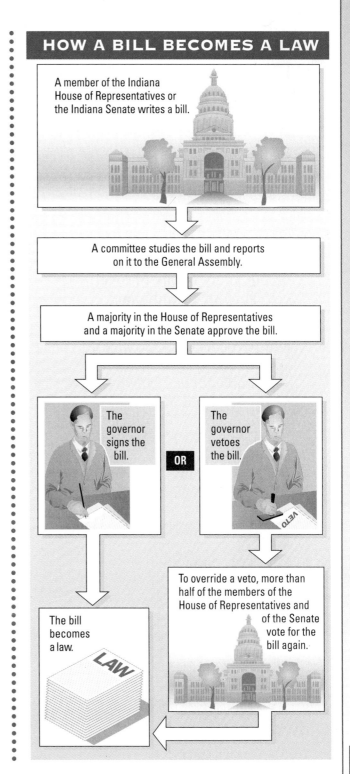

HOW A BILL BECOMES A LAW

A member of the Indiana House of Representatives or the Indiana Senate writes a bill.

A committee studies the bill and reports on it to the General Assembly.

A majority in the House of Representatives and a majority in the Senate approve the bill.

The governor signs the bill.

OR

The governor vetoes the bill.

The bill becomes a law.

LAW

To override a veto, more than half of the members of the House of Representatives and of the Senate vote for the bill again.

LOCAL GOVERNMENTS IN INDIANA

Link to Our World

What forms of local government make the laws where you live?

Focus on the Main Idea
Read to learn about the work of the many forms of local government in Indiana.

Preview Vocabulary

county seat
county
  commissioner
county council
township
  trustee
township
  board

common
  council
town board
Unigov
special
  district
school board

The Vanderburgh County courthouse in Evansville was built in 1890.

Hoosiers have governments for their cities, towns, and counties as well as for their state. These local governments make laws, see that laws are obeyed, and decide whether laws are fair in their own areas. Indiana has many local governments. There are 92 county governments, 1,008 township governments, 115 city governments, and 466 town governments. In one area a new kind of local government runs a city and a county together.

COUNTY GOVERNMENTS

After the Northwest Territory was created in 1787, the territory was organized into counties. Knox County was the first in what later became Indiana. Knox County included what later would be the entire state. Other counties were created out of Knox County. Later came Clark and Dearborn counties. Today, Indiana is divided into 92 counties. One town or city in each county serves as the county seat. The **county seat** is the center of government for that county. The leaders of county government meet at the county courthouse.

Each county is governed by a board made up of three **county commissioners**, who are elected by voters. The board does the work of the executive and legislative branches. It makes ordinances, or laws, for the county and makes sure they are obeyed. Voters in each county also elect people to form a **county council**. The main

INDIANA COUNTIES

1. Lake	32. Howard	63. Brown
2. Porter	33. Grant	64. Bartholomew
3. LaPorte	34. Blackford	65. Decatur
4. St. Joseph	35. Jay	66. Franklin
5. Elkhart	36. Fountain	67. Knox
6. Lagrange	37. Montgomery	68. Daviess
7. Steuben	38. Boone	69. Martin
8. Newton	39. Hamilton	70. Lawrence
9. Jasper	40. Madison	71. Jackson
10. Pulaski	41. Delaware	72. Jennings
11. Starke	42. Randolph	73. Ripley
12. Marshall	43. Vermillion	74. Dearborn
13. Fulton	44. Parke	75. Pike
14. Kosciusko	45. Putnam	76. Dubois
15. Whitley	46. Hendricks	77. Orange
16. Noble	47. Marion	78. Washington
17. DeKalb	48. Hancock	79. Scott
18. Allen	49. Henry	80. Jefferson
19. Benton	50. Wayne	81. Switzerland
20. White	51. Vigo	82. Ohio
21. Carroll	52. Clay	83. Gibson
22. Cass	53. Owen	84. Posey
23. Miami	54. Morgan	85. Vanderburgh
24. Wabash	55. Johnson	86. Warrick
25. Huntington	56. Shelby	87. Spencer
26. Wells	57. Rush	88. Perry
27. Adams	58. Fayette	89. Crawford
28. Warren	59. Union	90. Harrison
29. Tippecanoe	60. Sullivan	91. Floyd
30. Clinton	61. Greene	92. Clark
31. Tipton	62. Monroe	

PLACE The first county in Indiana was Knox County, created in 1790. The last was Tipton County, created in 1844.

■ Which counties border the state of Illinois?

duty of the county council is to decide how the county's money will be spent. The county council also makes sure that the board of county commissioners does not become too powerful.

Voters also elect seven county officials. In many counties the best known of these officials is the sheriff. The sheriff's job is to keep the county's citizens safe from crime.

Counties also have judges and courts—the judicial branch of government. Some counties share a court system made up of circuit and superior courts.

What is the job of the county commissioners?

TOWNSHIP GOVERNMENTS

Within each of Indiana's counties are several townships—the number depends on the county's size. Blackford, Brown, and Ohio counties have just 4 each, while LaPorte County has 21. There are 1,008 townships in Indiana altogether.

Each township has its own government, headed by a **township trustee**. The trustee is the executive branch of township government. Township laws are made by a **township board**. The board is the legislative branch of township government. There is no judicial branch in township government.

The township government has two main duties. One is to help people who do not have money for food and shelter. To get money to do this, the township government collects a tax on land and buildings. The second main duty of township government is to run the township's public school system, if there is one.

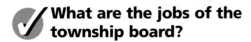 **What are the jobs of the township board?**

CITY AND TOWN GOVERNMENT

All cities or towns have governments that pass laws, make sure the laws are obeyed, and decide law cases. People living in cities and towns depend on their governments for services such as fire and police protection, libraries, and parks.

Cities in Indiana are governed by a mayor and a common council, also called a city council. The **common council** is the legislative branch of a city government. Members of the council are elected by voters to make laws for the city.

Towns in Indiana are governed by a mayor and a town board. The **town board** is the legislative branch. Voters elect three to seven members to the board to make laws for the town.

The mayor is the leader of the executive branch of government in a city or town. It is the mayor's job to make sure that the city or town laws are obeyed.

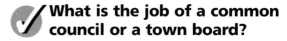 **What is the job of a common council or a town board?**

LEARNING FROM DIAGRAMS In the Unigov system, voters elect a mayor and a 29-member council. The mayor hires people to run the six main Unigov departments.
■ Which department would repair a broken traffic signal?

STRUCTURE OF UNIGOV

VOTERS

Mayor

City-County Council — make laws for city and county / reviews decisions of mayor and departments

Department of Public Safety
- fire
- police
- animal shelter

Department of Parks and Recreation
- land development
- park services

Department of Transportation
- road maintenance
- traffic systems

Department of Public Works
- sewers
- refuse collection

Department of Metropolitan Development
- housing
- historic preservation

Department of Administration
- government finances
- records

City department workers depend on taxes from citizens for their pay and the equipment they use.

UNIGOV

In 1970 the government of Indianapolis joined with the government of Marion County, where the city is located. The combined government they formed is called **Unigov**, for "unified government."

The legislative branch for the unified government is a 29-member city-county council, which makes laws for both the city and the county. It took the place of the Indianapolis common council.

In the Unigov plan there are no county commissioners. The mayor does their job. The mayor heads the executive branch of the Unigov, which is made up of six departments. These departments are in charge of police and fire services; keeping up parks, streets, and sewers; and running the government day to day. Each township within Unigov, however, has its own police, fire, and parks services; its own public school system; and its own maintenance crews.

What makes Unigov different from other local governments?

SPECIAL DISTRICTS

Indiana also has special districts. A **special district** is an area in which a certain problem, such as flooding, needs to be solved or a certain service, such as libraries, needs to be provided.

One kind of special district that most students know about is a school district, also called a school corporation. Voters in a school district elect a **school board**, whose members run the schools in that school district.

A special district may be smaller than a city or town, or it may be made up of a number of counties. Most special districts, however, are run in cooperation with county, township, or city and town governments.

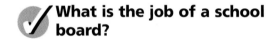

What is the job of a school board?

LESSON 2 REVIEW

Check Understanding

1. **Recall the Facts**   Name three forms of local government in Indiana.
2. **Focus on the Main Idea**   What do different forms of local government do?

Think Critically

3. **Personally Speaking**   Do you think the Unigov is a good plan for government?
4. **Cause and Effect**   How do decisions made by local governments affect you?

Show What You Know

Art Activity   Make a drawing to show the different forms of local government in action where you live. Display your drawing in the classroom.

Make Economic Choices

Why Is This Skill Important?

When you buy something at a store or decide what to order at a restaurant, you are making an economic choice. Some economic choices are difficult to make. To buy one thing, you may have to give up the chance to buy something else. Giving up one thing to get another is called a **trade-off**. What you give up is called the **opportunity cost** of what you get. Knowing about trade-offs and opportunity costs can help you make thoughtful economic choices.

Remember What You Have Read

Like people, governments have to make many economic choices. They, too, face trade-offs and opportunity costs.

It costs money for state and local governments to provide services, such as police and fire protection, road repair, and public libraries. Governments pay for these services with tax money they get from citizens. Often, however, governments do not have enough money to pay for everything that needs to be done.

Understand the Process

Imagine that you are the mayor of a town in Indiana. You have to make a choice. Should the town government pay to build a bike path, or should it use the money to build a basketball court?

1. **Think about the trade-offs.** To do this, you must think about the good and bad

changes each choice would bring. Building a bike path would make it safer for children and adults to ride their bicycles away from traffic. The trade-off is that it would not leave enough money to build a basketball court. Building a basketball court would give children and adults a safe place to play. The trade-off for that choice is that there would then not be enough money for building a bike path.

2. **Think about the opportunity costs.** Your town government does not have enough money to pay for both projects, so you will have to give up one. If you choose to build the bike path, the opportunity cost will be the new basketball court. If you choose to build the basketball court, the opportunity cost will be the new bike path. Which choice should you make?

Because you usually cannot have everything you want, you will often face opportunity costs as you trade off one product or service for another. This does not mean that the product or service you give up has no value. It means that at the time, another product or service has more value to you.

Think and Apply

Imagine that you have $2 to spend. You want to buy some comic books. But you also want to rent a movie. You do not have enough money for both. Explain to a partner the trade-offs and opportunity costs of your choices.

LESSON 3

HOOSIERS AND THE NATIONAL GOVERNMENT

Link to Our World

Why is it important to have good leaders in government?

Focus on the Main Idea
Read to learn about some national leaders from Indiana.

Preview Vocabulary
federal government
nominate

The national government, also called the **federal government**, is divided into three branches. It has an executive branch, a legislative branch, and a judicial branch. The executive branch is led by the President and Vice President. The legislative branch is made up of the two houses of Congress. The judicial branch has a Supreme Court and a court system. Many Hoosiers have served, and still serve, in all three branches of the national government.

Ribbon from William Henry Harrison's 1840 presidential campaign

HOOSIER PRESIDENTS

William Henry Harrison, known as "the Hero of Tippecanoe," had led Indiana through its earliest growth. The military leader served as governor of the Indiana Territory from 1800 to 1812. In 1840 Harrison was elected the ninth President of the United States. As Presidents did before 1937, he began to serve on March 4. He became ill soon after his first day as President and died in early 1841.

Abraham Lincoln is the best-known President who lived in Indiana. Lincoln grew up there during the pioneer days, not long after Indiana had become a state. He had been born in Kentucky, and he later settled in Illinois. In 1860 Lincoln was elected the sixteenth President. He led the United States during the Civil War, one of the hardest times the nation has ever faced.

Benjamin Harrison, the grandson of William Henry Harrison, became the twenty-third President of the

The five Hoosiers who have held the office of Vice President of the United States are (left to right) Schuyler Colfax, Thomas Hendricks, Charles W. Fairbanks, Thomas Marshall, and J. Danforth Quayle. The Vice President's office is located in the White House (above).

United States. Benjamin Harrison wanted to help soldiers who had been wounded in the Civil War and could not work. He got the government to give them enough money to live on. Benjamin Harrison served as President from 1889 to 1893.

In 1940, the year before the United States entered World War II, Hoosier Wendell L. Willkie of Elwood was **nominated**, or named, as a candidate for President. He ran against Franklin D. Roosevelt but lost the election by many votes.

 **What United States Presidents lived in Indiana?**

"MOTHER OF VICE PRESIDENTS"

Indiana has been given the nickname "Mother of Vice Presidents." Five Hoosiers have served in the national government as Vice President of the United States.

George Bush chose Hoosier J. Danforth Quayle as his running mate for the 1988 presidential election. When George Bush won, Dan Quayle became his Vice President. Quayle served from 1989 to 1993 as Vice President.

The other Hoosier Vice Presidents were Schuyler Colfax of South Bend, Thomas Hendricks and Charles W. Fairbanks of

Indianapolis, and Thomas Marshall of North Manchester. Colfax was the Vice President under Ulysses S. Grant from 1869 to 1873, Hendricks under President Grover Cleveland in 1885, Fairbanks under President Theodore Roosevelt from 1905 to 1909, and Marshall under Woodrow Wilson from 1913 to 1921.

✓ **What Vice Presidents have been from Indiana?**

OTHER WELL-KNOWN INDIANA LEADERS

Hoosiers have been leaders in the United States Congress, too. One of the state's best-known senators was Birch Bayh. First elected in 1962, he served three six-year terms. In 1976 he hoped to be nominated for President, but he did not get enough votes. His son Evan later became Indiana's governor.

Past and present Hoosier leaders in the United States Congress include (left to right) senators Richard G. Lugar and Daniel Coats and representatives Virginia Ellis Jenckes and Katie Beatrice Hall. The United States Capitol is shown below.

Today Indiana's senators are Daniel Coats and Richard G. Lugar. Coats became a senator in 1989. Lugar has been in office since 1976. Senator Lugar is a former mayor of Indianapolis. He is considered an expert on military matters, agriculture, and dealing with leaders from other countries.

So far, Indiana has not had a woman in the U.S. Senate, but it has had women in the House of Representatives. The first was Virginia Ellis Jenckes of Terre Haute. She ran her family's farm until she was elected in 1932. Knowing how farms are run helped her work in Congress to solve the economic problems of the Great Depression.

Indiana's first African American woman to be elected to the House of Representatives was Katie Beatrice Hall of Gary. She served from 1983 to 1985. Hall was one of the representatives who introduced into Congress the bill that made

Who?

Federal Workers

Many Hoosiers work in the agencies of the executive branch of the United States government. These agencies run the space program and banking and are involved in farm and home loans, interstate and international trade, and many other fields. Your letter carrier works for the federal government.

the birthday of Dr. Martin Luther King, Jr., a federal holiday.

 Name two Hoosiers who have served in Congress.

LESSON 3 REVIEW

Check Understanding

1. **Recall the Facts** Which three United States Presidents lived in Indiana?
2. **Focus on the Main Idea** What made some of the Hoosiers you read about in this lesson good leaders?

Think Critically

3. **Personally Speaking** Who represents your community in the United States House of Representatives?
4. **Past to Present** Compare present-day Indiana leaders with leaders of the past,

such as George Rogers Clark and Jonathan Jennings.

Show What You Know

 Writing Activity Imagine that you are running for election to the United States House of Representatives. Write a short speech to tell people why they should vote for you. Be sure to describe the things you will do to help the citizens. Give your speech to your classmates.

INDIANA CITIZENSHIP

Link to Our World

What does it mean to be a citizen?

Focus on the Main Idea
Read to learn about the rights and responsibilities of citizens of the United States and of Indiana.

Preview Vocabulary
responsibility
naturalized citizen
register
volunteer

Children under 18 years of age become citizens automatically when their parents do.

Since 1816, when Indiana became a state, Hoosiers have been citizens of the United States and also of the state of Indiana. The word *citizen* means "a member of a state or country." Citizens have rights that people who are not members of their state or country do not have. At the same time, citizens also have responsibilities. A **responsibility** is a duty.

BECOMING A CITIZEN

The United States Constitution says that "All persons born or naturalized in the United States . . . are citizens of the United States and of the State wherein they reside [live]."

People who are born in this country are citizens of the United States. A **naturalized citizen** is an immigrant who has become a citizen by taking the steps described in the law. When adults become United States citizens, any children they have under 18 years of age become citizens as well.

When an immigrant has lived in the United States for at least five years, he or she can follow three steps to become a naturalized citizen. First, the person must ask a judge in writing to become a citizen. Second, the person must pass a test to show that he or she under-stands United States history and how the United States government works. Third, the person must take part in a ceremony in which he or she promises to be loyal to the United States. Many of these ceremonies take place on September 17, Citizenship Day.

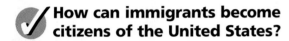
How can immigrants become citizens of the United States?

THE RIGHTS OF CITIZENS

Citizens of Indiana have the rights listed in both the United States and Indiana constitutions. Citizens have the right to vote and the right to hold public office. They have the right to travel through their home state and all of the United States. Citizens have freedom of speech, freedom of the press, freedom of religion, and freedom to gather in groups. New laws passed by the United States Congress and the Indiana General Assembly can give citizens other rights.

Governments cannot take away a citizen's constitutional rights, but governments can place certain limits on them. The United States government says that a citizen must be at least 18 years old to vote. State governments can say that a citizen must **register**, or sign up, to vote.

People who are not citizens have many of the same rights as citizens. However, they cannot vote, hold public office or certain other jobs, or be a member of a trial jury.

What documents give Indiana citizens their rights?

THE RESPONSIBILITIES OF CITIZENS

With rights come responsibilities. With the right to vote comes the responsibility to vote. With freedom of speech and of the press comes the responsibility to be an informed citizen.

Some responsibilities are stated in laws. United States and Indiana laws state that it is a citizen's responsibility to pay taxes, obey laws, and be loyal. Some people also take on responsibilities that help make their communities better places to live. **Volunteers**, or people who work

Hoosiers are citizens both of the United States and of Indiana.

Hoosiers have always had the volunteer spirit. The volunteers at left were teachers for the Indianapolis Red Cross during World War I. Today, the volunteers above help build low-cost houses for people who need them.

without pay, help out in places such as schools and hospitals. Some volunteers take part in community cleanup projects. Volunteering to help an older neighbor with yard work is another way to show responsibility as a citizen.

 What are some responsibilities that citizens have?

LESSON 4 REVIEW

Check Understanding

1. **Recall the Facts**   At what age can citizens vote in the United States?
2. **Focus on the Main Idea**   What are some rights and responsibilities of citizens of the United States?

Think Critically

3. **Think More About It**   Why do you think people need to be responsible citizens?

4. **Cause and Effect**   How do responsible citizens affect the country and the state?

Show What You Know

 **Poster Activity**   Make a poster showing ways people can act as responsible citizens today. You might use pictures of people who are showing responsibility as citizens. Display your poster in the classroom.

REVIEW

CONNECT MAIN IDEAS

Use this organizer to show that you understand how the chapter's main ideas are connected. Copy the organizer onto a separate sheet of paper. Then complete it by listing the parts of each level of government, the work each part does, and the role of Indiana's citizens in government.

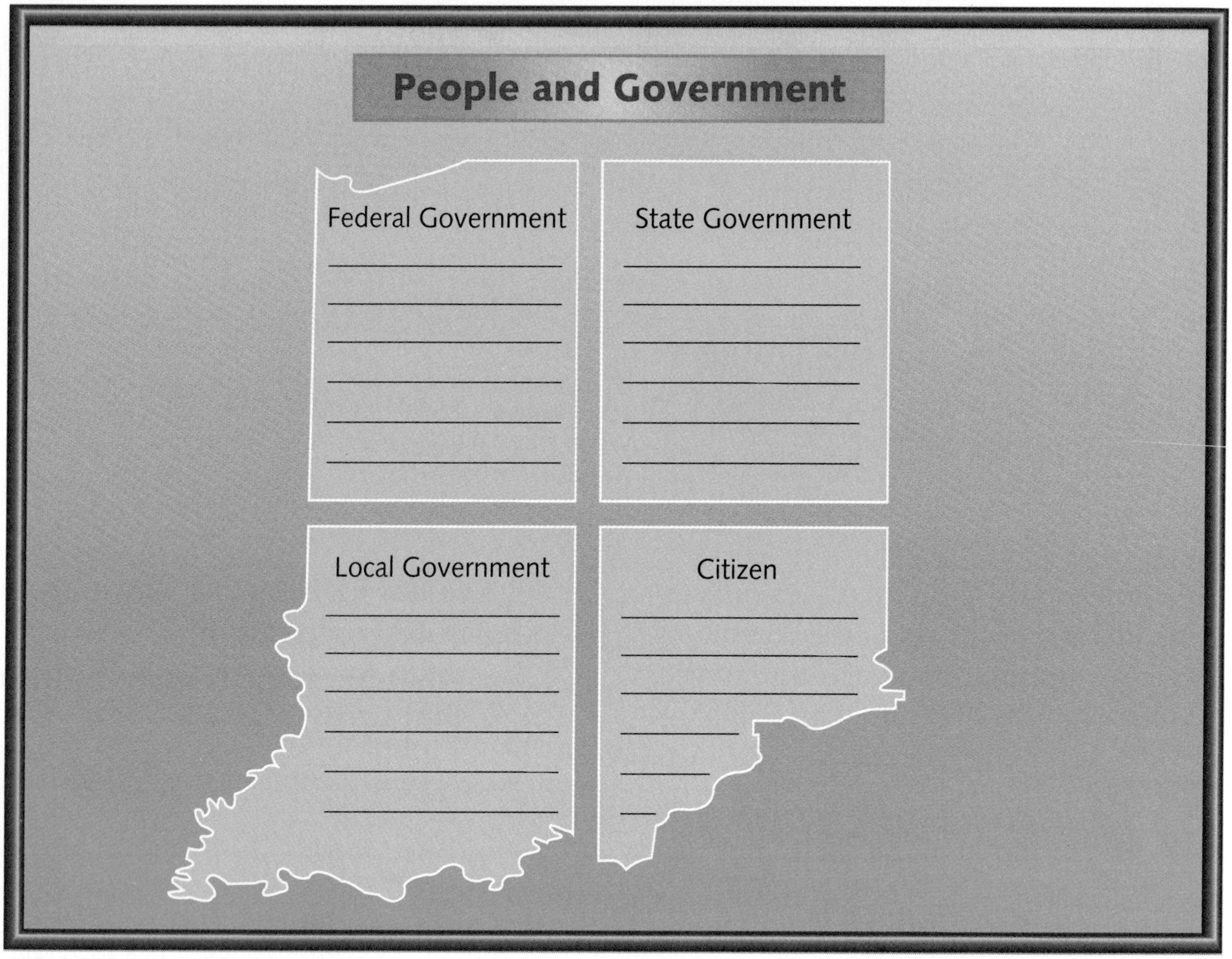

People and Government

Federal Government

_____
_____
_____
_____
_____
_____

State Government

_____
_____
_____
_____
_____
_____

Local Government

_____
_____
_____
_____
_____
_____

Citizen

_____
_____
_____
_____
_____
_____

WRITE MORE ABOUT IT

1. **Write a Journal Entry** Imagine that you have just become a naturalized citizen. Write a journal entry that describes the steps you went through and how you feel about being a citizen. Share your entry with a classmate.

2. **Write a Comparison** Choose two current leaders at different levels of government. Write a paragraph about each person that describes what he or she does. Then write a third paragraph that compares the responsibilities of the two leaders.

On a separate sheet of paper, write the word or phrase that completes each of the sentences that follow.

Bill of Rights   **legislative branch**
executive branch   **naturalized citizen**
judicial branch   **Unigov**

1. The list of rights in the Indiana Constitution is called the _____.

2. The _____ of the state government in Indiana makes laws.

3. The governor is the head of the _____ of the Indiana state government.

4. Courts and judges that hear and decide law cases make up the _____ of the Indiana state government.

5. _____ is the combined government of the city of Indianapolis and Marion County.

6. An immigrant who has become a United States citizen is a _____.

CHECK UNDERSTANDING

1. Name some of the rights of citizens listed in the Indiana Bill of Rights.

2. What is the main work of the Indiana General Assembly?

3. What job does the governor do?

4. What is the highest court in Indiana?

5. Name three forms of local government in Indiana.

6. Who is the head of the executive branch of city government?

7. What are some of the responsibilities of citizens?

1. **Think More About It** How is the Indiana Constitution similar to the United States Constitution?

2. **Explore Viewpoints** Why do some immigrants want to become citizens of the United States?

3. **Personally Speaking** Do you think you will vote when you are old enough to do so? Explain your answer.

APPLY SKILLS

How to Follow a Flow Chart Think about something you do often, such as getting ready for school or playing a game. List the steps you follow when performing the task. Then make a flow chart of the task, placing the steps in order. Add arrows and a title to complete your flow chart.

How to Make Economic Choices Imagine that you need to choose between buying a video game or a new pair of soccer shoes. How would you go about making this economic choice? What would be the trade-offs and the opportunity costs?

READ MORE ABOUT IT

I Never Wanted to Be Famous by Eth Clifford. Houghton Mifflin. This book tells the story of a young boy who goes from his hometown in Indiana to Washington, D.C. While there, he meets his representative and visits the home of the President.

Our Constitution by Linda Carlson Johnson. Millbrook. This book tells about the United States Constitution and the ideas it contains.

In Peers We Trust

TEEN COURT

Indiana has a new way of keeping law and order—teen court! This court is for young people who admit to infractions such as traffic violations and theft. They can be tried by their peers, young people their own age, instead of by adults in the state juvenile court.

Like regular court, teen court is made up of many people doing many jobs. The difference is that all of them, except for the judge, are students. The clerks, court deputies, attorneys, and jurors are teenage volunteers.

When court is held, the young attorneys, or lawyers, for each side present their views and suggest a sentence, or punishment, for the crime. Most sentences require the young person to repay the community with service. He or she might work for the town library or animal shelter or do odd jobs for an older adult. Later, he or she must take a turn as a juror in teen court.

Teen court judge Douglas Haney says, "Oftentimes a jury of their peers is more in tune with their real motives and attitudes and is able to come back with a sentence that's appropriate for someone their age."

The young person has about five weeks to complete his or her sentence. If the sentence is not completed, the case goes to regular court.

In teen court young people learn how the court system works. Says one teenager, "Students learn about law and get to contribute to the community." Many of Indiana's 92 counties now have teen courts.

Teen court judge Douglas Haney listening to teen attorneys

Teen court in session

THINK AND APPLY

Find out more about teen courts and other community projects in which young citizens can take part. Report your findings to the class.

BUILDING CITIZENSHIP

STORY CLOTH

Follow the pictures shown in this story cloth to help you review Unit 4.

Summarize the Main Ideas

1. Most of Indiana's people were born in the state, but they represent cultures from all over the world.

2. Hoosiers earn their livings in many ways. They make products, sell products, mine and farm, and provide services.

3. Hoosiers are working to improve education, to keep their cities safe and clean, and to protect the environment.

4. The state government of Indiana has three branches—the executive, the legislative, and the judicial.

5. Local government in Indiana takes the form of county governments, township governments, city or town governments, Unigov, and special districts.

6. Hoosiers have served, and still serve, in all branches of the national government.

7. Citizens of Indiana have the rights given in the United States and Indiana constitutions. They also have responsibilities, such as voting and helping make their communities better places to live.

Create a Mural Create a mural that shows how citizens can take part in different levels of government, from local to state to national. Invite other classes to your classroom, and give them a tour of government in Indiana.

UNIGOV
INDIANAPOLIS - MARION COUNTY

UNIT 4
REVIEW

COOPERATIVE LEARNING WORKSHOP

Remember
- Share your ideas.
- Cooperate with others to plan your work.
- Take responsibility for your work.
- Show your group's work to the class.
- Discuss what you learned by working together.

Activity 1
Plan a Presentation
Work with a group of classmates to plan a presentation about one of the cultural groups that lives in Indiana. Find out more about the group, such as its special foods, clothing, and holidays. Make drawings or models to show what you learned. Share your presentation with the rest of the class.

Activity 2
Make a Poster
In a group, make a poster that shows the best ways to use the natural resources of your community. You can draw or cut out pictures to put on your poster. Add a title and a message that will help people understand your poster.

Activity 3
Perform a Simulation
Work with several other classmates to prepare a skit in which the main characters are members of the branches of Indiana state government. There should be at least one character from each branch—for example, a state senator, the governor, and a justice of the Indiana Supreme Court. Write a scene in which the characters talk about their jobs in state government. Make name tags that give the government branch and job title for each character.

Activity 4
Design a Brochure
As a class, create a brochure that explains the rights and responsibilities of United States citizens. Draw or find pictures to illustrate the brochure.

USE VOCABULARY

For each group of terms, write one or two sentences that explain how they are related.

1. conserve, reclaim

2. human resource, informed citizen

3. legislative branch, budget

4. executive branch, veto power

5. responsibility, naturalized citizen

CHECK UNDERSTANDING

1. About how many people live in Indiana?

2. In which kind of industry do most Hoosiers earn their livings?

3. Why is recycling important?

4. What are some rights listed in the Indiana Bill of Rights?

5. Who leads the executive branch of the Indiana state government?

6. What is the job of a common council or town council?

7. Who are the present-day senators from Indiana in the federal government?

8. What are some responsibilities of United States citizens?

THINK CRITICALLY

1. **Cause and Effect** How might a growing population in Indiana affect the state's businesses?

2. **Link to You** What are four things you can do every day to protect the environment where you live?

3. **Explore Viewpoints** Why do you think some people and businesses choose not to recycle?

4. **Personally Speaking** What job in government would you like to have? Why?

APPLY GEOGRAPHY SKILLS

How to Use a Population Map

Study the map below, and answer the questions about population density.

1. In what part of the Middle West is population density the greatest?

2. How does the population density of Indiana compare with that of the other states in the Middle West?

Indiana state capitol

FOR YOUR REFERENCE

First state capitol, Corydon

CONTENTS

**HOW TO GATHER
AND REPORT INFORMATION**   **R2**

ALMANAC

    FACTS ABOUT INDIANA   **R8**

    FACTS ABOUT INDIANA COUNTIES   **R10**

    FACTS ABOUT INDIANA GOVERNORS   **R14**

**SOME FAMOUS PEOPLE IN
    INDIANA HISTORY**   **R16**

GAZETTEER   **R20**

GLOSSARY   **R24**

INDEX   **R29**

Soldiers and Sailors Monument

HOW TO GATHER AND REPORT INFORMATION

To write a report, make a poster, or do many other projects in your social studies class, you may need information that is not in your textbook. You can gather this information from reference books, electronic references, or community resources. The following guide can help you gather information from many sources and report what you find.

HOW TO USE REFERENCE TOOLS

Reference works are collections of facts. They include books and electronic resources, such as almanacs, atlases, dictionaries, and encyclopedias. Books in libraries are organized through a system of numbers. Every book in a library has its own number, called a call number. The call number on the book tells where in the library the book can be found. In a library a reference book has an *R* or *REF* for *reference* on its spine along with the call number. Most reference books are for use only in the library. Many libraries also have electronic reference materials on CD-ROM and the Internet.

WHEN TO USE AN ENCYCLOPEDIA

An encyclopedia is a good place to begin to look for information. An encyclopedia has articles on nearly every subject. The articles are arranged in alphabetical order by subject. Each article gives basic facts about people, places, and events. Some electronic encyclopedias allow you to hear music and speeches and see short movies related to the subject.

WHEN TO USE A DICTIONARY

A dictionary gives information about words. Dictionaries explain the meanings of words and show how the words are pronounced. A dictionary is a good place to check the spelling of a word. Some dictionaries also include the origins of words and lists of foreign words, abbreviations, well-known people, and place names.

WHEN TO USE AN ATLAS

You can find information about places in an atlas. An atlas is a book of maps. Some atlases have road maps. Others have maps of countries around the world. Some atlas maps show where certain crops are grown and where certain products are made. Others show the populations of different places. Ask a librarian to help you find the kind of atlas you need.

WHEN TO USE AN ALMANAC

An almanac is a book or an electronic resource containing facts and figures. It shows information in tables and charts. The population of a city or the largest industries of a country are the kinds of facts given in an almanac.

The subjects in an almanac are grouped in broad categories, not in alphabetical order. To find a certain subject, such as health and sports, you need to use the index, which lists the subjects in alphabetical order. Most almanacs are brought up to date every year. So an almanac can give you the latest information on a subject.

HOW TO FIND NONFICTION BOOKS

Unlike fiction books, which tell stories that are made up, nonfiction books give facts about real people, places, and events. In a library all nonfiction books are placed in order on the shelves according to their call numbers.

You can find a book's call number by using a card file or a computer catalog. To find this number, however, you need to know the book's subject, author, or title. Here are some entries for a book about Tecumseh.

Subject Card

INDIANS OF NORTH AMERICA--BIOGRAPHY.

973.04 Kent, Zachary.
KEN   Tecumseh / Zachary Kent. -- Chicago :
        Childrens Press, c1992.

        31 p. : ill. (some col.), map ; 25 cm.
(Cornerstones of freedom)

        ISBN 0-516-06660-9

Author Card

973.04   Kent, Zachary.
KEN   Tecumseh / Zachary Kent. -- Chicago :
        Childrens Press, c1992.

        31 p. : ill. (some col.), map ; 25 cm.
(Cornerstones of freedom)

        ISBN 0-516-06660-9

        1. Tecumseh, Shawnee Chief, 1768-1813--
Juvenile literature. 2. Shawnee Indians--
Biography--Juvenile literature. 3. Shawnee
Indians--History--Juvenile literature. 4.
Tecumseh, Shawnee Chief, 1768-1813. 5.
Shawnee Indians--Biography. 6. Indians of

Title Card

TECUMSEH/

973.04 Kent, Zachary.
KEN   Tecumseh / Zachary Kent. -- Chicago :
        Childrens Press, c1992.

        31 p. : ill. (some col.), map ; 25 cm.
(Cornerstones of freedom)

        ISBN 0-516-06660-9

E99.S35T162 1992   973'.04
                                92-8217 /AC

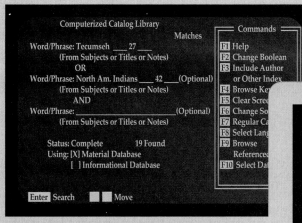

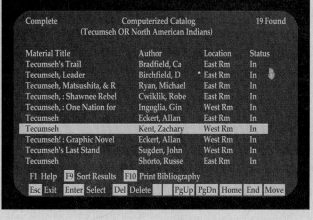

Computer Catalog

HOW TO FIND PERIODICALS

Libraries have special sections for periodicals—newspapers and magazines. A periodical, which is usually published every day, week, or month, is a good source for the most up-to-date information and for topics not yet covered in books. In a library, the latest issues of periodicals are usually displayed on a rack. Older issues are stored away, sometimes on film.

Most libraries have an index that lists magazine articles by subject. The most widely used indexes are the *Children's Magazine Guide* and the *Readers' Guide to Periodical Literature.* The entries in these guides are in alphabetical order by subject and author, and sometimes by title. Abbreviations are used for many parts of an entry, such as the name of the magazine and the date of the issue. Here is a sample entry for an article about Tecumseh.

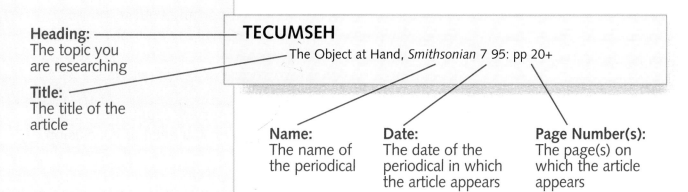

Heading:
The topic you are researching

Title:
The title of the article

TECUMSEH

The Object at Hand, *Smithsonian* 7 95: pp 20+

Name:
The name of the periodical

Date:
The date of the periodical in which the article appears

Page Number(s):
The page(s) on which the article appears

HOW TO CONDUCT AN INTERVIEW

Conducting interviews, or asking people questions, is a good way to get facts and points of view on a topic.

PLANNING AN INTERVIEW

1. Make a list of people to interview. Think about who the experts are on the subject you are researching.
2. Call or write to each person to ask for an interview. Identify yourself, and let the person know what you want to talk about.
3. Ask the person you will interview to set a time and place to meet.

BEFORE THE INTERVIEW

1. Read more about your topic and, if possible, about the person you are interviewing. That way you will be better able to talk with the person.
2. Make a list of questions to ask.

DURING THE INTERVIEW

1. Listen carefully. Do not interrupt or argue with the person.
2. Take notes as you talk with the person, and write down the person's exact words.
3. If you want to use a tape recorder, first ask the person if you may do so.

AFTER THE INTERVIEW

1. Before you leave, thank the person you interviewed.
2. Follow up by writing a thank-you note.

HOW TO CONDUCT A SURVEY

A good way to get information about the views of people in your community is to conduct a survey.

1. Identify your topic, and make a list of questions. Write the questions so that they can be answered with "yes" or "no" or with "for" or "against." You may also want to give a "no opinion" or "not sure" choice.
2. Make a tally sheet to use for recording your responses.
3. Decide how many people you will ask and where you will conduct your survey.
4. During the survey, carefully record each person's responses on the tally sheet.
5. When you have finished your survey, count your responses and write a summary statement or conclusion that your survey supports.

How to Write for Information

You can write a letter to ask for information about a certain topic. When you write, be sure to do these things:

- Write neatly or use a word processor.
- Say who you are and why you are writing.
- Make your request specific and reasonable.
- Provide a self-addressed, stamped envelope for the answer.

You may or may not get a reply, but if you do, you may find it was worth your time to write.

How to Write a Report

You may be asked to write a report on the information you have gathered. Knowing how to write a report will help you make good use of the information you have collected. You should take the following steps when writing a report.

Gather and Organize Your Information

- Gather information about your topic from reference books, electronic references, or community resources.
- Take notes as you find information that you need for your report.
- Review your notes to make sure you have all the information you want to include.
- Organize your information in an outline.
- Make sure the information is in the order in which you want to present it.

Draft Your Report

- Review your information. Decide if you need more.
- Remember that the purpose of your report is to share information about your topic.
- Write a draft of your report. Put all your ideas on paper. Present your ideas in a clear and interesting way.

Revise

- Check to make sure that you have followed the order of your outline. Move sentences that seem out of place.
- Add any information that you feel is needed.
- Add quotations to show people's exact words.
- Reword sentences if too many follow the same pattern.

Proofread and Publish

- Check for errors.
- Make sure nothing has been left out.
- Make a clean copy of your report.

ALMANAC

FACTS ABOUT INDIANA

Did You Know?

Except for Hawaii, Indiana is the smallest state west of the Appalachian Mountains.

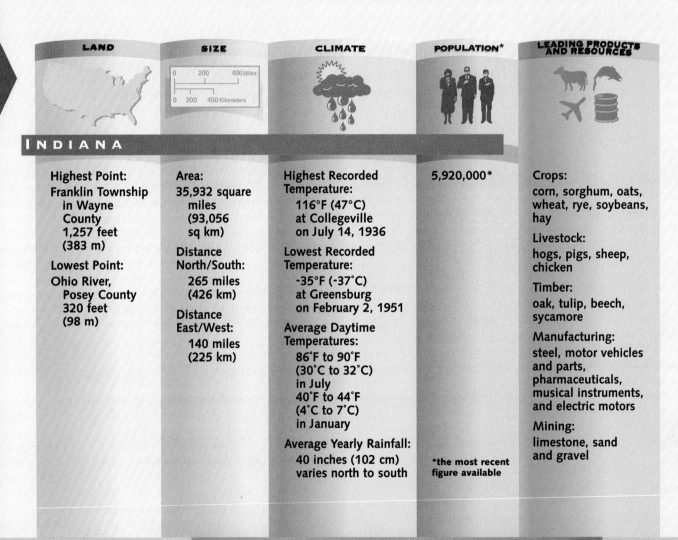

LAND	SIZE	CLIMATE	POPULATION*	LEADING PRODUCTS AND RESOURCES
Highest Point: Franklin Township in Wayne County 1,257 feet (383 m) **Lowest Point:** Ohio River, Posey County 320 feet (98 m)	**Area:** 35,932 square miles (93,056 sq km) **Distance North/South:** 265 miles (426 km) **Distance East/West:** 140 miles (225 km)	**Highest Recorded Temperature:** 116°F (47°C) at Collegeville on July 14, 1936 **Lowest Recorded Temperature:** -35°F (-37°C) at Greensburg on February 2, 1951 **Average Daytime Temperatures:** 86°F to 90°F (30°C to 32°C) in July 40°F to 44°F (4°C to 7°C) in January **Average Yearly Rainfall:** 40 inches (102 cm) varies north to south	5,920,000* *the most recent figure available	**Crops:** corn, sorghum, oats, wheat, rye, soybeans, hay **Livestock:** hogs, pigs, sheep, chicken **Timber:** oak, tulip, beech, sycamore **Manufacturing:** steel, motor vehicles and parts, pharmaceuticals, musical instruments, and electric motors **Mining:** limestone, sand and gravel

INDIANA

Indianapolis is the largest city in Indiana. Its population is more than 750,000. One of every five Hoosiers lives in the Indianapolis metropolitan area.

THE UNITED STATES

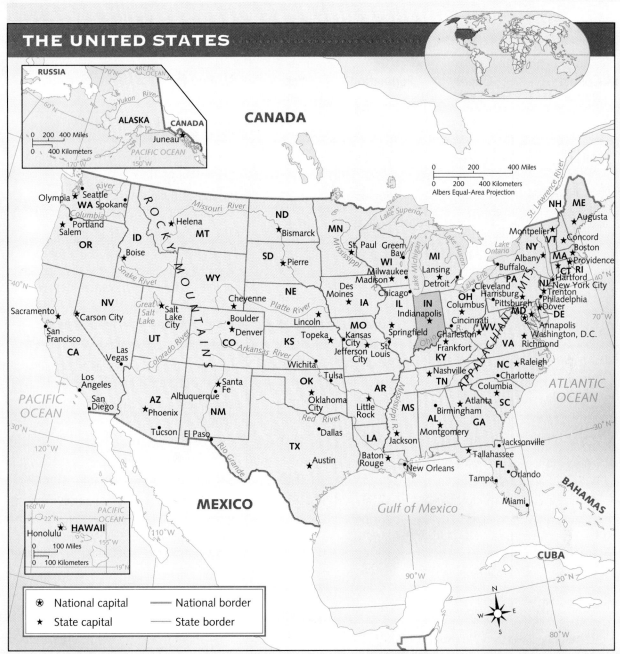

RUSSIA

70°N

ARCTIC OCEAN

Yukon River

60°N

ALASKA

CANADA

Juneau

PACIFIC OCEAN

0 200 400 Miles
0 400 Kilometers

150°W

CANADA

River

Olympia ★ Seattle
WA Spokane
Columbia
★ Portland
Salem
OR

Missouri River

ID
Helena
MT
Boise

R O C K Y   M O U N T A I N S

Snake River

40°N

ND
Bismarck

SD
Pierre

WY

NE

Cheyenne ★
Platte River

MN
St. Paul
Green Bay

Lake Superior

Milwaukee
Madison ★
WI

MI
Lansing
Detroit

Lake Huron

Lake Michigan

Des Moines
IA

Chicago

Lake Ontario
Lake Erie

Buffalo

NH **ME**
Augusta

Montpelier ★ **VT** ★ Concord
Boston
Albany ★ **MA**
NY **CT** RI Providence
Hartford
NJ New York City
PA
Harrisburg ★ Trenton
Pittsburgh ★ Philadelphia
MD Dover
DE

St. Lawrence River

70°W

0 200 400 Miles
0 200 400 Kilometers
Albers Equal-Area Projection

Sacramento ★
NV
Carson City ★

San Francisco

CA

Los Angeles

PACIFIC OCEAN

San Diego

Great Salt Lake
Salt Lake City ★
UT

Colorado River

Las Vegas

AZ
Phoenix ★

Tucson

Boulder ★
Denver
CO
Arkansas River

★ Santa Fe
Albuquerque
NM

El Paso

120°W 110°W

Lincoln ★

KS
Topeka ★
Wichita

OK
Oklahoma City ★

MO
Jefferson City ★
Kansas City

Tulsa

Red River

Dallas

TX

Austin ★

Rio Grande

30°N

MEXICO

Springfield
St. Louis

IL
IN
Indianapolis ★

Ohio R.

Columbus ★
OH
Cincinnati

Frankfort ★
KY

Nashville ★
TN

Mississippi R.

AR
Little Rock ★

MS
Jackson ★

LA
Baton Rouge ★

New Orleans

Cleveland
WV
Charleston ★

VA
Richmond ★

A P P A L A C H I A N   M T S

NC
Charlotte
Raleigh ★

Columbia ★
SC

Atlanta ★
GA
Birmingham

AL
Montgomery ★

Jacksonville

Tallahassee ★
FL
Orlando

Tampa

Miami

Gulf of Mexico

90°W

Annapolis ★
Washington, D.C. ✪

70°W

ATLANTIC OCEAN

40°N

30°N

BAHAMAS

CUBA

20°N

80°W

160°W 22°N PACIFIC OCEAN
Honolulu ★ **HAWAII**
155°W
0 100 Miles
0 100 Kilometers 19°N

N
W E
S

Legend:
✪ National capital — National border
★ State capital — State border

The state capitol is in Indianapolis. The site for Indiana's capital city was chosen in 1821. The government started work there in 1825.

Indiana has more than 1,500 elementary schools.

ALMANAC

FACTS ABOUT INDIANA COUNTIES

County Name	County Seat	Population*	Year Organized	Named for
Adams	Decatur	32,123	1836	John Quincy Adams, a President of the United States
Allen	Fort Wayne	307,685	1823	John Allen, a liberator of Fort Wayne in the War of 1812
Bartholomew	Columbus	66,965	1821	Joseph Bartholomew, a hero of the Battle of Tippecanoe
Benton	Fowler	9,594	1840	Thomas H. Benton, a U.S. senator from Missouri
Blackford	Hartford City	13,991	1839	Isaac Newton Blackford, the first Speaker of Indiana's House of Representatives, and later, a justice of the state supreme court
Boone	Lebanon	40,911	1830	Daniel Boone, an American pioneer
Brown	Nashville	14,809	1836	Jacob Brown, a hero of the War of 1812
Carroll	Delphi	19,493	1828	Charles Carroll of Maryland, a signer of the Declaration of Independence
Cass	Logansport	38,520	1828	Lewis Cass, a governor of the Michigan Territory
Clark	Jeffersonville	90,868	1801	George Rogers Clark, a hero of the American Revolution
Clay	Brazil	25,761	1825	Henry Clay, a U.S. senator from Kentucky
Clinton	Frankfort	32,307	1830	DeWitt Clinton, a governor of New York
Crawford	English	10,309	1818	William Crawford, a leader in the American Revolution; or William H. Crawford, a U.S. secretary of the treasury
Daviess	Washington	28,252	1816	Joseph Hamilton Daviess, a soldier in the Battle of Tippecanoe
Dearborn	Lawrenceburg	43,255	1803	Henry Dearborn, a U.S. secretary of war
Decatur	Greensburg	24,775	1821	Stephen Decatur, a hero of the War of 1812
DeKalb	Auburn	37,508	1837	Johann DeKalb, an officer in the American Revolution
Delaware	Muncie	119,243	1827	Delaware Indians
Dubois	Jasper	38,179	1817	Toussaint Dubois, an officer in the Battle of Tippecanoe
Elkhart	Goshen	163,992	1830	Elkhart Indians
Fayette	Connersville	26,444	1818	Marquis de Lafayette, a French officer in the American Revolution
Floyd	New Albany	69,094	1819	John Floyd, a governor of Virginia; or Davis Floyd, the county's first circuit court judge
Fountain	Covington	17,996	1825	James Fountain, an officer at the Battle of Maumee

*The population figures give the most recent estimates.

County Name	County Seat	Population*	Year Organized	Named for
Franklin	Brookville	20,280	1811	Benjamin Franklin, a leader in the American Revolution
Fulton	Rochester	19,652	1836	Robert Fulton, an American engineer and inventor who built the country's first money-making steamboat
Gibson	Princeton	32,138	1813	John Gibson, a governor of the Indiana Territory
Grant	Marion	73,779	1831	Samuel and Moses Grant of Kentucky
Greene	Bloomfield	32,238	1821	Nathanael Greene, an officer in the American Revolution
Hamilton	Noblesville	134,257	1823	Alexander Hamilton, a leader in the American Revolution and the first U.S. secretary of the treasury
Hancock	Greenfield	49,427	1827	John Hancock, the first signer of the Declaration of Independence
Harrison	Corydon	31,891	1808	William Henry Harrison, the first governor of the Indiana Territory, and later, a President of the United States
Hendricks	Danville	84,105	1823	William Hendricks, a governor of Indiana
Henry	New Castle	48,968	1821	Patrick Henry, a leader in the American Revolution
Howard	Kokomo	82,995	1844	Tilghman Howard, an Indiana representative
Huntington	Huntington	36,408	1834	Samuel Huntington, a Connecticut delegate to the Continental Congress and a signer of the Declaration of Independence
Jackson	Brownstown	39,530	1815	Andrew Jackson, a hero of the War of 1812, and later, a President of the United States
Jasper	Rensselaer	27,375	1838	William Jasper, a soldier in the American Revolution
Jay	Portland	21,785	1836	John Jay, the first chief justice of the United States
Jefferson	Madison	30,536	1811	Thomas Jefferson, a President of the United States
Jennings	Vernon	25,512	1816	Jonathan Jennings, the first governor of Indiana
Johnson	Franklin	99,022	1822	John Johnson, an Indiana supreme court justice
Knox	Vincennes	40,069	1790	Henry Knox, an officer in the American Revolution and the first U.S. secretary of war
Kosciusko	Warsaw	67,956	1837	Thaddeus Kosciusko, a Polish patriot and an officer in the American Revolution
LaGrange	LaGrange	31,225	1832	Marquis de Lafayette's country home near Paris, France
Lake	Crown Point	481,635	1837	Lake Michigan

*The population figures give the most recent estimates.

County Name	County Seat	Population*	Year Organized	Named for
LaPorte	LaPorte	109,626	1832	The French term for "the door" or "the port"
Lawrence	Bedford	44,364	1818	James Lawrence, a hero of the War of 1812
Madison	Anderson	132,766	1823	James Madison, a President of the United States
Marion	Indianapolis	818,014	1822	Francis Marion, a hero of the American Revolution
Marshall	Plymouth	44,206	1836	John Marshall, a chief justice of the United States
Martin	Shoals	10,582	1820	John P. Martin of Kentucky; Thomas E. Martin of Kentucky; or Jeremiah Martin, a Kentucky volunteer in the War of 1812
Miami	Peru	34,498	1834	Miami Indians
Monroe	Bloomington	113,830	1818	James Monroe, a President of the United States
Montgomery	Crawfordsville	35,698	1823	Richard Montgomery, an officer in the American Revolution
Morgan	Martinsville	60,999	1822	Daniel Morgan, a soldier in the American Revolution
Newton	Kentland	14,130	1859	John Newton, a soldier in the American Revolution
Noble	Albion	39,971	1836	James Noble, a U.S. senator from Indiana
Ohio	Rising Sun	5,452	1844	Ohio River
Orange	Paoli	18,848	1816	Prince William IV of Orange; Orange County, North Carolina
Owen	Spencer	19,223	1819	Abraham Owen, a hero of the Battle of Tippecanoe
Parke	Rockville	15,867	1821	Benjamin Parke, an Indiana judge
Perry	Cannelton	18,997	1814	Oliver Hazard Perry, a hero of the War of 1812
Pike	Petersburg	12,631	1817	Zebulon M. Pike, an officer in the War of 1812 and an American explorer
Porter	Valparaiso	138,243	1836	David Porter, an officer in the War of 1812
Posey	Mt. Vernon	26,344	1814	Thomas Posey, a governor of the Indiana Territory
Pulaski	Winamac	13,003	1822	Casimir Pulaski, a Polish patriot and an officer in the American Revolution
Putnam	Greencastle	32,519	1822	Israel Putnam, an officer in the American Revolution
Randolph	Winchester	27,143	1818	Thomas Randolph, a soldier in the Battle of Tippecanoe and an Attorney General of the Indiana Territory; or Randolph County, North Carolina
Ripley	Versailles	26,418	1818	Eleazar Wheelock Ripley, an officer in the War of 1812

The population figures give the most recent estimates.

County Name	County Seat	Population*	Year Organized	Named for
Rush	Rushville	18,488	1822	Benjamin Rush, a signer of the Declaration of Independence
St. Joseph	South Bend	255,431	1830	St. Joseph River
Scott	Scottsburg	22,138	1820	Charles Scott, an officer in the American Revolution and a governor of Kentucky
Shelby	Shelbyville	42,183	1822	Isaac Shelby, a governor of Kentucky
Spencer	Rockport	20,144	1818	Spier Spencer, a hero of the Battle of Tippecanoe
Starke	Knox	22,334	1850	John Stark, an officer in the French and Indian War and in the American Revolution
Steuben	Angola	29,272	1837	Friedrich von Steuben, a trainer of soldiers in the American Revolution
Sullivan	Sullivan	19,297	1817	Daniel Sullivan, a soldier in the American Revolution
Switzerland	Vevay	8,136	1814	Country of Switzerland
Tippecanoe	Lafayette	134,425	1826	Battle of Tippecanoe; Tippecanoe River
Tipton	Tipton	16,347	1844	John Tipton, a U.S. senator from Indiana
Union	Liberty	7,278	1821	Union of the United States
Vanderburgh	Evansville	167,445	1818	Henry Vanderburgh, a leader of the Northwest Territory Legislative Council in 1799, and later, a judge in the Indiana Territory
Vermillion	Newport	16,753	1824	Big Vermillion River
Vigo	Terre Haute	107,140	1818	Francis Vigo, a supplier of money and goods for the American Revolution
Wabash	Wabash	34,822	1835	Wabash River
Warren	Williamsport	8,200	1827	Joseph Warren, an officer in the American Revolution
Warrick	Boonville	48,625	1813	Jacob Warrick, a hero of the Battle of Tippecanoe
Washington	Salem	25,453	1814	George Washington, the first President of the United States
Wayne	Richmond	72,398	1811	Anthony Wayne, an officer in the American Revolution and at the Battle of Fallen Timbers, and a signer of the Treaty of Greenville
Wells	Bluffton	26,293	1837	William A. Wells, a scout for Anthony Wayne
White	Monticello	24,202	1834	Isaac White, an officer at the Battle of Tippecanoe
Whitley	Columbia City	29,040	1839	William Whitley of Kentucky

*The population figures give the most recent estimates.

ALMANAC

FACTS ABOUT INDIANA GOVERNORS

Governor	(birth/death)	Place of Birth	Political Party	Term
Governors of the Indiana Territory				
William Henry Harrison	(1773–1841)	Berkeley, Virginia	Whig	1800–1812
John Gibson	(1740–1822)	Lancaster, Pennsylvania	Dem.– Rep.*	1812–1813
Thomas L. Posey	(1750–1818)	Alexandria, Virginia	Dem.– Rep.*	1813–1816
Governors of the State of Indiana				
Jonathan Jennings	(1784–1834)	Hunterdon County, New Jersey	Dem.– Rep.*	1816–1822
Ratliff Boon	(1781–1844)	North Carolina or Georgia	Dem.– Rep.*	1822
William Hendricks	(1782–1850)	Ligonier, Pennsylvania	Dem.– Rep.*	1822–1825
James Brown Ray	(1794–1848)	Jefferson County, Kentucky	Dem.– Rep.*	1825–1831
Noah Noble	(1794–1844)	Clark County, Virginia	Dem.– Rep.*	1831–1837
David Wallace	(1799–1859)	Mifflin County, Pennsylvania	Whig	1837–1840
Samuel Bigger	(1802–1846)	Warren County, Ohio	Whig	1840–1843
James Whitcomb	(1795–1852)	Windsor, Vermont	Democratic	1843–1848
Paris C. Dunning	(1806–1884)	Greensboro, North Carolina	Democratic	1848–1849
Joseph A. Wright	(1809 or 1810–1867)	Washington, Pennsylvania	Democratic	1849–1857
Ashbel P. Willard	(1820–1860)	Oneida County, New York	Democratic	1857–1860
Abram A. Hammond	(1814–1874)	Vermont	Democratic	1860–1861
Henry S. Lane	(1811–1881)	Montgomery County, Kentucky	Republican	1861
Oliver P. Morton	(1823–1877)	Salisbury, Indiana	Republican	1861–1867
Conrad Baker	(1817–1885)	Franklin County, Pennsylvania	Republican	1867–1873
Thomas A. Hendricks	(1819–1885)	Zanesville, Ohio	Democratic	1873–1877
James D. Williams	(1808–1880)	Pickaway County, Ohio	Democratic	1877–1880
Isaac P. Gray	(1828–1895)	Chester County, Pennsylvania	Democratic	1880–1881
Albert G. Porter	(1824–1897)	Lawrenceburg, Indiana	Republican	1881–1885
Isaac P. Gray	(1828–1895)	Chester County, Pennsylvania	Democratic	1885–1889
Alvin P. Hovey	(1821–1891)	Mt. Vernon, Indiana	Republican	1889–1891
Ira J. Chase	(1834–1895)	Rockport, New York	Republican	1891–1893
Claude Matthews	(1845–1898)	Bath County, Kentucky	Democratic	1893–1897
James A. Mount	(1843–1901)	Montgomery County, Indiana	Republican	1897–1901
Winfield T. Durbin	(1847–1928)	Lawrenceburg, Indiana	Republican	1901–1905
J. Frank Hanley	(1863–1920)	St. Joseph, Illinois	Republican	1905–1909
Thomas R. Marshall	(1854–1925)	North Manchester, Indiana	Democratic	1909–1913
Samuel M. Ralston	(1857–1925)	Tuscarawas County, Ohio	Democratic	1913–1917
James P. Goodrich	(1864–1940)	Winchester, Indiana	Republican	1917–1921
Warren T. McCray	(1865–1938)	Kentland, Indiana	Republican	1921–1924

*Democratic-Republican

Governor	(birth/death)	Place of Birth	Political Party	Term
Emmett F. Branch	(1874–1932)	Martinsville, Indiana	Republican	1924–1925
Ed Jackson	(1873–1954)	Kokomo, Indiana	Republican	1925–1929
Harry G. Leslie	(1878–1937)	Lafayette, Indiana	Republican	1929–1933
Paul V. McNutt	(1891–1955)	Franklin, Indiana	Democratic	1933–1937
M. Clifford Townsend	(1884–1954)	Blackford County, Indiana	Democratic	1937–1941
Henry F. Schricker	(1883–1966)	North Judson, Indiana	Democratic	1941–1945
Ralph F. Gates	(1893–1978)	Columbia City, Indiana	Republican	1945–1949
Henry F. Schricker	(1883–1966)	North Judson, Indiana	Democratic	1949–1953
George N. Craig	(1909–)	Brazil, Indiana	Republican	1953–1957
Harold W. Handley	(1909–1972)	LaPorte, Indiana	Republican	1957–1961
Matthew E. Welsh	(1912–1995)	Detroit, Michigan	Democratic	1961–1965
Roger D. Branigin	(1902–1975)	Franklin, Indiana	Democratic	1965–1969
Edgar D. Whitcomb	(1917–)	Hayden, Indiana	Republican	1969–1973
Otis R. Bowen	(1918–)	Rochester, Indiana	Republican	1973–1981
Robert D. Orr	(1917–)	Ann Arbor, Michigan	Republican	1981–1989
Evan Bayh	(1955–)	Terre Haute, Indiana	Democratic	1989–1997

Some Famous People in Indiana History

This list gives facts about the famous people in Indiana history that you met in this book. The page number tells where you can read about each person. Also listed are some other famous Hoosiers you might like to know about.

A

Adams, John Ottis *1851–1927* Artist from Amity. He was best known for his statues and landscape paintings.

Ade, George *1866–1944* Newspaper writer and essayist born in Kentland. He worked for the *Chicago Daily News*. p. 229

Allen, Joseph P. *1937–* Space-shuttle astronaut from Crawfordsville. p. 207

Anspaugh, David *1946–* Movie director and producer from Decatur. His movies *Hoosiers* and *Rudy* are both set in Indiana.

Apperson brothers Elmer and Edgar Apperson started one of the first automobile factories in Indiana. They were partners with Elwood Haynes. p. 182

B

Bacon, Hiram *1800–1880* Indianapolis station-master on the Underground Railroad. p. 166

Ball brothers Edmund, William, Lucius, George, and Frank Ball owned one of the nation's largest glassmaking factories, in Muncie. They gave money to start Ball State University. p. 177

Bayh, Birch *1928–* U.S. Senator from Indiana who served in Congress from 1963 to 1981. p. 259

Bayh, Evan *1955–* Indiana governor from 1989 to 1997. He is the son of Birch Bayh. p. 259

Bell, Lawrence *1894–1956* Founder of Bell Aircraft Corporation, maker of helicopters, America's first jet airplane, and the *Bell X-1*, the first jet airplane to fly faster than the speed of sound.

Bird, Larry *1956–* Professional basketball player from French Lick. He was the National Basketball Association's Most Valuable Player three years in a row, from 1984 to 1986. p. 230

Black, Edward *1800s* Union army drummer from Hagerstown. He was one of the youngest Hoosiers in the Civil War. p. 167

Blue Jacket *1700s* Shawnee leader defeated at the Battle of Fallen Timbers. p. 106

Borman, Frank *1928–* Astronaut from Gary. He orbited the moon in *Apollo 8* in 1968. p. 206

Botts, Walter *1900–1972* Model for the famous Uncle Sam poster by James Montgomery Flagg, which urged Americans to enlist in the U.S. Army during World War I. He was born in Sullivan.

Brokenburr, Robert L. *1886–1974* African American state senator who worked to pass civil rights laws in Indiana. p. 205

C

Carmichael, Hoagy (KAR•my•kuhl, HOH•gee) *1899–1981* Songwriter from Bloomington. p. 230

Chapman, John *1774–1845* Pioneer who traveled through the Middle West planting apple seeds and tending apple orchards. He is known to most as Johnny Appleseed.

Clark, George Rogers *1752–1818* Leader of American forces that defeated the British at Fort Sackville, Vincennes, during the American Revolution. This victory helped the Americans gain control of the Northwest Territory. p. 84

Coats, Daniel *1943–* U.S. Senator from Indiana. p. 260

Coffin, Katherine *1803–1881* An Underground Railroad worker also known as Aunt Katie. She and her husband, Levi, were stationmasters and helped runaway slaves escape. p. 165

Coffin, Levi *1789–1877* One of Indiana's best-known stationmasters on the Underground Railroad. p. 165

Colfax, Schuyler *1823–1885* Vice President from South Bend. He served under President Ulysses S. Grant from 1869 to 1873. p. 258

Conn, C. G. *1844–1931* Entrepreneur from Elkhart. After the Civil War, he started one of the first companies in the country to make musical instruments. p. 178

Conner, William *1777–1855* Pioneer in central Indiana. Today his settlement, Conner Prairie, is a living history museum. p. 150

D

Davis, Jim *1945–*   Artist from Marion. He created the comic strip "Garfield."

Dean, James *1931–1955* Movie actor born in Marion.

Debs, Eugene *1855–1926* Railroad union leader from Terre Haute. He ran for President in 1900, 1904, 1908, 1912, and 1920.

Dreiser, Theodore *1871–1945* Author from Terre Haute and brother of Paul Dresser. Paul Americanized the family name.

Dresser, Paul *1858–1906* Songwriter from Terre Haute. He wrote "On the Banks of the Wabash, Far Away," Indiana's state song. p. 222

Duesenberg brothers Fred and August, Indianapolis automobile makers. p. 184

E

Eads, James Buchanan *1820–1887* Engineer and inventor from Lawrenceburg. He designed armored boats during the Civil War and the first iron bridge across the Mississippi River.

F

Fairbanks, Charles W. *1852–1918* Vice President from Indianapolis. He served under President Theodore Roosevelt from 1905 to 1909. p. 258

Forsyth, William *1854–1935* Artist from Indianapolis. He helped start the Herron School of Art in Indianapolis, Indiana's oldest and largest art school. p. 230

G

Gary, Elbert H. *1846–1927* Head of the United States Steel Corporation when the company built a mill and town in the Calumet region. The city of Gary is named for him. p. 178

Goldsmith, Stephen *1946–* Mayor of Indianapolis.

Grissom, Virgil ("Gus") *1926–1967* Astronaut from Mitchell. He was the second American in space. p. 206

Gruelle, John Barton *1880–1938* Artist and writer from Indianapolis. He wrote the Raggedy Ann and Raggedy Andy stories, about a pair of rag dolls.

H

Hall, Katie Beatrice *1938–* First African American woman from Indiana elected to the U.S. Congress. She was one of several members of Congress who introduced the bill that made the birthday of Dr. Martin Luther King, Jr., a federal holiday. p. 260

Hamilton, Henry *1740?–1796* British general who was defeated at Fort Sackville by George Rogers Clark in the American Revolution. p. 83

Harper, Ida Husted *1851–1931* Newspaper reporter from Fairfield. She worked to help women gain the right to vote. p. 192

Harris, Chapman *1800s* African American conductor on the Underground Railroad. He ferried runaway slaves across the Ohio River. p. 165

Harrison, Benjamin *1833–1901* Twenty-third President of the United States. He fought in the Civil War. Later, as President, he helped Civil War soldiers get payments from the government. p. 257

Harrison, William Henry *1773–1841* Ninth President of the United States. Earlier he led American soldiers at the Battle of Tippecanoe. He was also a commander in the War of 1812 and the first governor of the Indiana Territory. p. 109

Harroun, Ray *1878–1968* Winner of the first Indianapolis 500 automobile race, in 1911. p. 184

Hatcher, Richard *1933–* Mayor of Gary from 1968 to 1988. He was one of the first African Americans elected as mayor of a large United States city. p. 246

Haynes, Elwood *1857–1925* Inventor from Kokomo. He test-drove one of the first automobiles. p. 182

Hendricks, Thomas *1819–1885* Vice President from Indianapolis. He served under President Grover Cleveland in 1885. p. 258

I

Indiana, Robert *1928–* Artist from New Castle. p. 230

J

Jackson, Janet *1966–* Musician from Gary. p. 230

Jackson, Michael *1958–* Musician from Gary. p. 230

Jenckes, Virginia Ellis *1877–1975* First Indiana woman in the House of Representatives, elected in 1932. She was from Terre Haute. p. 260

Jennings, Jonathan *1784–1834* First governor of the state of Indiana. He was one of the main writers of the state constitution in 1816. p. 118

K

Kautsky, Frank *1888?–1959* Grocer who sponsored one of the first professional basketball teams in Indiana. p. 204

Kelley, Oliver H. *1826–1913* Founder of the Grange organization for farmers. p. 175

Knight, Bob *1940–* Coach of the Indiana University basketball team since 1971. p. 230

L

La Salle, René-Robert Cavelier (luh•SAL) *1643–1687* First European to reach what is now Indiana. He also explored the Mississippi River valley and claimed the land for France. p. 72

Lauter, Sara *?–1963* Leader from Indianapolis who worked to help women gain the right to vote. p. 192

Letterman, David *1947–* Television host and comedian from Indianapolis.

Lilly, Eli *1839–1898* Business leader in Indianapolis. The pharmaceutical company he started in 1876 became one of the world's largest. p. 180

Lincoln, Abraham *1809–1865* Sixteenth President of the United States. He grew up in Indiana. p. 128

Little Turtle *1752–1812* Chief of the Miamis who defeated American soldiers at Kekionga in 1791. p. 105

Long, Shelley *1949–* Movie and television actor.

Lugar, Richard G. *1932–* U.S. Senator from Indiana and former mayor of Indianapolis. p. 260

M

Mapes, Arthur Franklin *1913–1986* Poet who wrote the state poem, "Indiana."

Marshall, Thomas *1854–1925* Vice President from North Manchester. He served under President Woodrow Wilson from 1913 to 1921. p. 259

McCormick, Cyrus *1809–1884* Inventor of a reaping machine for harvesting wheat. p. 173

McNutt, Paul V. *1891–1955* Governor of Indiana during the Great Depression. p. 194

Mellencamp, John *1951–* Musician from Seymour. p. 230

Morgan, John Hunt *1825–1864* Confederate general who led soldiers into southern Indiana during the Civil War. p. 168

Morisson, Sarah Parke *1833–1919* First woman in the nation to graduate from a state university—Indiana University in Bloomington in 1869.

Morton, Oliver P. *1823–1877* Governor of Indiana during the Civil War. p. 167

O

Oliver, James *1823–1908* Inventor of the chilled iron plow. He owned the largest plow factory in Indiana. p. 173

Owen, Robert *1771–1858* Wealthy entrepreneur. He bought the community of Harmonie from George Rapp in 1824 and renamed it New Harmony. p. 131

Owen, Robert Dale *1801–1877* Son of New Harmony's Robert Owen. He was the principal writer of Indiana's current constitution. He also wrote a letter to President Abraham Lincoln calling for an end to slavery. p. 169

P

Pauley, Jane *1950–* Television newscaster from Indianapolis.

Pontiac *1720–1769* Ottawa chief who led Indian attacks on British forts in 1763. p. 80

Porter, Cole *1893–1964* Songwriter from Peru, Indiana. Many of his songs were written for musical shows. p. 230

Purdue, John *1802–1876* Community leader in Lafayette. He gave money and land to the state's first agricultural school, built in Lafayette. It was later named Purdue University. p. 174

Pyle, Ernie *1900–1945* Newspaper reporter from Dana. He wrote about the experiences of soldiers in World War II. p. 203

Q

Quayle, J. Danforth *1947–* Vice President from Huntington. He served under President George Bush from 1989 to 1993. p. 258

R

Ralston, Alexander *1771–1827* Surveyor of the site selected for Indiana's capital, Indianapolis, in 1821. p. 122

Rapp, George *1757–1847* Minister who, with his followers, started the community of Harmonie in 1814. p. 131

Redenbacher, Orville (RED•uhn•bah•ker) *1907–1995* Entrepreneur born in Brazil, Indiana. He began one of the most successful popcorn businesses in the United States. p. 54

Richardson, Henry J., Jr. *1902–1983* African American lawyer who worked to end segregation in Indiana's schools. p. 205

Riley, James Whitcomb *1849–1916* Known as the Hoosier Poet. He wrote more than 1,000 poems about the state he loved, Indiana. He was born in Greenfield and lived in Indianapolis. p. 229

Robertson, Oscar *1938–* Basketball player from Indianapolis. He was co-captain of the 1960 Olympic basketball team and was a star in the National Basketball Association. p. 230

Rockne, Knute (RAHK•nee, NOOT) *1888–1931* Coach of the Notre Dame University football team in the early 1900s. p. 230

Ross, Jerry *1948–* Space-shuttle astronaut from Crown Point. p. 207

Rudolph, Wilma *1940–1994* Olympic track and field champion. She won three gold medals at the 1960 Olympics. p. 231

S

St. Clair, Arthur *1736–1818* First governor of the Northwest Territory. p. 105

Sanders, "Colonel" Harland *1890–1980* Entrepreneur born in Henryville. He started the famous Kentucky Fried Chicken fast-food restaurants.

Sewall, May Wright *1844–1920* Leader from Indianapolis who worked to help women gain the right to vote. p. 192

Slocum, Frances *1773–1847* Pioneer who lived much of her life with the Delawares.

Steele, Theodore C. *1847–1926* Artist from Owen County. He painted nine of the portraits in the Governors' Portraits Collection. p. 230

Stratton-Porter, Geneva *1868–1924* Author whose books show her love of nature and geography. She is known to most as Gene Stratton-Porter. p. 32

Studebaker brothers Clem and Henry Studebaker were wagonmakers from South Bend. They later became leading manufacturers of automobiles. p. 183

T

Tarkington, Booth *1869–1946* Author who described life in Indianapolis. Some of his books were written for young people. p. 229

Taylor, "Major" Marshall *1878–1932* Bicyclist from Indianapolis. He was one of the best-known African American athletes at the beginning of the 1900s. p. 230

Teale, Edwin Way *1899–1980* Author who wrote about nature and the outdoors. p. 126

Tecumseh (tuh•KUM•suh) *1768–1813* Shawnee leader of Indians in the Northwest Territory. He wanted to form a strong Indian confederation. p. 110

Tenskwatawa (ten•SKWAHT•uh•wah) *1768–1834* Shawnee leader known as the Prophet. He worked with his brother Tecumseh. p. 111

Townsend, James M. *1841–1913* Minister and teacher who lived in Evansville and Richmond. He was the first African American elected to the Indiana General Assembly.

V

Vawter, Will *1871–1941* Artist from Greenfield. He drew many of the pictures for James Whitcomb Riley's books of poetry.

Vonnegut, Kurt, Jr. *1922–* Author from Indianapolis.

Von Tilzer, Albert *1878–1956* Musician from Indianapolis. He wrote the music for the classic baseball song "Take Me Out to the Ball-Game."

Voss, Janice *1956–* Space-shuttle astronaut from South Bend. She was the first woman from Indiana chosen to fly in space. p. 207

W

Walker, Madam C. J. *1867–1919* Indianapolis entrepreneur from Louisiana. She started her own business making hair care products for women. She became one of the country's wealthiest women. p. 180

Wallace, Lew *1827–1905* Author from Brookville. He was also a Civil War general.

Wayne, Anthony *1745–1796* General of the U.S. Army. He led the victory over the Miamis at the Battle of Fallen Timbers in 1794. He was known to his soldiers as Mad Anthony. p. 106

West, Jessamyn *1902–1984* Author of many books with Indiana settings. p. 229

White, Ryan *1971–1990* High school student who died of AIDS. Before his death in Cicero, he worked to educate people about the disease.

White Beaver *1600s* Native American guide. He led La Salle into what is now Indiana in 1679. p. 73

Williams, Donald E. *1942–* Space-shuttle astronaut from Lafayette. p. 207

Williams, Matt *1951–* Writer and television producer from Evansville.

Willkie, Wendell L. *1892–1944* Candidate for President in 1940. The Elwood citizen lost the election to Franklin D. Roosevelt. p. 258

Wooden, John *1910–* Former basketball player and coach from Martinsville. He played at Purdue University and became the basketball coach at the University of California, Los Angeles. p. 230

Wright, Wilbur *1867–1912* He and his brother, Orville, flew the first powered aircraft at Kitty Hawk, North Carolina, in 1903. Wilbur was born on a farm near New Castle. p. 193

GAZETTEER

The Gazetteer is a geographical dictionary that will help you locate places discussed in this book. The page number tells where each place appears on a map.

A

Anderson A city in eastern Indiana, near Mounds State Park; the county seat of Madison County. (40°N, 86°W) p. 64

Angel Mounds State Historic Site A historic site near Evansville, where visitors can see earthworks built by Mound Builders about 1,000 years ago. (38°N, 87°W) p. 64

Angola (an•GOH•luh) The county seat of Steuben County, in northeastern Indiana. (42°N, 85°W) p. 25

Attica (AT•ih•kuh) A city in Fountain County, in western Indiana. (40°N, 87°W) p. 146

B

Bass Lake A lake in Starke County, in northern Indiana. p. A15

Bedford A city in southern Indiana, near Bluespring Caverns; the county seat of Lawrence County. (39°N, 86°W) p. 41

Beech Grove A city in Marion County, in central Indiana. (40°N, 86°W) p. 25

Big Blue River A tributary of the East Fork White River. p. A15

Bloomington The county seat of Monroe County, in south-central Indiana; home of Indiana University. (39°N, 87°W) p. 146

Blue River A river in southern Indiana and a tributary of the Ohio River. p. 39

Bluespring Caverns A cavern in southern Indiana; one of the longest underground rivers in the United States flows through this cavern. (39°N, 86°W) p. 41

Boonville The county seat of Warrick County, in southwestern Indiana. (38°N, 87°W) p. 64

Bourbon A town in Marshall County, in northern Indiana. (41°N, 86°W) p. A14

Brookville Lake A large lake in southeastern Indiana. p. A15

Brownsburg A town in Hendricks County, in central Indiana. (40°N, 86°W) p. 25

C

Cagles Mill Lake A large lake in south-central Indiana. p. A15

Carmel A town in Hamilton County, in central Indiana. (40°N, 86°W) p. 25

Cecil M. Harden Reservoir A reservoir in western Indiana; formed by a dam built across Raccoon Creek. p. A15

Central Till Plain A natural region covering the central part of Indiana. p. 35

Charlestown A city in Clark County, in southern Indiana. (38°N, 86°W) p. 219

Clarksville A town in Clark County, in southern Indiana. (38°N, 86°W) p. 110

Columbia City The county seat of Whitley County, in northeastern Indiana. (41°N, 85°W) p. 25

Columbus The county seat of Bartholomew County, in south-central Indiana. (39°N, 86°W) p. 54

Connersville The county seat of Fayette County, in eastern Indiana. (40°N, 85°W) p. 54

Corydon The county seat of Harrison County, in southern Indiana; capital of Indiana Territory, 1813–1816; capital of the state of Indiana until 1825. (38°N, 86°W) p. 110

Crawfordsville The county seat of Montgomery County, in west-central Indiana. (40°N, 87°W) p. 54

D

Decatur (dih•KAY•tuhr) The county seat of Adams County, in eastern Indiana. (41°N, 85°W) p. 54

E

Eagle Creek Reservoir A reservoir in Marion County, in central Indiana. p. 25

East Chicago A city in Lake County, in northeastern Indiana; located on Lake Michigan. (42°N, 87°W) p. 219

East Fork White River A tributary of the White River. p. 39

Eel River A tributary of the White River. p. A15

Elkhart A city in Elkhart County, in northern Indiana. (42°N, 86°W) p. 146

Evansville The county seat of Vanderburgh County, in southwestern Indiana; located on the Ohio River. (38°N, 88°W) p. 37

F

Falls of the Ohio An area of rapids on the Ohio River; near where Louisville, Kentucky, and Jeffersonville, Indiana, are now located. (38°N, 86°W) p. 84

Flatrock River A tributary of the East Fork White River. p. A15

Fontanet A town in Vigo County, in western Indiana. (40°N, 87°W) p. 25

Fort Harrison A fort built on the Wabash River, near what is now Terre Haute. (39°N, 87°W) p. 110

GAZETTEER

Fort Miami An early trading post and fort built by the French in 1721, near present-day Fort Wayne. (41°N, 85°W) p. 79

Fort Ouiatenon (wee•AHT•uh•nohn) The first French trading post in Indiana; it was built in 1717 near present-day Lafayette. (40°N, 87°W) p. 79

Fort Sackville The name given to the fort at Vincennes after it was captured by Henry Hamilton's army during the American Revolution. p. 84

Fort St. Joseph An early fort built near present-day South Bend. (42°N, 86°W) p. 80

Fort Wayne The county seat of Allen County, in northeastern Indiana; site of the early Miami Indian settlement called Kekionga. (41°N, 85°W) p. 37

Fountain City A town in Wayne County, in eastern Indiana. (40°N, 85°W) p. 165

Frankfort The county seat of Clinton County, in central Indiana. (40°N, 87°W) p. 25

French Lick A town in Orange County, in southern Indiana. (39°N, 87°W) p. A14

G

Gary A city in Lake County, in northwestern Indiana; located on Lake Michigan, it is an important steel-producing center. (42°N, 87°W) p. 37

Geist Reservoir A reservoir in central Indiana. p. 25

Goshen (GO•shuhn) The county seat of Elkhart County, in northern Indiana. (42°N, 86°W) p. 54

Great Lakes Plain A broad, lowland plain covering the northern one-third of Indiana. p. 35

Greencastle The county seat of Putnam County, in west-central Indiana. (40°N, 87°W) p. 146

Greenfield The county seat of Hancock County, in central Indiana. (40°N, 86°W) p. 25

Greenwood A city in Johnson County, in central Indiana. (40°N, 86°W) p. 25

Griffin A town in Posey County, in southwestern Indiana. (38°N, 88°W) p. 95

H

Hammond A city in Lake County, in northwestern Indiana. (42°N, 87°W) p. 54

Hardy Lake A lake in southeastern Indiana. p. A15

Hoosier National Forest A national forest in southern Indiana; the state's largest forest. p. 41

Huntington The county seat of Huntington County, in northeastern Indiana. (41°N, 85°W) p. 54

Huntington Lake A large lake in northern Indiana; formed by a dam built across the Wabash River. p. A15

I

Indianapolis The state capital of Indiana since 1825, and the state's largest city; the county seat of Marion County, in central Indiana. (40°N, 86°W) p. 37

Iroquois River (IR•uh•kwoy) A river that begins in northwestern Indiana and flows into the Kankakee River, in Illinois. p. 39

J

Jasper The county seat of Dubois County, in southwestern Indiana. (38°N, 87°W) p. 43

Jeffersonville The county seat of Clark County, in southern Indiana; located on the Ohio River across from Louisville, Kentucky. (38°N, 86°W) p. 43

K

Kankakee River (kaing•kuh•KEE) A large river that begins in northern Indiana and flows southwest into Illinois. p. 39

Kekionga (kee•kee•ohn•GUH) A settlement built by the Miamis at the headwaters of the Maumee River, where the city of Fort Wayne is presently located. p. 84

Kendallville A city in Noble County, in northeastern Indiana. (41°N, 85°W) p. 25

Kokomo (KOH•kuh•moh) The county seat of Howard County, in north-central Indiana. (40°N, 86°W) p. 37

L

La Crosse A town in LaPorte County, in northern Indiana. (41°N, 87°W) p. 25

Lafayette (lah•fee•ET) The county seat of Tippecanoe County, in west-central Indiana; home of Purdue University. (40°N, 87°W) p. 37

Lake Freeman A lake in northern Indiana; formed by a dam built across the Tippecanoe River. p. A15

Lake Manitou (MAN•uh•too) A lake in Fulton County, in northern Indiana. p. A15

Lake Michigan One of the five Great Lakes; forms part of Indiana's northern border. p. 25

Lake Shafer A lake in White County, in northwestern Indiana; formed by a dam built across the Tippecanoe River. p. A15

Lake Wawasee (wah•wuh•SEE) A large lake in Kosciusko County, in northern Indiana. p. 39

LaPorte The county seat of LaPorte County, in northern Indiana. (42°N, 87°W) p. 181

Laughery Creek A tributary of the Ohio River. p. A15

Lawrenceburg The county seat of Dearborn County, in southeastern Indiana; located on the Ohio River. (39°N, 85°W) p. 54

Leavenworth (LEH•vuhn•wuhrth) A town in Crawford County, in southern Indiana. (38°N, 86°W) p. 165

Little Pigeon Creek A tributary of the Ohio River. p. A15

Logansport The county seat of Cass County, in north-central Indiana. (41°N, 86°W) p. 146

Lost River A tributary of the East Fork White River. p. A15

M

Madison The county seat of Jefferson County, in southeastern Indiana; located on the Ohio River. (39°N, 85°W) p. 43

Marion The county seat of Grant County, in north-central Indiana. (41°N, 86°W) p. 25

Maumee River (maw•MEE) A river that begins in northeastern Indiana and flows into the state of Ohio. p. 39

Maxinkuckee Lake (max•in•KOO•kee) A lake in Marshall County, in northern Indiana. p. A15

Michigan City A port city in LaPorte County, in northern Indiana; located on Lake Michigan. (42°N, 87°W) p. 54

Mississinewa Lake (mih•suh•SIN•uh•wah) A lake in northern Indiana; formed by a dam built across the Mississinewa River. p. A15

Mississinewa River (mih•suh•SIN•uh•wah) A tributary of the Wabash River. p. 39

Mitchell A city in Lawrence County, in southern Indiana. (39°N, 86°W) p. 146

Monroe Lake A large lake in southern Indiana; formed by a dam built across a tributary of the East Fork White River. p. 39

Monticello (mahnt•uh•SEL•oh) The county seat of White County, in northwestern Indiana; located on the Tippecanoe River. (41°N, 87°W) p. 43

Mooresville A town in Morgan County, in central Indiana. (40°N, 86°W) p. 25

Morse Reservoir A large reservoir in central Indiana, north of Indianapolis; formed by a dam built across a tributary of the East Fork White River. p. 39

Moscow A town in Rush County, in east-central Indiana. (39°N, 86°W) p. 25

Mounds State Park A state park near Anderson, where visitors can see earthworks built by Mound Builders more than 2,000 years ago. p. 64

Mount Vernon The county seat of Posey County, in southwestern Indiana; located on the Ohio River. (38°N, 88°W) p. 64

Muncie The county seat of Delaware County, in east-central Indiana; home of Ball State University. (40°N, 85°W) p. 43

Muscatatuck River (muhs•kuh•TAH•tuck) A tributary of the East Fork White River. p. A15

N

Napoleon (nuh•POH•lee•uhn) A town in Ripley County, in southeastern Indiana. (39°N, 85°W) p. 25

New Albany The county seat of Floyd County, in southern Indiana; located on the Ohio River across from Louisville, Kentucky. (38°N, 86°W) p. 54

New Harmony A town in Posey County, in southwestern Indiana; founded in 1814 as Harmonie by George Rapp and his followers, who were called Harmonists; the town was sold to Robert Owen in 1825 and renamed New Harmony. (38°N, 88°W) p. 25

Noblesville The county seat of Hamilton County, in central Indiana. (40°N, 86°W) p. 37

O

Ohio River A large river that forms Indiana's southern border. p. 39

Orleans A town in Orange County, in southern Indiana. (39°N, 86°W) p. A14

Owensville A town in Gibson County, in southwestern Indiana. (38°N, 88°W) p. 95

P

Paoli (pay•OH•lee) The county seat of Orange County, in southern Indiana. (39°N, 86°W) p. 25

Patoka Lake (puh•TOH•kuh) A lake on the Patoka River in southern Indiana. p. 39

Patoka River (puh•TOH•kuh) A tributary of the Wabash River. p. 39

Peru The county seat of Miami County, in north-central Indiana. (41°N, 86°W) p. 54

Pigeon Creek A tributary of the Ohio River. p. A15

Pigeon River A river in northeastern Indiana that flows into St. Joseph of the Lake River. p. A15

Pine Lake A lake in LaPorte County, in northeastern Indiana. p. A15

Plainfield A town in Hendricks County, in central Indiana. (40°N, 86°W) p. 25

Plymouth The county seat of Marshall County, in northern Indiana. (41°N, 86°W) p. 25

Portland The county seat of Jay County, in eastern Indiana. (40°N, 85°W) p. 54

Prairie Creek Reservoir A reservoir in eastern Indiana. p. A15

Princeton The county seat of Gibson County, in southwestern Indiana. (38°N, 88°W) p. 95

Prophetstown (PRAHF•uhts•taun) An Indian village that was built on the Tippecanoe River, near where Lafayette is today; it served as the capital of Tecumseh's Indian confederation. p. 111

R

Raccoon Creek A tributary of the Wabash River. p. A15

Rensselaer (REN•suh•luhr) The county seat of Jasper County, in northwestern Indiana. (41°N, 87°W) p. 54

Richmond The county seat of Wayne County, in eastern Indiana. (40°N, 85°W) p. 37

Rochester The county seat of Fulton County, in northern Indiana. (41°N, 86°W) p. 25

Rushville The county seat of Rush County, in east-central Indiana. (40°N, 85°W) p. 25

S

St. Bernice A town in Vermillion County, in western Indiana. (40°N, 88°W) p. 25

St. Joseph of the Lake River A river that flows across northern Indiana. p. A15

St. Joseph River A river in eastern Indiana and a tributary of the Maumee River. p. 39

St. Marys River A tributary of the Maumee River. p. 39

Salamonie Lake (SAL•uh•moh•nee) A lake in northern Indiana; formed by a dam built across the Salamonie River. p. A15

Salamonie River (SAL•uh•moh•nee) A tributary of the Wabash River. p. 39

Salem The county seat of Washington County, in southern Indiana. (39°N, 86°W) p. 25

Salt Creek A tributary of the East Fork White River. p. 41

Scottsburg The county seat of Scott County, in southeastern Indiana. (39°N, 86°W) p. 25

Shelbyville The county seat of Shelby County, in central Indiana. (40°N, 86°W) p. 54

Shoals (SHOHLZ) The county seat of Martin County, in southwestern Indiana. (39°N, 87°W) p. 25

South Bend The county seat of St. Joseph County, in northern Indiana; home of the University of Notre Dame. (42°N, 86°W) p. 35

Southern Hills and Lowlands A natural region that covers much of south-central Indiana. p. 35

Speedway A town in Marion County, in central Indiana; site of the Indianapolis Motor Speedway. (40°N, 86°W) p. 25

Sugar Creek A tributary of the East Fork White River. p. A15

Sugar Creek A tributary of the Wabash River. p. A15

T

Ten O'Clock Line A boundary line set up by the Treaty of Fort Wayne that separated United States land from Indian land. p. 110

Terre Haute (TER•uh HOHT) The county seat of Vigo County, in western Indiana; home of Indiana State University. (39°N, 87°W) p. 37

Tippecanoe River (tih•pee•kuh•NOO) A tributary of the Wabash River. p. 39

V

Vernon The county seat of Jennings County, in southeastern Indiana. (39°N, 86°W) p. 146

Versailles (vuhr•SAYLZ) The county seat of Ripley County, in southeastern Indiana. (39°N, 85°W) p. 25

Vincennes (vin•SENZ) The county seat of Knox County, in southwestern Indiana; site of an early fort and the first permanent European settlement in Indiana; capital of Indiana Territory until 1813. (39°N, 88°W) p. 43

W

Wabash (WAW•bash) The county seat of Wabash County, in northern Indiana. (41°N, 86°W) p. 146

Wabash River (WAW•bash) The longest river in Indiana; flows west across the state from Ohio before turning south and forming part of the Indiana-Illinois border. p. 39

Warsaw The county seat of Kosciusko County, in northern Indiana. (41°N, 86°W) p. 54

Washington The county seat of Daviess County, in southwestern Indiana. (39°N, 87°W) p. 146

Westfield A town in Hamilton County, in central Indiana. (40°N, 86°W) p. 165

White River A river that flows southwest across southern Indiana and is a tributary of the Wabash River. p. A15

Whitewater River A river in southeastern Indiana that flows into Ohio. p. 39

Whiting (WYT•ing) A city in Lake County, in northwestern Indiana; located on Lake Michigan. (42°N, 87°W) p. 219

Wildcat Creek A tributary of the Wabash River. p. A15

Williamsport The county seat of Warren County, in western Indiana. (40°N, 87°W) p. 146

GLOSSARY

The Glossary contains important social studies words and their definitions. Each word is respelled as it would be in a dictionary. When you see this mark ´ after a syllable, pronounce that syllable with more force than the other syllables. The page number at the end of the definition tells where to find the word in your book.

add, āce, câre, pälm; end, ēqual; it, īce; odd, ōpen, ôrder; tŏŏk, pōol; up, bûrn; yōō as u in fuse; oil; pout; ə as a in above, e in sicken, i in possible; o in melon, u in circus; check; ring; thin; this; zh as in vision

A

agency (ā´jən•sē) A group of state officials who make sure laws are obeyed. p. 249

agriculture (ag´ri•kul•chər) Farming. p. 174

ally (al´ī) A partner, friend, or helper, especially in time of war. p. 79

amendment (ə•mend´mənt) Any addition or change to the Constitution. p. 192

automobile (ô•tə•mə•bēl´) A vehicle that can move by itself, powered by its own engine; a car. p. 182

aviation (ā•vē•ā´shən) The making and flying of airplanes. p. 193

B

band (band) A small group of families that lived and worked together long ago. p. 61

barge (bärj) A large, flat-bottomed boat. p. 236

bill (bil) A plan for a new law. p. 251

Bill of Rights (bil uv rīts) A list of rights and freedoms for citizens. p. 247

bituminous (bə•tōō´mə•nəs) Soft coal. p. 54

boundary line (boun´drē līn) An imaginary line that tells where a border is. p. 110

broadleaf (brôd´lēf) A tree that has wide, flat leaves that fall off each year before the winter. p. 55

budget (buj´it) A written plan for spending and saving money. p. 248

C

canal (kə•nal´) A narrow waterway built to connect other waterways or bodies of water. p. 143

cargo (kär´go) Goods being shipped. p. 236

cause (kôz) Something that makes something else happen. p. 115

cavalry (kav´əl•rē) Soldiers on horses. p. 168

census (sen´səs) An official government count of people. p. 109

centennial (sen•ten´ē•əl) The one-hundredth anniversary of a special event. p. 184

century (sen´chər•ē) A period of 100 years. p. 71

citizen (sit´ə•zən) A member of a country, a state, or a city or town. p. 19

civics (siv´iks) The study of citizenship. p. 23

civil (siv´əl) Of or about citizens, or people who are not part of the military. p. 69

civil rights (siv´əl rīts) The rights of citizens to be treated equally. p. 205

civil war (siv´əl wôr) A fight between groups of citizens of what was once one country. p. 167

claim (klām) Land that you say is yours. p. 128

climate (klī´mit) The kind of weather a place has most often, year after year. p. 42

colonist (kol´ə•nist) A person who lives in a colony. p. 78

colony (kol´ə•nē) A settlement set up and ruled by another country. p. 72

commercial farm (kə•mûr´shəl färm) A farm owned by a company. p. 234

common council (kom´ən koun´səl) The legislative branch of city government in Indiana. p. 254

commute (kə•myōōt´) To travel to and from. p. 204

compass rose (kum´pəs rōz) The direction marker on a map. p. 25

compromise (kom´prə•mīz) To give up some of what you want in order to reach an agreement. p. 123

Confederacy (kən•fed´ər•ə•sē) The group of Southern states that made up the Confederate States of America during the Civil War. p. 167

confederation (kən•fed•ə•rā´shən) A large group made up of several smaller groups that have the same goals and want to work together. p. 105

conflict (kon´flikt) A fight or disagreement. p. 105

Congress (kong´gris) The part of the United States government that makes the nation's laws. p. 104

conserve (kən•sûrv´) To save a resource. p. 240

constitution (kon•stə•too´shən) A plan of government that describes the basic laws and tells how the government is to work. p. 119

consumer good (kən•soo•mər good) A product made for personal use. p. 193

convention (kən•ven´shən) A special meeting or assembly held for a certain purpose. p. 120

cooperate (kō•op´ə•rāt) To work together. p. 62

Corn Belt (kôrn belt) A region in the middle part of the United States. It grows more corn than any other region in the world. p. 234

council (koun´səl) A group of advisers. p. 69

county commissioner (koun´tē kə•mish´ən•ər) One of the people who govern the county by making ordinances, or laws, for the county and by making sure the laws are obeyed. p. 252

county council (koun´tē koun´səl) The group of people who decide how the county's money will be spent. p. 252

county seat (koun´tē sēt) The town or city that is the center of government for a county. p. 252

culture (kul´chər) A group's way of dressing, speaking, behaving, and believing. p. 63

D

dam (dam) A wall built across a river to help control flooding. p. 41

debt (det) The owing of money. p. 210

deed (dēd) A document that describes a piece of land and tells who owns it. p. 104

defense plant (di•fens´ plant) A factory that makes things needed to defend a country. p. 202

delegate (del´ə•git) Someone chosen by people to represent them at a meeting. p. 119

demand (di•mand´) A desire. p. 210

democracy (di•mok´rə•sē) A government that is run by the people it governs. p. 238

depression (di•presh´ən) A time when there are few jobs and people have little money. p. 193

diverse economy (di•vûrs´ i•kon´ə•mē) An economy with many kinds of industries. p. 210

downstream (doun´strēm´) In the direction of a river's current. p. 142

drought (drout) A period with little rain. p. 44

E

earthworks (ûrth´wûrkz) Huge mounds, or piles, of earth made by people. p. 64

economy (i•kon´ə•mē) The ways people use resources and make choices to meet their needs. p. 23

effect (i•fekt´) What results from a cause. p. 115

enabling act (in•ā´bling akt) A special law that let a territory become a state. p. 119

entrepreneur (än•trə•prə•nûr´) A person who starts and runs a business. p. 179

environment (in•vī´rən•mənt) The place in which people live. p. 20

equator (i•kwā´tər) An imaginary line that runs east and west around the middle of the Earth. p. 36

executive branch (ig•zek´yə•tiv branch) The branch of government that sees that laws are carried out. p. 249

export (eks´pôrt) To send something to be sold in other places. p. 236

extinct (ik•stingkt´) No longer living. p. 63

F

fable (fā´bəl) A story that teaches a lesson. p. 229

fact (fakt) A statement that can be checked and proved true. p. 195

federal government (fed´ər•əl guv´ərn•mənt) The national government. p. 257

fertile (fûr´təl) Good for growing crops. Describes rich soil. p. 53

flatboat (flat´bōt) A large wooden boat with a flat bottom and square ends. p. 85

flow chart (flō chärt) A drawing that shows the order in which things happen. p. 251

fork (fôrk) A branch of a river. p. 39

free enterprise (frē en´tər•prīz) An economic system in which people are free to start and run their own businesses. p. 179

free state (frē stāt) A state in which slavery was not allowed. p. 164

frontier (frun•tir´) The edge of settled land. p. 84

G

geography (jē•og´rə•fē) The study of the Earth's surface and the way people live on it. p. 22

glacier (glā´shər) A mass of ice. p. 33

government (guv´ərn•mənt) A system for deciding what is best for people living in a large group. p. 69

Grange (grānj) The name of a club for farm families; an old word meaning "farm"; the first national farm organization in the United States. p. 175

grid (grid) Numbered lines on a map that cross each other to form a pattern of squares. p. 25

gristmill (grist´mil) A mill for grinding grain. p. 131

H

habitat (hab´ə•tat) A place where an animal naturally finds food and shelter. p. 56

headwaters (hed´wô•tərz) The upper part of a river. p. 67

hemisphere (hem•ə•sfir´) A half of the Earth. p. 36

high-tech (hī•tek´) Having to do with the technology of computers and electronics. p. 210

Hispanic (his•pan´ik) A person whose family comes from one of the Spanish-speaking countries. p. 227

history (his´tə•rē) The study of the past. p. 23

hub (hub) A center of activity. p. 145

human resource (hyoo´mən rē´sôrs) A worker and the knowledge and skills he or she brings to a job. p. 238

humid (hyoo´mid) Having a lot of moisture. p. 45

I

immigrant (im´ə•grant) A person who moves to a country from another country. p. 179

industry (in´dəs•trē) All businesses with one kind of product or one kind of service. p. 176

informed citizen (in•fôrmd sit´ə•zən) A citizen who understands why things happen in the community, the state, the nation, and the world. p. 239

inset map (in´set map) A small map within a larger map. p. 25

interstate highway (in´tər•stāt hī´wā) A highway that goes from one state in the United States to another. p. 236

isolated (ī´sə•lāt•əd) Far from others. p. 172

J

judicial branch (joo•dish´əl branch) The branch of government made up of courts and judges who hear and decide law cases. p. 249

jury trial (joor´ē trī´əl) A trial in which a group of citizens decides if a person accused of a crime is guilty or not guilty. p. 250

L

lake effect (lāk i•fekt´) The effect of the Great Lakes on the weather near them; it brings more snow to northern Indiana than to southern Indiana. p. 45

latitude (la´tə•tood) An imaginary line that runs east and west around the Earth. p. 36

legislative branch (le´jus•lā•tiv branch) The branch of government that makes, or passes, laws. p. 248

leisure time (lē´zhər tīm) Time away from work. p. 204

limestone (līm´stōn) A hard rock used for making buildings. p. 55

line (līn) A transportation route. p. 145

location (lō•kā´shən) Where a place is. p. 37

locomotive (lō•kə•mō´tiv) A train engine. p. 144

loft (lôft) The part of a cabin between the ceiling and the roof. p. 130

longitude (lon´jə•tood) An imaginary line that runs north and south around the Earth through the North Pole and the South Pole. p. 36

M

majority (mə•jôr´ə•tē) More than half. p. 249

manufacturing (man•yə•fak´chər•ing) The making of products in factories. p. 176

map key (map kē) A part of a map that explains what the symbols on the map stand for. Also called a map legend. p. 25

map scale (map skāl) A part of a map that compares a distance on a map to a distance in the real world. p. 25

map title (map tī´təl) Words on a map that tell the subject of a map. p. 24

marsh (märsh) A lowland area with wet soil and tall grasses. p. 34

memorial (mə•môr´ē•əl) Anything created to honor a person or an event. p. 185

metropolitan area (met•rə•pol´ə•tən âr´ē•ə) A large city plus all the suburbs, towns, and smaller cities around it. p. 239

military (mil´ə•ter•ē) Having to do with an army or with war. p. 69

mineral (min´ər•əl) A natural resource found in the ground. p. 54

moraine (mə•rān´) A hill formed of stony soil carried by glaciers and left behind when they melt. p. 34

mouth (mouth) The place where a river flows into a larger body of water. p. 38

N

naturalized citizen (nach´ər•əl•īzd sit´ə•zən) An immigrant who has become a citizen by taking the steps described in the law. p. 261

natural region (nach´ər•əl rē´jən) A part of the Earth that has one major kind of natural feature, such as mountains, hills, or plains. p. 33

natural resource (nach´ər•əl rē•sôrs) Something found in nature that people can use. p. 53

navigable (nav´ə•gə•bəl) Deep enough for travel by boats. Describes some rivers. p. 143

needleleaf (nēd´əl•lēf) A tree that has thin, sharp leaves like needles. p. 56

nominate (nom´ə•nāt) To name as a candidate to run in an election. p. 258

O

opinion (ə•pin´yən) A statement that tells what a person thinks or believes. p. 195

opportunity cost (op•ər•tōō´nə•tē kôst) What you give up to get something else. p. 256

orbit (ôr´bit) To circle. p. 206

ordinance (ôr´də•nəns) An order, a law, or a set of laws. p. 103

P

permanent (pûr´mən•ənt) Lasting a long time. p. 76

pharmaceutical (fär•mə•sōō´ti•kəl) A medicine. p. 180

pictograph (pik´tə•graf) A graph that uses symbols to stand for amounts. p. 237

pioneer (pī´ə•nir) One of the first settlers in a place. p. 84

pollute (pə•lōōt´) To spoil the environment. p. 55

population (pop•yə•lā´shən) The number of people who live in a place. p. 147

population density (pop•yə•lā´shən den´sə•tē) The number of people living in an area of a certain size. p. 232

portage (pôr´tij) An overland route between two bodies of water. p. 68

prairie (prâr´ē) Flat grasslands. p. 57

precipitation (pri•sip´ə•tā•shən) Rain, sleet, hail, or snow. p. 43

preserve (pri•zûrv´) To save. p. 185

primary source (prī´mer•ē sôrs) A source that gives the real words and pictures of people who actually saw an event. p. 170

prime meridian (prīm mə•rid´ē•ən) The starting point for measuring lines of longitude, imaginary lines that run north and south around the Earth. The line of longitude marked 0°. p. 36

proclamation (prok•lə•mā´shən) An order from a leader to the citizens of a place. p. 81

Q

quarry (kwô´rē) A large open pit from which stone is cut. p. 235

R

reclaim (ri•klām´) To make something usable by people again. p. 235

recycle (rē•sī´kəl) To use materials again instead of wasting them. p. 203

refinery (ri•fī´nər•ē) A factory where resources such as oil are made into products people can use. p. 177

register (rej´is•tər) To sign up, or enter one's name, to vote. p. 262

represent (rep•ri•zent´) To speak for people. p. 118

reservoir (re´zər•vwär) A lake that stores water held back by a dam. p. 41

resolve (ri•zolv´) To settle. p. 123

responsibility (ri•spon•sə•bil´ə•tē) A duty. p. 261

retreat (ri•trēt´) To turn back from battle. p. 107

revolution (rev•ə•lōō´shən) A sudden, violent change in government and in people's lives. p. 83

rights (rīts) Freedoms or legal claims. p. 76

river system (riv´ər sis´təm) A river and all its tributaries. p. 39

route (rōōt) A path that a person takes to get from one place to another. p. 77

rural (rŏŏr´əl) Of or about the countryside. p. 229

S

St. Lawrence Seaway (sānt lôr´əns sē´wā) A waterway that was built by Canada and the United States. Its canals link the St. Lawrence River, Lake Ontario, and Lake Erie. p. 209

sand dune (sand dōōn) A hill built up from sand that the wind has swept from beaches. p. 34

scarce (skârs) Hard to find. p. 63

school board (skōōl bôrd) A group of people elected by voters in a school district to make decisions about running the schools. p. 255

sea level (sē lev´əl) At the same height as the surface of the oceans. p. 35

secondary source (sek´ən•der•ē sôrs) A source written at a later time by someone who did not see an event. p. 170

section (sek´shən) In American western lands long ago, a piece of land 1 mile (about 2 km) square. p. 104

segregation (seg•rə•gā´shən) Keeping people in separate groups based on race or culture. p. 205

self-sufficient (self´sə•fish´ənt) Able to produce everything needed to live, without help from others. p. 172

service industry (sûr´vis in´dəs•trē) An industry that does things for people but does not make goods. p. 210

sharecropper (shâr´krop•ər) A person who rents farmland and pays the rent with a share of the crops raised on the land. p. 179

shortage (shôr´tij) A short supply that is not enough for everyone. p. 190

site (sīt) A place. p. 121

slave (slāv) A person who is owned as the property of another person. p. 104

slave state (slāv stāt) A state in which people could own slaves. p. 163

sod (sod) Soil in which grass is growing. p. 173

source (sôrs) The place where a river begins. p. 38

special district (spesh´əl dis´trikt) A district that deals with one problem or service. p. 255

specialize (spesh´əl•īz) To work at one job only. p. 63

stagecoach (stāj´kōch) A covered passenger wagon pulled by horses. p. 142

status symbol (stat´əs sim´bəl) An object that is a sign of wealth or importance. p. 76

stockade (sto•kād´) A wall of strong posts built for protection. p. 85

suffrage (su´frij) The right to vote. p. 192

supply (sə•plī´) The amount available. p. 211

surplus (sûr´pləs) Extra supply. p. 172

surrender (sə•ren´dər) To give up. p. 86

T

tax (taks) The money a government collects to pay for the services it provides. p. 82

temperature (tem´prə•chər) The measure of how warm or cold a place is. p. 42

territory (ter´ə•tôr•ē) Land that is owned by a country but is not part of any state. p. 87

till (til) A thick layer of soil left behind by glaciers. p. 34

time line (tīm līn) A graph that shows the order of events and the amount of time between them. p. 71

tornado (tôr•nā´dō) A funnel-shaped storm of swirling winds. p. 45

town board (toun bôrd) The legislative branch of town government in Indiana. p. 254

township (toun´ship) A piece of land 6 miles (about 10 km) square. p. 104

township board (toun´ship bôrd) The group of citizens that makes township laws. p. 253

township trustee (toun´ship trus•tē´) A person who heads the government of a township. p. 253

trace (trās) A trail. p. 141

trade (trād) The exchange of goods. p. 64

trade-off (trād´ôf) The giving up of one thing to get another. p. 256

treaty (trē´tē) A written agreement between two or more groups. p. 79

tribe (trīb) A group of many bands of people that share land and a way of life. p. 63

tributary (tri´byə•ter•ē) A river or creek that flows into a larger river or creek. p. 38

turning point (tûrn´ing point) An event that causes an important change to take place. p. 107

U

Underground Railroad (un´dər•ground rāl´rōd) A system of escape routes along which runaway slaves knew they could find help in getting to free land. p. 166

unemployment (un•im•ploi´mənt) The number of people without jobs. p. 194

Unigov (yoo´nə•guv) The plan of unified government that joins Marion County and Indianapolis. p. 255

Union (yoon´yən) The United States of America. p. 167

unite (yoo•nīt´) To bring together. p. 80

upstream (up•strēm´) Against a river's current. p. 142

V

veto power (vē´tō pou´ər) The power to stop a new law by refusing to sign it. p. 249

volunteer (vol•ən•tir´) A person who works without pay. p. 262

voyageur (voi´ə•zhoor) A French word meaning "traveler." A person hired to carry furs or other goods to be sold. p. 75

W

war bond (wôr bond) A paper that stands for a loan of money to a government to help pay for the costs of a war. p. 190

weather (weth´ər) The temperature, precipitation, and wind in a place. p. 42

INDEX

Page references for illustrations are set in italic type. An italic m indicates a map. Page references set in boldface type indicate the pages on which vocabulary terms are defined.

A

Adams, John, 109
Ade, George, 229
African Americans
  civil rights and,
    205–206, *205*
  Ku Klux Klan and,
    191, *191*
  migration to North,
    179, *179*
  Indiana Black Expo,
    228, *228*
  in military, *208*
  population of, 227
  settlements of, 158,
    m159
  as sharecroppers, 179
  in U.S. Congress, *259*,
    260
  voting rights of, 121
  See also Slaves and
    slavery
Agencies, **249**
  federal, 260, *260*
Agriculture (farming),
  174, *222*, 235
  commercial farms,
    234
  crops, 53–54, *m54*, 63,
    63, 68, 172, 173,
    234–235, *m234*
  debt in, 210
  drought and, 44
  of early people, 63
  Grange and, 175, *175*
  growing season for,
    43, *m43*
  isolated farms, 172
  machines in, 173, *173*,
    178
  new ideas about, 174
  number of farms, 173
  pioneer farms, 172, *172*
  rural life in 1930s,
    196–201
  sharecroppers in, 179
  soil for, 53–54, *53*
  surpluses in, 172
Airplanes, 193, *193*, *195*,
  236
Allen, Joseph P., 207
Allies, **79**
Amendment, **192**

American Indians. *See*
  Indians, American
American Revolution,
  82–87, *m84*, *86*, *87*
Amish, 228–229, *229*
Angel Mounds State
  Historic Site, 64–65,
  m64, *65*
Animals
  early, 61, 62, *62*
  extinction of, 63
  as natural resource,
    56–57, *56*, *57*
Anthem, national,
  224–225
Apollo 1 spacecraft, 206
Apollo 8 spacecraft, 206
Apperson, Edgar, 182
Apperson, Elmer, 182
Arrowheads, 72
Artists, 230
Asian Americans, 227
Astronauts, 188, *188*,
  206–207, *206*, *207*
Atlantis space shuttle,
  207
Automobile, **182**–184,
  182, *183*, *184*, 193, 202,
  204, 210, 239–240
Automobile parts, 183
Aviation, **193**, *193*, *195*,
  236
Ax, *82*

B

Bacon, Hiram, 166
Bacon's Swamp, *m165*,
  166
Ball brothers, 177
Ball State University, 177
Bands, **61**
Barges, 209, **236**
Basketball, 204, 214–215,
  214, *215*, 230–231
Battleships, 113, 203, *203*
Bayh, Birch, 259
Bayh, Evan, 239, *248*, 259
Beanblossom Bluegrass
  Festival, 228
Beaver hats, 74, *74*
Bedford, *m25*, 235
Bill, 251
Bill of Rights, 247

Bird, Larry, 230
Birds, **56**, 57
Bituminous (coal), **54**
Blackford County, 253,
  m253
Blade, stone, *61*
Bloomington, *m25*, 235
Bluegrass music, 228
Blue Jacket (Indian
  leader), 106
Blue River, *m39*
Bluespring Caverns, 35,
  m41
Boats and ships
  barges, 209, **236**
  battleships, 113, 203,
    203
  canal boats, 143–144,
    144
  canoes, 67, *67*
  cargo ships, *209*
  flatboats, 84–**85**,
    98–101, 128, 131, *143*
  steamboats, 142–143,
    143, *m181*
  submarine, *203*
  in War of 1812, 113
Border states, *m166*
Borman, Frank, 206
Boundary line, 109–**110**,
  m110, *m119*
Britain
  in American
    Revolution, 83–87,
    m84, *86*, *87*
  exploration and settle-
    ment by, 78–81, *m79*,
    m81
  forts of, *m80*, 83, 84,
    85, 105, 106, 114
  in French and Indian
    War, 79–80
  trade with Indians,
    78–79, 105
  treaty with Indians, 79
  in War of 1812, 113–114,
    m114
  in World War I, 189
  in World War II, 202
Broadleaf (tree), **55**,
  55–56, *56*
Brokenburr, Robert Lee,
  205, 206
Brown, William Wells,
  166

Brown County, 253,
  m253
Budget, **248**
Buffalo Trace, 141
Burns Harbor, 209
Bush, George, 258

C

Cabins, 68, *128*, 129–130,
  129, *164*
Cahokia, 64, 85
Calumet region, 178,
  179, 233
Camp Morton, 167
Canal, 143–144, *144*,
  m146
Canal boats, 143–144, *144*
Canoe, 67, *67*
Capital, 121–122, *122*, 248
Capitol, Indiana, 220
Capitol, U.S., 259
Cardinal (state bird), *56*
Cargo, **236**
Cargo ships, *209*
Carmichael, Hoagy, 230
Cataract Falls, 29
Cause, **115**
  and effect, 115
Cavalry, **168**
Cavelier, René–Robert,
  72
Caves, 35, *41*, *m41*
Celebrations, 184–185,
  185, 227–228, *228*
Census, **109**
  of 1800, 109
  of 1814, 118
  of 1990, 227
Centennial, 184–185, *185*
Central Till Plain, 33,
  34–35, *34*, *m35*
Century, **71**
Change, **20**
Charlestown, *m25*, 118
Children, enslaved, 163
Cities, 176–180
  government of, 254
  growth of, 176, 178
  immigrants in, 179
  industries in, 176–178,
    177, *178*, 182–184,
    183, *184*
  problems of, 239–240

Citizen, 19
  informed, **239**
  naturalized, **261**–262, *261*
  responsibilities of, 261, 262–263, *262*
  rights of, 262. *See also* Rights
Civics, 23
Civil, 69
  chiefs, 69
Civil rights, 205–206, *205*
Civil War, *m166*, **167**–171, *167, 168, 170*
Claim, 128
Clark, George Rogers, 60, *60*, 84–86, *m84*, 103, 238
Clark County, 252, *m253*
Clarksville, 103
Cleveland, Grover, 259
Climate, 42–45
Coal, 54–55, *m54, m181*, 235, *235*
Coats, Daniel, 258, *259*
Coffin, Katherine ("Aunt Katie"), 165, 170
Coffin, Levi, 165, *165*, 170
Colfax, Schuyler, 258, *258*, 259
Collegeville, 43
Colonists, 78
Colony, 72–73
Columbus, 233
Commercial farms, 234
Commonality, 19
Common council, 254
Commute, 204
Compass rose, 25, *m25*
Compromise, 123
Computers, 210–211
Confederacy, *m166*, **167**
Confederation, 105
  of Indian tribes, 105–106, 110–113, 114
Conflict, 20, 105
  compromise to resolve, 123
  in Northwest Territory, 105–108, *106*, 110–114, *113, m114*, 116–117
  See also Wars
Congress, 104
  Indiana (General Assembly), *19*, 120, *120*, 121–122, 210, 248, *248*

United States, 104, 118–119, 259–260, *259*
Conn, C. G., 178
Conner Prairie, 150–151
Conserve, 240–241
Constitution, 119
  of Indiana, 119–121, *121*, 247–248
  of United States, 192, 247
Constitutional convention (Indiana), 120–121
Constitutional Elm, 120, *120, 231*
Consumer goods, 193, 233
Continuity, 20
Convention, 120
  constitutional, 120–121
  Women's Rights, 192
Cooperate, 20, **62,** 66, *66*
  cooperation, 20
Corduroy roads, 141, 142
Corn, 53, *63*, 68, 234, *m234*
Corn Belt, 234, *m234*, 235
Corydon, *m110*, 119–120, *119*, 121, *168, 171*
Cotton, *m181*
Council, 69
  common, **254**
  county, **252**–253
Council Oak meeting, 73
County commissioners, 252
County council, 252–253
County governments, 252–253, *252, m253*
County seat, 252
Courts, 249–250, *250*
  Appeals, 250
  Supreme (Indiana), 120, 121, 250, *250*
  teen, 266, *267*
Crime, 240
Crops, 53–54, *m54*, 234–235
  corn, *63*, 68, 172, 234, *m234*
  of early people, 63, *63*
  soybeans, 234, *m234*
  wheat, 172, 173
Crossroads of America, 145
Culture, 23, *63*, 227–228, *228*

D

Dams, 41
Dearborn County, 252, *m253*

Debt, 210
Declaration of Independence, 83, *83*
Deed, 104
Defense plants, 202–203
Delaware people, 69, 70, *m70*, 73, 79, 105, 107
Delegates, 119, 121
Demand, 210
Democracy, 238
Demoiselle, chief of Miami tribe, 79
Depression, 193–194, *194*
Diagrams, 140, *140*
Disease, 76, 79
Diverse economy, 210
Diversity, 19
Downstream, 142
Dresser, Paul, 222–223, 229–230
Drought, 44
Drummers, in Civil War, 167, *167*
Duesenberg, August, 184
Duesenberg, Fred, 184
Duesenberg automobile, 183–184
Duncan, John, 243
Dunes, 34, *34*

E

Earthworks, 64–65, *64, 65*
Eastern Woodland Indians, 67
Economic choices, 256
Economy, 23, 233–236, *234*
  budget and, 248
  diverse, 210
  Great Depression and, 193–194, *194*
  unemployment and, 194, 210
Education, improving, 238–239
  See also Schools
Edwards, Bill, 243
Eel River, *m39*
Effect, 115
  cause and, 115
Elkhart, 178, *m181*, 233
Emancipation Proclamation, 169
Employment, 194, 210
Enabling act, 119
England. *See* Britain
Entrepreneur, 179–180, *180*

Environment, 20
  human interactions with, 20
  preservation of, 185
  protecting, 90–91, *90, 91*, 240–241, *241*
Equator, 36, *m36*
Erie, Lake, 40, 114, 144, 209
Evansville, *m25*, 144, 164, 176, 211, 233
Evergreens, 56
Executive branch of government, 249, *249*
Exploration
  British, 78–81
  French, 72–74, *73, m77*
Export, 236, *236*
Extinct, 63

F

Fable, 229
Fact, 195
Factories. *See* Manufacturing
Fairbanks, Charles W., 258–259, *258*
Fallen Timbers, Battle of, 106–107, *106*
Falls of the Ohio, *m77*, 103
Farming. *See* Agriculture
Feast of the Hunters' Moon, 228, *228*
Federal government, 257
  Congress, **104,** 118–119, 259–260, *259*
  Hoosiers in, 257–260
  Northwest Territory and, 104
  organization of, 257
Fertile, 53
Fertilizers, 174
Flatboat, 84–85, 98–101, 128, 131, *143*
Floods, 44, *44*
Flow chart, 251, *251*
Flower (state), *57*
Food gatherers, 63
Food products, 233
Forest conservation, 241
  See also Trees
Forest products, *m54*, 56
Fork (of river), **39,** *m39*
Forsyth, William, 230, 231
Fort Detroit, *m80*, 83, 85, 114
Fort Greenville, 106–108

Fort Harrison, *m25,* 112
Fort Miami (British),
　m80, 106, 107
Fort Miami (French), 75,
　79, *m79,* 80
Fort Ouiatenon, 75, 79,
　80, *m80,* 228
Fort Pitt, *m80,* 84
Forts
　American, 107, 112
　British, *m80,* 83, 84, 85,
　　105, 106, 107, 114
　French, 73, 75–76, *75,*
　　79, 80
Fort Sackville, *m84,* 85,
　86–87
Fort Wayne
　building of, 107
　city of, 37, *m37,* 40, 67,
　　75, 107, 144, 178, 211
　industry in, 178
　Treaty of, 110, 112
France
　exploration and settle-
　　ment by, *19, 72–76,*
　　73, 75, m77, m79
　forts built by, 73,
　　75–76, *75, 79,* 80
　trade with Indians, 72,
　　74–76, *74,* 79
Franklin Township, 34–35
Free enterprise, 179
Free states, 164
French and Indian War,
　79–80
Frontier, 84
Fulton, Robert, 142
Fur trade, 74–76, *74,*
　78–79, 105

G

Gary, *m25,* 178, 179, 202,
　206
Gary, Elbert H., 178
Gas, natural, *m54,* 55,
　176–177, *177*
General Assembly, *19,*
　120, 121–122, 210, 248,
　248
Geography, 22
　lakes, 33, 40–41
　latitude and longitude,
　　36–37, *m36, m37*
　rivers, 30–31, 38–40,
　　38, m39, 40, 41, *m41*
　shape of land, 33–35,
　　33, 34, m35
**George III, king of
　England,** 81

**Germany, in World War
　I,** 189–190
Glaciers, 33, *33*
Glass, *176, 177, m181*
Government, 23, 69,
　247–255
　city, 254
　constitution and,
　　119–121, *121,* 247–248
　county, 252–253, *252,*
　　m253
　executive branch of,
　　249, *249*
　federal, 104, **257**–260
　judicial branch of,
　　249–250, *249, 250*
　legislative branch of,
　　121–122, 210, **248,**
　　248, 249
　of Miami people, 69, *69*
　state, 120–122, *121, 122,*
　　247–250, *248, 249, 250*
　town, 254
　township, 253–254
　Unigov, *254,* **255**
Governor, 249
Grange, *175, 175*
Grant, Ulysses S., 259
Graphs
　line, *147, 147*
　pictographs, **237,** *237*
Gravel roads, 142
Great Britain. *See* Britain
Great Depression,
　193–194, *194*
Great Lakes, 33, 40,
　113–114, 143–144,
　209, 236. *See also
　individual lakes*
Great Lakes Plain, 33,
　34, *34, m35*
Greenville, Treaty of,
　107–108, *107, 108,*
　109–110
Gresham, James, *190*
Grid, 25, *m25, 37*
Grissom, Virgil ("Gus"),
　188, 206, *206*
Gristmills, 131, 134–139,
　140
Group projects, 66, *66*
Growing season, 43, *m43*
Gypsum, 55

H

Habitats, 56–57, *57*
Hall, Katie Beatrice, *259,*
　260

Hamilton, Henry, 83, 84,
　m84, 85, 86
Haney, Douglas, 266, *267*
Harmonie, 131
Harmonists, 131
Harper, Ida, 192
Harris, Chapman, 165
Harrison, Benjamin,
　257–258
**Harrison, William
　Henry,** 109, *109,* 110,
　112–113, 116–117, 238,
　257
Harrodsburg, 41
Hatcher, Richard, 206,
　246, *246*
Hatchet, *82*
Haynes, Elwood, 182,
　183, *183*
Headwaters, 67
Helmet, *189*
Hemispheres, *27, 27,* **36,**
　m36
Hendricks, Thomas,
　258–259, *258*
Henry, Patrick, 84
High-tech, 210
　businesses, 210–211
Hispanics, 227, 228
History, 23
Home Guard, 168
Hoosier National Forest,
　241
**House of Representatives
　(Indiana),** 248. *See also*
　General Assembly
Housing
　log cabins, 129–130, *129*
　of Miamis, *68*
　rock shelters, 62
　slave cabins, *164*
Hub, 145
Human resources, 238
Humid, 45
**Hunters' Moon, Feast of
　the,** 228, *228*
Hunting, 61, 62, 68, 76
Huron, Lake, *m114*

I

Illinois, 26, *m166*
Illinois River, 40, 73, 74
Illinois tribe, 73, 75
Immigrant, 179, 261–262
**Independence,
　Declaration of,** 83, *83*
Indiana, *m25, m37*
　centennial of, 184–185,
　　185

Congress (General
　Assembly) of, *19,*
　120, *120,* 121–122,
　210, 248, *248*
　government of. *See*
　　Government
　location of, 26–27,
　　26–27
　Presidents from,
　　257–258
　statehood for, 118–122
　state bird of, *56*
　state flower of, *57*
　state motto of, 145
　state song of, 222–223,
　　230
　state tree of, *56*
　townships and sections
　　in, 104, *m104*
　Vice Presidents from,
　　258–259, *258*
Indiana, Robert, 230
Indiana Black Expo, 228,
　228
**Indiana Dunes State
　Park,** *34*
Indiana Pacers (basket-
　ball team), 204
Indianapolis, *m25,* 240
　automobile industry
　　in, 183–184, *183, 184*
　in Civil War, 167–168
　end of World War II
　　in, 204
　population of, 239
　service industries in,
　　211, *211*
　as state capital,
　　121–122, *122,* 248
　travel to, 142, 145, *145,*
　　m155
　Underground
　　Railroad in, 166
　Union Station in, *145,*
　　211, *211*
　Women's Rights
　　Convention in, 192
Indianapolis, **USS,** 203,
　203
Indianapolis 500, *183,* 184
**Indianapolis International
　Airport,** 236
Indiana State Fair, 174,
　174
Indiana Territory, 109–114
　boundaries of,
　　109–110, *m110, m119*
　changes in, 109–110
Indiana University, 120
Indians, American
　agriculture of, 63

in American
Revolution, 83–84
celebrations of, 228,
228
confederation of,
105–106, 110–113,
114
conflict with, 105–108,
106, 110–114, *113,*
m114, 116–117
cooperation among,
62, *66*
disease among, 76, 79
earliest, 61–65
food gathering by, 63
in French and Indian
War, 79–80
French explorers and,
72–76, *73*
historical routes of,
m62
hunting by, 61, 62, 68,
76
land owned by, 103,
109–110, *m110,*
112–113, 116–117
Mound Builders, 29,
64–65, *m64, 65*
population of, 227
rights of, 76, 103, 121
settlements of, 68, *68,*
m70, 71, *m81,*
111–112, *111*
trade with British,
78–79, 105
trade with French, 72,
74–76, *74, 79*
treaty with British, 79
tribes of, **63,** 80. *See*
also individual groups
in War of 1812, 113, 114
Individualism, 20
Industry, 176
automobile, 182–184,
182, 183, 184, 193,
202, 210
aviation, **193,** *193*
consumer good, **193,**
233
diversity of, 233–236,
234
entrepreneurs in,
179–180, *180*
during Great
Depression, 193–194
high-tech, **210**–211
service, **210,** 211, *211,*
233–234
steel, 178, *178, m181,*
193, 202, 210, 233, *233*
See also Manufacturing

Informed citizen, 239
Inset map, 25
Interactions, within
different environments,
20
Interdependence, 20
Interstate highway, 236
Iowa, 26
Iroquois people, 70, 73
Iroquois River, *m39*
Isolated, 172
farms, 172

J

Jackson, Cornelia,
158–161
Jackson, Janet, 230
Jackson, Michael, 230
Jackson, Selena, 158–161
Japan, in World War II,
202, 203, *204*
Jeffersonville, 166, 178
Jenckes, Virginia Ellis,
259, 260
Jennings, Jonathan,
118–120, *118,* 121, 238
Johnson, Oliver, 130
Judicial branch of gov-
ernment, 249–250, *250*
Jury trial, 250

K

Kankakee River, *m39,*
40, 73, 74
Kansas, 26
Kaskaskia River, 85
Kautsky, Frank, 204
Kekionga, 67–68, *m70,*
75, 85
Kelley, Oliver H., 175
Kentucky, 127
Key, Francis Scott, 224–225
Kickapoo people, 70, *m70*
King, Martin Luther, Jr.,
206, 260
Klawitter, Bob, 243
Knight, Bob, *214,* 230
Knox County, 252, *m253*
Kokomo, *m25,* 182
Ku Klux Klan (KKK),
191, *191*

L

Lafayette, *m25,* 111
Lake effect, 45

Lakes, 33, 40–41
formation of, 33, 40
reservoirs, 41
See also individual lakes
Land
claim to, 128
deed to, 104
distribution after
American
Revolution, 103
ownership of, 103,
109–110, *m110,*
112, 116–117
shape of, 33–35, *33, 34,*
m35
subdivisions of town-
ships and sections,
104, *m104*
Land Ordinance of 1785,
104
LaPorte, 44
LaPorte County, 253, *m253*
La Salle, Sieur de, 72–74,
73, m77
Latitude, 36–37, *m36, m37*
Lauter, Sara, 192
Laws
in Constitution, 120–121
legislative branch of
government and, 248
process of making, *251*
on statehood, 104
Legislative branch of
government, 121–122,
210, **248,** *248, 249*
Leisure time, 204
Lenape people, 69
License plate, *90*
Lilly, Eli, 180, *180*
Limestone, *m54,* **55,** *55,*
235
Lincoln, Abraham
in Civil War, 167, 169
early life of, 127–129,
128, 257
Lincoln, Nancy, 127–129,
131
Lincoln, Tom, 127–129
Line, 145
Line graph, 147, *147*
Little Pigeon Creek,
128–130
Little Turtle
(Michikinikwa),
105–106, *105,* 107, *107,*
110, 238
Location, 37
Locomotive, 144, *145*
Loft, 130
Longitude, 36–37, *m36,*
m37

Lost River, 41
Louis XIV, king of
France, 74
Lowlands region, 33, 35,
m35
Lugar, Richard G., *259,*
260

M

Madison, 145, 166, 176
Mahler, Andrew, 241
Maize (corn), *63*
Majority, 249
Mammoths, 61
Manufacturing, 176–178,
177, 178, 233, *233,*
234
in World War I, 189
in World War II,
202–203, *m219*
See also individual
industries
Map key, *m24,* **25,** *m25*
Maps
movement on, 133,
m133
physical, 24, *mA15*
political, 24, *m24*
population, *m232*
product, 181, *m181*
reading, 24–25, *m25*
Map scale, 25, *m25*
Map title, 24, *m24*
Marengo cave, 35
Marion County, 255
Marshall, Thomas, *258,*
259
Marshes, 34, 56
Mastodons, 61, *62*
Maumee River, *m39,* 40,
67, 68, 75, 85, 106, 107,
144
Mayor, 254
McCormick, Cyrus, 173
McCormick's reaper, 173
McCullough, Elizabeth,
188
McNutt, Paul V., 194
Medical research, *210*
Mellencamp, John, 230
Memorial, 185
Meridian, prime, 36,
m36
Metal arrowheads, *72*
Metropolitan area,
239–240, *240. See also*
Cities
Miami people, 67–69, *68,*
69, m70, 73, 78–79, 83,
105

Michigan, 26
Michigan, Lake, *m39*, 44, 73, 177, 209
Michigan City, 143
Michigan Road, 142, *m146*
Michigan Territory, 109
Michikinikwa (Little Turtle), 105–106, *105*, 107, *107*, 110, 238
Middle West, 26
Milan High School, 214, *215*
Mile marker, *141*
Military, 69
Minerals, 54–55, *m54*, 55
Mining, 235, *235*
Minnesota, 26
Mississinewa River, 39, *m39*
Mississippi River, 40, 74, *m77*, 85
Missouri, 26
Monroe, Lake, *m39*, 41
Moon landing, 206
Moraines, 34
Morgan, John Hunt, 168–169, *168*, 170, 171
Morgan's raid, 168–169, 171
Morse Reservoir, *m39*
Morton, Oliver P., 167, 168
Motto, (state), 145
Mound Builders, 29, 64–65, *m64*, 65, 66
Mounds State Park, 64, *m64*
Mount Vernon, 209
Mouth (of river), 38
Muncie Central High School, 214
Museums, 185
Music, 222–225, 228, 229–230
Musical instruments, 178, *m181*, 227, 228, 233
Musket balls, *78*
Musselman, Helen, 202

N

National Road, 142, *142*, *m146*
Native Americans. *See* Indians, American
Natural gas, *m54*, 55, 176–177, *177*
Naturalized citizen, 261–262, *261*
Natural region, 33

Natural resources, 53–57, *m54*, *m181*
 animals, 56–57, *56*, *57*
 coal, 54–55, *m54*, *m181*, 235, *235*
 conservation of, 240–241
 minerals, 54–55, *m54*, 55
 natural gas, *m54*, 55, 176–177, *177*
 oil, *m54*, 177, *177*
 preservation of, 185
 soil, 53–54, *53*, 173, 240
 trees, *m54*, 55–56, *56*, 120, 241
 use of, 242–243
Navigable, 143
 river, 143
Navy, 113–114
Nebraska, 26
Needleleaf (tree), 56, 56
New Albany, *m25*, 141, 176
New France colony, 72, 73
New Harmony, *m25*, 131–132, *132*
New York state, 103
Nicholson, Meredith, 18
Nineteenth Amendment (women's suffrage), 192
Noblesville, 37, *m37*
Nominate, 258
North America, 27, *27*
North Dakota, 26
Northeast, 26
Northern Hemisphere, 36, *m36*
North Pole, 36, *m36*
Northwest Ordinance, 104–105
Northwest Territory, 87, 103–114
 conflict in, 105–108, *106*, 110–114, *113*, *m114*, 116–117
 slavery in, 104
 townships and sections in, 104, *m104*

O

Ohio, 26
Ohio County, 253, *m253*
Ohio River, 35, 39–40, *39*, *m39*, 44, 76, 103, 120, 143–144, 164, 165, 176, 209, 236

Ohio River valley, 73
Ohio Territory, 109
Oil, *m54*, 177, *177*
Oktoberfest, 228
Oliver, James, 173, 178
Oliver's plow, 173, *173*, 178
Ontario, Lake, 209
"On the Banks of the Wabash, Far Away" (state song), 222–223, 230
Opinion, 195
Opportunity cost, 256
Orbit, 206
Ordinance, 103–105
Orr, Robert D., 226
Ottawa people, 80
Otters, 56, *57*
Owen, Robert, 131, *132*
Owen, Robert Dale, 169, *169*
Owenites, 131–132

P

Painters, 230, *231*
Parades, 184, *185*, *191*
Parks
 Cataract Falls, *29*
 Mound Builder sites, 64–65, *m64*, 65
 preservation of natural resources and, 185
 Tillery Hill, 242–243
Patoka Lake, *m39*, 242–243
Patoka River, *m39*
Pearl Harbor attack, 202
Peasley, W. J., 144
Peony (state flower), *57*
Permanent, 76
 settlement, 76
Perry, Oliver Hazard, 113–114
Pharmaceuticals, 180
Physical maps, 24, *mA15*
Piankashaw people, 70, *m70*
Pictographs, 237, *237*
Pigeon River, *m39*
Pioneers, 84
 farms of, 172, *172*
 life of, 97–101, 134–138
 log cabins of, 129–130, *129*
 road building by, 141–142, *141*, *142*, *m146*
 schools of, 130, *130*
 settlements of, 127–132, *128*, *130*, *132*, *m133*, 150–151

Plains
 Central Till, 33, 34–35, *34*, *m35*
 Great Lakes, 33, 34, *34*, *m35*
Plank roads, 141, 142
Plow, 173, *173*, 178
Plump, Bobby, 214
Point of view, 208
Police, 239
Political maps, 24, *m24*
Pollute, 55, 240
Pontiac, 80, 238
Pontiac's War, 80, *m80*
Poplar, yellow (state tree), *56*
Population, 147
Population density, 232
Population map, *m232*
Population statistics, 147, *147*, 182, 210, 227, 232, 239, *m271*. *See also* Census
Portage, 68
Porter, Cole, 230
Portland, 176
Port of Indiana, 209
Ports, 209, 236
Posey County, 35
Potawatomi people, 70, *m70*, 105
Poultry, 235
Power, sources of, 54–55
Prairies, 57
Precipitation, 43–44, *44*
Preserve, 185
Presidents (Hoosier), 257–258
Primary sources, 170, 171
Prime meridian, 36, *m36*
Problem solving, 52
Proclamation, 81
 of 1763, 81, *m81*
Product map, 181, *m181*
Prophet (Tenskwatawa), 111–112, *112*
Prophetstown, 111–112, *m111*
Purdue, John, 174
Purdue University, 174
Pyle, Ernie, 203, *203*

Q

Quakers, 165
Quarry, 235
Quayle, J. Danforth (Dan), 258, *258*

R

Railroads, 144–145, *145, m146,* 236
    Underground, 164–**166,** *m165*
Rainfall, 43–44, *44*
Ralston, Alexander, 122
Rapp, George, 131
RCA Dome, 211, 214, *240*
Reaper, 173
Reclaim, 235
Recycle, 203, 240, *241*
Red Cross, *263*
Refinery, 177, *177*
Register, 262
Religions, 165, 228–229, *229*
Represent, 118
Research, medical, *210*
Reservoir, 41
Resolve, 123
Resources. *See* Human resources; Natural resources
Responsibility, 261
    of citizens, 261, 262–263
Retreated, 107
Revolution, 83
    American, 82–87, *m84, 86, 87*
Reynolds, William, 243
Richardson, Henry J., Jr., *205,* 206
Richmond, 142, 233
Rights, 76
    Bill of, **247**
    of citizens, 262
    civil, **205**–206, *205*
    in Constitution, 120, 121, 247
    of Indians, 76, 103
    voting, 121, 191–192, *191, m192*
    of women, 121, 191–192, *191, m192*
Riley, James Whitcomb, 229
River otters, 56, *57*
Rivers, 30–31, 38–40, *38, m39, 40,* 41, *m41,* 143
River system, 39, *m39*
Roads
    automobiles and, 184, 239–240
    early, 141–142, *141, 142, m146, m155*
    interstate highways, **236**
    traffic on, 239–240

Roberts, Ishmael, 158
Robertson, Oscar, *215,* 230
Rockne, Knute, 230
Rock shelters, 62
Roosevelt, Franklin D., 194, 202, 258
Roosevelt, Theodore, 259
Ross, Jerry, 207
Route, 77, *m77*
Rudolph, Wilma, 231
Rural, 229
    areas, 196–201, 229
    See also Agriculture

S

Sackville, Lord, 85
St. Clair, Arthur, 105, 106
St. Joseph River, *m39,* 40
St. Lawrence Seaway, 209
St. Marys River, *m39,* 40
Salamonie River, 39, *m39*
Sales tax, 210
Salt Creek, 41
Sand dunes, 34, *34*
Scarce, 63
School board, 255
School districts, 255
Schools
    improving, 238–239, *238*
    pioneer, 130, *130*
    sports in, 214, *215*
    universities, 120, 174, 177
Scythe, *172*
Sea level, 35
Secondary sources, 170
Sections, 104, *m104*
Segregation, 205–206, *205*
Self-sufficient, 172
Senate (Indiana), 248
    See also General Assembly
Service industries, 210, 211, *211,* 233–234
Settlements
    of African Americans, 158, *m159*
    British, 78–81, *m79, m81*
    French, 72, 75–76, *75, m79*
    of Indians, 67, 68, *m70, 71, m81,* 111–112, *111*
    permanent, **76**
    pioneer, 127–132, *128, 129, 130, 132, m133,* 150–151
    Spanish, *m81*

Sewall, May Wright, 192
Sharecropper, 179
Shawnee people, 69, *m70,* 73, 79, 83, 102, *102,* 105, 107, 110–113
Shelbyville, 144
Shepard, Alan B., 206
Sheriff, 253
Shortage, 190
Site, 121
Slave, 104
Slaves and slavery, 104, 163–166, *164*
    children as, 163
    Civil War and, 167, 169
    end of, 169
    escapes by, 158–161, 164–166, *m165*
    in Indiana, 121, 128, 164
    in Kentucky, 127
    in Northwest Territory, 104
    Underground Railroad and, 164–166, *m165*
Slave states, 163
Snow, 43–44, *43*
Social studies
    ideas in, 19–20
    reading, 21
    subjects of, 22–23
Society of Friends, 165
Sod, 173
Soil, 53–54, *53,* 173, 240
    fertile, 53
Songs
    national anthem, 224–225
    state song, 222–223, 230
Source (of river), 38
Sources
    primary, **170,** 171
    secondary, **170**
South Bend, 40, 73, 178, 182, 211
South Dakota, 26
Southeast, 26
Southern Hemisphere, 36, *m36*
Southern Hills, 33, 35, *m35*
South Pole, 36, *m36*
Southwest, 26
Soybeans, 234, *m234*
Space program, *188,* 206–207, *206, 207*
Space shuttle, *207*
Spain, settlements of, *m81*

Special district, 255
Specialize, 63
Sports, 204, 214–215, *214, 215,* 230–231
Sports coaches, 230
Stagecoach, 142
Standard Oil Company of Ohio, 176–177
"Star–Spangled Banner, The" (national anthem), 224–225
State fair, 174, *174*
Statehood
    for Indiana, 118–122
    laws on, 104
State roads, 141–142
Status symbol, 76
Steamboats, 142–143, *143, m181*
Steam turbines, 55
Steele, Theodore C., 230
Steel industry, 178, *178, m181,* 193, 202, 210, 233, *233*
Step Ahead plan, 239
Stockade, 85
Stone blade, *61*
Stratton–Porter, Geneva ("Gene"), 32, *32,* 33
Strip mining, 235, *235*
Studebaker, 182–183, *184*
Studebaker, Clem, 183
Studebaker, Henry, 183
Submarine, *203*
Suffrage, 191–**192,** *191, m192*
Sulfur, 55
Superior, Lake, 209
Supply, 211
Supreme Court (Indiana), 120, 121, 250, *250*
Surplus, 172
Surrender, 86, *87*
Surveyor, 84, *103*
Symbols
    on product maps, 181, *m181*
    status, **76**

T

Tarkington, Booth, 229
Tax, 82
    American Revolution and, 82
    General Assembly and, 248
    sales, 210
Taylor, Marshall, *230*

Teale, Edwin Way, 34, 126
Tecumseh, 102, *102,* 110–113, 114, 116–117, 238
Teen court, 266, *267*
Temperature, 42–43, *m43*
Ten O'Clock Line, 110
Tenskwatawa (the Prophet), 111–112, *112*
Terre Haute, *m25,* 112, 142, 144
Territory, 87
Thames River, 114
Till, 34
Tillery Hill Park, 242–243
Time line, 71, *71*
Tippecanoe, Battle of, *m110,* 112–113, *113*
Tippecanoe River, 39, *m39, 111*
Tools
　metal, *72*
　stone, *61*
Tornado, 45, *45,* 46–51, *m95*
Town board, 254
Town government, 254
Township board, 253
Township governments, 253–254
Township trustee, 253
Townships, 104, *m104*
Traces, 141
Trade, 64
　British and, 78–79, 105
　among early people, 64
　French and, 72, 74–76, *74,* 79
　in fur, 74–76, *74,* 78–79, 105
　with Indians, 72, 74–76, *74,* 78–79, 105
　among pioneers, 128
Trade-off, 256
Trading posts, 75–76
Traffic, 239–240
Transportation, *m146,* 235–236
　by airplane, 193, *193, 195,* 236
　by automobile, **182**–184, *182, 183, 184,* 193, 202, 204, 210, 239–240
　by boat. *See* Boats and ships
　for exports, 236
　by rail, 144–145, *145, m146,* 236

by road, 141–142, *141, 142, m146, m155,* 184, 236
　by stagecoach, 142
Treaty, 79
　of Fort Wayne, 110, 112
　of Greenville, 107–108, *107, 108,* 109–110
　of Paris of 1763, 79
Trees, 55–56, *56*
　broadleaf, **55**–56, *56*
　conservation of, 241
　Constitutional Elm, 120
　needleleaf, **56**
　state tree, *56*
Tribes, 63, 80
Tributary, 38–39, *m39*
Trucks, transportation by, 236
Tulip tree (state tree), *56*
Turbines, 55
Turning point, 107

U

Underground Railroad, 164–**166,** *m165*
Unemployment, 194, 210
Unigov, *254,* **255**
Union, *m166,* **167**
Union Station (Indianapolis), *145,* 211, *211*
United, 80
　tribes, 80
United States, *m24*
　Capitol of, *259*
　federal workers in, 260, *260*
　government of. *See* Federal government
　regions of, 26
United States Steel Corporation, 178, 233
Universities, 120, 174, 177
University, Indiana, 120
Upstream, 142

V

Vandalia, Illinois, 142
Vanderburgh County Courthouse, 252
Veto power, 249
Vice Presidents (Hoosier), 258–259, *258*

Viewpoint, 208
Vincennes, 76, *m79,* 85–86, 109, 112, 116, 118, 119–120, 141
Virginia, 103
Volunteers, 262–263, *263*
Voss, Janice E., 207, *207*
Voting pins, *247*
Voting rights, 121, 191–192, *191, m192*
Voyageurs, *74, 75*

W

Wabash and Erie Canal, 143–144
Wabash River, 30–31, 38–39, *38, m39,* 68, 75, 76, 143, 144, 222–223, 228
Wabash River valley, 68, 75
Walker, Madam C. J., 162, *162,* 180
War bonds, 189–190, *190*
Wars
　American Revolution, 82–87, *m84, 86, 87*
　Civil War, *m166,* **167**–171, *167, 168, 170*
　of 1812, 113–114, *m114*
　French and Indian, 79–80
　in Northwest Territory, 105–108, *106,* 110–114, *113, m114,* 116–117
　surrender in, 86, *87*
　World War I, 189–190, *189, 190*
　World War II, 202–203, *202, 203, 204, m219*
Washington, George, 106
Wawasee, Lake, *m39,* 41
Wayne, Anthony, *105,* 106, 107, 108
Wayne County, 34–35
Wea people, 70, *m70,* 75
Weapons
　arrowheads, *72*
　British gifts to Indians, 83
　musket balls, *78*
　war club, *96*
Weather, 42–45, *42, m43, 44, 45, m95*
West, 26
West, Jessamyn, 229

Western Hemisphere, 27, *27*
Westfield, 166
Wetlands, 56–57
Wheat, 172, 173
White River, 39, *m39*
Whitewater River, *m39,* 40
Williams, Donald E., 207
Willkie, Wendell L., 258
Wilson, Woodrow, 189, 259
Wind, 45, *45,* 46–50
Wisconsin, 26
Women
　in business, 162, *162,* 180, *226*
　in literature, 229
　in Miami government, 69, *69*
　in space program, 207, *207*
　in sports, 231
　in U.S. Congress, 259, 260
　voting rights of, 121, 191–192, *191, m192*
　in World War I, 189, *190*
　in World War II, 203
Women's Rights Convention, 192
Wooden, John, 230
Works Progress Administration (WPA), *194*
World War I, 189–190, *189, 190*
World War II, 202–203, *202, 203, 204, m219*
Wright, Orville, 193
Wright, Wilbur, 193
Writers, 229
Wyandotte Cave, 35
Wyandot tribe, 107

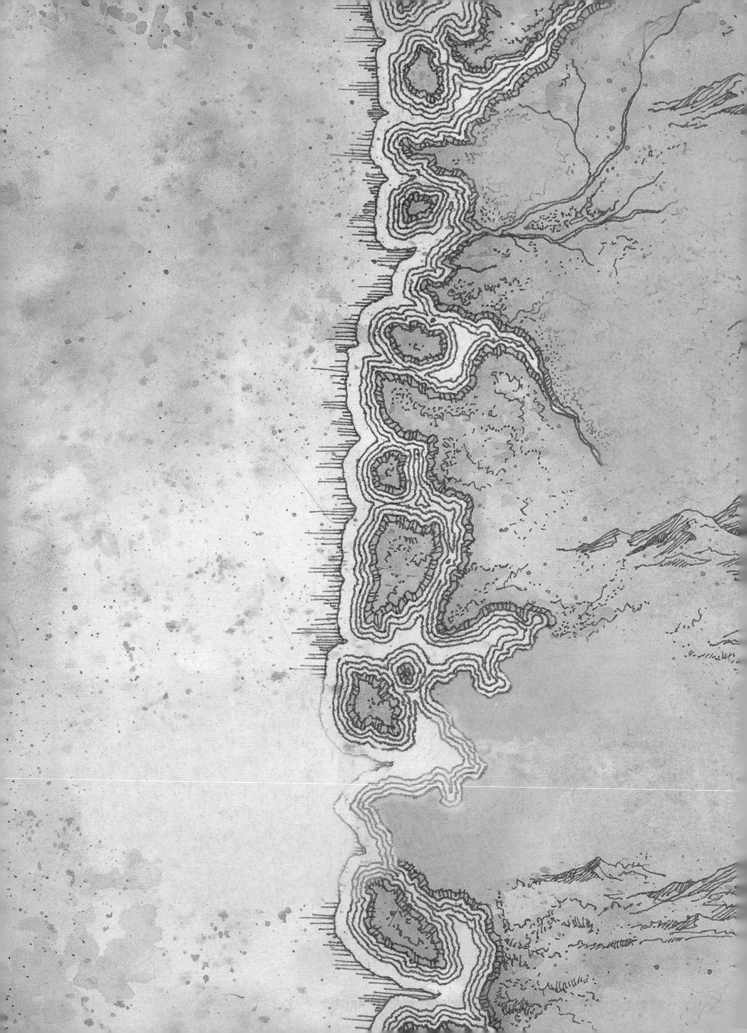